THE APE OF SORROWS

From Stranger To Destroyer:
The Inside Story Of Humans

iUniverse, Inc.
New York Bloomington

The Ape of Sorrows

From Stranger to Destroyer: The Inside Story of Humans

Grateful acknowledgement is made to Lucian Freud and © The artist for permission
to reproduce "Small Portrait 2001" on the cover of this book.

iUniverse books may be ordered through booksellers or by contacting:

iUniverse
1663 Liberty Drive
Bloomington, IN 47403
www.iuniverse.com
1-800-Authors (1-800-288-4677)

ISBN: 978-0-595-49558-0 (pbk)
ISBN: 978-0-595-49360-9 (dj)
ISBN: 978-0-595-61150-8 (ebk)

Printed in the United States of America
iUniverse rev. date: 9/25/2009

Dachiell

CONTENTS

INTRODUCTION

Maurice Rowdon died while bringing *THE APE OF SORROWS* to completion. This book, his most ambitious project, describes the human not in terms of his own stories, his "histories" of himself, but his mutations and adaptations, demonstrating with example after example that the human is valiant because he is an eroded creature. He argues that religions and civilizations are a clear reflection of his constant and essential self-revisions, as if only hermetic practices give him a structure of sanity.

Although the bulk of *THE APE OF SORROWS* was written between 1985 and 1998 it presents a totally new perspective of the human and its provocative message remains unassailable by time. Indeed the turbulence of this young twenty-first century seems to have caught up to the author's vision. In light of the state of the planet, many of us are wondering about our collective sanity (or at least that of our neighbors) and are now inclined to review our status of being the highest and wisest of all the animal kingdom with skepticism.

Maurice Rowdon was an astute observer and visionary. In his book *PERIMETER WEST* published in 1956, he described menacing yet absent frontier posts around a nameless German city which became the reality of Berlin with the construction of The Wall in 1961. Welt und Wort described the book at the time to be "the most important novel to come to us out of England since 1945". In his acclaimed *ITALIAN SKETCHES* (1963) he casually wrote that cars would eventually be banned from city centers and politics in the future would be determined by environmental issues.

He spent four decades in Italy where his observations on Italian life, culture and society were acclaimed as so "piercingly accurate and so far under the skin of everyday appearances that it is really a new appraisal almost of a new country". Of THE FALL OF VENICE (1970), a critic wrote "one cannot help concluding that to fall is happier than to rise". His original historian's insight and his bold exploration of the past, as illustrated in his LORENZO THE MAGNIFICENT (1974) and LEONARDO DA VINCI (1975), led him to an uncanny understanding of the direction our world was bound to follow.

His book on animal intelligence, THE TALKING DOGS, (1978) was reviewed as "documented—painstakingly, impressively and convincingly" and "its implications, not only for our relationship with the animal kingdom as a whole, but for our own future as a race, cannot and should not be ignored".

The reader of THE APE OF SORROWS will find the same meticulous attention paid to this revolutionary study of the human. The author called it "the first study of the human animal by an animal". To write it, he said, "I shall have to stop thinking like a human. Now there's obviously a contradiction here—between being an animal and being a human. For me it's the contradiction between a real and a surrogate being. And I don't want to be surrogate."

The reader is to know that wherever the author referred to "this century" he was writing about the twentieth century. Chronic ill health stalled the book's completion until 2007 when he took it up again to include statistics relating to the twenty-first century but he passed away before he was able to revise accordingly. In respect of his work I have chosen to alter nothing of the original text.

D.A. Rowdon

FOREWORD

I take History to mean everything the human has ever thought about himself—even when his own actions have been deeply mysterious to him. Sometimes he has spoken his thoughts to others and they have traveled by word of mouth, sometimes he has written them (on parchment and later paper), and today he "publishes" to the world at large. So History is a mine of thought, its changing sorrows a pageant of the heartbreaking and crass, the tragic and beautiful.

In my first year at Oxford I knew I wished to devote myself to this strange study, especially to its "modern" period, which was apparently after the "medieval" period. Historians invented all these strange time-categories for us quite as if human life was on the bubble all the time. It also seemed that historians were quite powerful people, starting in ancient Greece with Herodotus ("The Father of History"), whose book was aptly enough all about human war.

I was well aware that one historian could flatly contradict another even about an event recalled by everybody. Take British historians on the bitter argument about the "Enclosures" at the end of the eighteenth century, namely the wild or "common" land where the poorest could traditionally graze their cattle. That ancient right was gradually stolen by the rich. So it depended on where you the historian belonged socially—to the "upper" or less "upper" class.

Take historians on the "Luddites", those members of a highly secret organization in the early nineteenth century who wrecked the "new" silk looms because they were producing bogus silk at half the price. Some historians cursed these rebels while others stood up for them.

My college at Oxford was the least endowed one you could find in town. To make things worse it was a Victorian building in the Streaky Bacon style of red brick, and it was a good walk away from the truly great colleges like Christchurch, Magdalen and Balliol, which, when you slept in them, were so well endowed that the old stones whispered their centuries to you.

But I chose Keble precisely to avoid those biggies—I'd already tried for a scholarship at Peterhouse, Cambridge, and missed it (literally) by one line, and I got a commiserating letter of great charm from the history tutor there. So I wasn't going to take any chances at Oxford.

And, strange to tell, my choice of Keble was the best I could have made. In the shape of the Reverend John Stewart, Dean of the college, and my tutor Donald Mackinnon, I found two friends who knew far more about my life and particularly my future than I did. They were the first to tell me that I was a writer and that I must write a book (I published my first soon after).

Donald took my viva voce, namely the first conversation you have with your college when you present yourself to it for the first time. There and then he made a bargain with me. He said he was happy that I should continue History for my first year and take a degree in it (a short "war" degree, as World War Two was on) but could he persuade me to study Philosophy under him when I came back from the war? And I found myself saying yes—without the slightest understanding of how history could be connected with philosophy, of all studies.

To my astonishment I learned more History from Philosophy than I could believe. Philosophy asked me to consider what I meant by the word "facts", namely what History is all about. It asked me even more severely what I meant by "indisputable" facts, since anything and everything was open to dispute. "Truth", "reasoning", "analysis"—all the things claimed by History—were drawn from the study of Logic, which again belongs securely to Philosophy.

And Donald gave me the worst task that could befall anyone studying the subject for the first time. He invited me to bury myself (this is exactly how it felt) for no fewer than three years in Immanuel Kant's *Critique of Pure Reason* (quite as if anybody had ever said, inside philosophy or out, that any such thing as Pure Reason existed).

It wasn't the length of time that troubled me, for three years is minimal for the understanding of any philosophy, but the fact that what Kant was saying or trying to say remained foreign to me even after those three years (it was a great boost to my morale that Nietzsche once described him as a "catastrophic spider").

To shock my body back into life after just a day of Kant I would go out to a field where a lady, once a history don, kept ponies on whom you had to ride without saddle or bridle or reins. Now these ponies had a sense of humor. At a mighty gallop they hurtled you towards a row of dense prickly bushes and tossed you into them head first. It was a treat for me in that it simultaneously shook me free of Kant and punished me for studying him.

To my surprise (now) Philosophy never marred the humanity of my two guides, John Stewart and Donald Mackinnon. For I believe that a lack of humanity is visible in Aristotle and indeed almost every philosopher you are likely to read.

Only T.H.Bradley, of all the Oxford philosophers, was to my mind blessed with unfailing humanity. It was why he talked conversationally in his work. Yet Donald never so much as mentioned him. There was a reason for this. Bradley lived in the dark Victorian age, when talking openly and clearly on any academic subject was almost an assault on the Queen's obsession with respectability (which governed all but the greatest writers of her time).

Oxford not only ignored Bradley, it declined to publish his first book (an act almost unheard of where philosophy tutors were concerned). It was perhaps the very sanity of his words, his easy conversational and direct style that hurt. But mostly it was the core of what he said: that we humans base our lives on ridiculous assumptions about ourselves, and that the chief of these assumptions is that we "lead" our own lives.

On the contrary, he said, we are provided with everything we know—not only our assumptions but our understanding and knowledge, our simple power to differentiate between above and below, inner and outer, light and dark. These are entirely made for us. We no more "lead" our own lives than we invent our own legs.

When I first read his book I was satisfied as by no other philosophy. I knew that everything of importance that had happened to me, every exhilarating discovery, every important journey I'd taken, had come to me, not me to it.

Only the great Arnold J. Toynbee put this same notion forward in terms of History. He said that no history could happen unless you enquired first what civilization you were talking about, and what religion you were talking about. These and not so-called "facts" were history's only real subject. He showed how the human mind inherited ideas so habitual generation by generation that they became automatic, and these were passed on from parent to child as "feelings", automatic ones. It is here (life can be very tricky this way) that philosophy pops up. For philosophy is also an examination of feeling.

So it was that more and more I ceased trying to consciously direct my life. I let myself be led. After I came down from Oxford I was invited to become a lecturer in English literature at Baghdad University and within days of the invitation I flew to Baghdad. From there I went to live in Rome and wrote more books, many on Italy. I started writing about famous figures like Leonardo da Vinci and Lorenzo the Magnificent. My work was serving, I suppose, a secret quest—to examine again and again what it is to be human.

Out of the blue, a family friend suggested I go and see an Indian guru who taught Hatha Yoga. For twelve years I practiced Yoga and daily pranayama, that is Hatha breathing, as he taught it. Everything to do with breathing fascinated me as I began to realize that it is the principal key to human life. From this came my breathing system which I called Oxygenesis. My technique was designed to stimulate the inborn intelligence-systems that lie waiting in our bodies to be used. I practiced it in Europe and then in California, where I intended to stay three months and remained for the best part of ten years.

Everything came to me in this way, already charted out for me. It was in San Rafael, Ca. that I was privileged to meet a great celebrity—Koko the lowland gorilla, who communicated in the American Sign Language with Dr Penny Patterson as her guide, philosopher and friend. The day was exquisitely warm, with golden light pouring down on the tall trees. Koko had a spacious beautifully turfed outdoor cage and a cozy, reclusive indoor one.

I went straight to her and "exchanged" the breath with her. She wanted to be free to be closer to me and rattled the bars of her cage, glancing at Penny with her silent language "Why do we have to be separated by all this?"

When I bent down to her it was I who felt the poor devil, while she was whole and herself. Yet she was in the cage.

Thus were sown the seeds of this book, which I began in 1985 and ended but recently.

Maurice Rowdon

ONE

The Monkey Wars

Back in 1932 the anatomist Solly Zuckerman published a book about animal behavior called *The Social Life of Monkeys and Apes*. Already by that year it was popular knowledge that Sigmund Freud regarded the sex instinct as a key to human behavior. His terms "repression" and "inhibition" and "inferiority complex" were beginning to figure in common speech, often as personal insults.

Solly Zuckerman's book emphasized two points—that monkeys and apes were motivated first and foremost by sex and secondly that they had no capacity for social responses such as humans had.

His reason for saying this was a sexual brawl at the monkey house in the London zoo, which he witnessed. In fact this brawl turned into something of a massacre of the kind humans are good at. All trace of hierarchy in the group, all domination by males, collapsed. Disemboweling, sexual mutilation—the things we humans are used to hearing about in a human context—happened within the monkey enclosure.

The title of the book was thus a bit odd—it was about the social life of monkeys but clearly this lot didn't have any.

I remember first reading Zuckerman's book in my early teens and seeing his monkeys exactly as he did. That is, my thoughts were divided into two watertight areas, the one occupied by humans such

1

as myself and my family, the other occupied by a group of monkeys who for no reason other than that they were monkeys assaulted each other in a—well—bestial manner. As for human wars, that was a complicated subject no human, let alone a dirty little monkey (words my mother used playfully to me when I was small), could resolve.

Also human wars were conducted *in an organized way*. You couldn't imagine monkeys having strategic plans and putting these plans into practice from an army headquarters linked by radio to the front line.

The differences between humans and monkeys were too obvious, starting from the monkey's unfortunate jaw line to his splaying feet and, well, sometimes, if you waited long enough at the Monkey House he would masturbate right in front of you.

I put these thoughts down because, far from disappearing from the human mind with the onset of the first chin stubble or menstruation, they in fact supply the quite unconscious background of *most of what we think.*

The interest aroused by Zuckerman's book thus rested on two quite opposite appeals—first the shocking one that we were no better than monkeys, since we too had sex and sometimes got rough about it. And secondly the comforting one that we were decidedly better then monkeys because we could rise above our sex instinct ("sublimation" was another Freudian word coming in at the time) and turn sexual energy to powerful account, especially in the matter of creating society, with its institutions that outlasted us—a convoluted idea, even if it had any meaning at all.

Five years before he published his book Zuckerman was appointed research assistant at the London zoo. His chosen subject was the nature of the menstrual cycle and its effect on animal behavior. It was this that took him to observe the sexual life of a group of hamadryas (baboons) in one of the zoo enclosures. He kept a detailed account of the primate war conducted within that enclosure between 1927 and 1928.

Now back in 1925 the zoo authorities had placed one hundred baboons into an oval rock-work enclosure one hundred feet by sixty feet, so that each baboon had, so to speak, a place for himself or herself of solely one foot by six inches. There were artificially heated cave shelters for sleeping. All but six of these baboons were male, meaning that the male population outnumbered the female by no fewer than sixteen times.

Between June and December 1925 there were twenty-seven deaths, but only one of these was directly caused by fighting, there being many diseases a zoo monkey (like a human) may die from— pleurisy, emphesema, enteritis, peritonitis, pancreatitis, nephritis, septicemia, pneumonia, pulmonary abscess, pericarditis.

In 1926 two males and one female were killed by other monkeys. By July 1927 the population that remained numbered only fifty-seven. This was a remarkably high mortality rate but no one considered that this might be due to captivity, namely the forced erosion of faculties designed for an altogether different habitat. Clearly, if there are only iron bars and cement structures to respond to you have a perfect setting for the kind of alienation the human is prone to when in solitary confinement in a prison. The distress eats deep into the auto-immune system. Virtually a new creature (remarkably like the distressed human creature) develops. But for Zuckerman there was no difference between a "wild" animal and a zoo one.

Suddenly a large new batch of females was introduced. By the following year, due to fighting, the population was down to fifty-one males and fifteen females, and by the end of that year nine more males and four more females were dead.

In January 1930 the population was thirty males and nine females, and of these three males and four females died after fighting. So there were twenty-seven males and five females, out of an original population of one hundred.

"The fight in which the last of these females lost her life," says Zuckerman, "was so protracted and repellent...that the decision was made to remove the five surviving females."

Of the dead females from the new batch thirty had been killed in fights and showed extensive lacerations in the genital and anal areas. The injuries sometimes appeared too slight to cause death and may have come from exhaustion, since fights often went on for several days.

Had Zuckerman visited the front-line trenches of the Western Front but fifteen years before he could have witnessed similarly repellent holes and lacerations in human bodies machine-gunned, shelled, blast-shaken and shrapnel-fragmented repeatedly even after death. He would have heard such screams as to make him think that monkey behavior was more, not less controlled, than the human.

On the contrary, even a second world war not twenty years after this first one failed to sober him up. In fact he became scientific advisor to the British government in 1939 and, later, quite an expert on portable lethal weapons, nuclear this time.

Thankfully the monkeys didn't have the wherewithal to blow up the entire London zoo—and London with it.

* * *

Zuckerman's monkey book was presented as scientific material and accepted and praised as such not only at the time of its publication but for decades afterwards. Yet his observations cover a minute part of what was actually observable in those primate wars, despite the fact that they took place not in the wild but inside a zoo enclosure, under his very nose.

No one at the zoo, least of all he, seemed interested in *why* the monkey wars were taking place, *why* they should involve sex and usually only sex. The possibility that the males wanted sex was obvious. But still sex wasn't the most important factor. Careful observation— and a proper study of other people's fieldwork—would have shown Zuckerman that the real explanation lay in the fact that the baboons were already deeply disturbed by their alienation from their rightful habitat. Stripped of this they had to construct something essentially fragile, exactly as humans were once obliged to do in *their* lack of an original habitat, where the fruits of the trees and the roots of the earth were unavailable to them. And in fact those monkeys showed social powers at least equal to those of humans, who conducted war on their own species at the drop of a hat.

At that time, in the 1930s, human prisons were sexually segregated, and there were no examples ready to hand of social collapses similar to those among the baboons. That has changed now. In June, 1989, for example, a batch of females was introduced to the detention facility at Clayton, Ca. A riot was the result. It only died down when the women had been removed to a remote building, and contact between the sexes was once more regulated.

As to the mutilation of the female monkeys it looked very much like a version of human dementia or "walking" psychosis, and with identical causes. A zoo means the absence of the right inherited habitat but this doesn't mean that a zoo animal fails to respond to the new environment. He will respond intensely or otherwise according to the degree of closeness to the old habitat which the new one attains. The same happens among humans. Put them among strangers speaking a foreign language, or in a new landscape previously unpopulated, and their responses will be low *in intensity*. In turn this is likely to provoke touchy nervous reactions, and sometimes blind outbursts and murderous behavior. The more distant the outside world is from an animal's proper habitat the more he or she it will react spitefully. But when it can easily evoke responses in fellow animals, and can expect and enjoy those responses, all will be well.

In other words those monkeys were going the human way but, being imprisoned, they had no power to effect even that small degree of social stability attained by humans.

For we too created a society by mental effort. We too, in the lack of our rightful, namely original or "fixed" habitat, could only govern ourselves with difficulty. This is why we need law enforcement, judicial systems, bills of rights which are written down or passed from generation to generation as a largely unwritten "constitution" (meaning simply "system"). They replace the old instinctive memory, when the habitat we found around us was what precisely fitted our nervous systems (including our digestive organs), and thus our ways of moving, eating, sleeping, drinking, we being provided with everything we biologically expect.

Society in the human sense is therefore *an emergency measure*. But for Zuckerman it showed that humans had "gone beyond" biology, were no longer animals, had superseded an old and unwanted state. A vast abyss separated animals from humans. He called this abyss "culture", meaning not art or learning simply but civilization. He saw human society as a deliberate rejection of animal life, rather as a schoolboy might say to himself, "I'm going to give up disgusting habits".

Yet he saw the monkey wars as he would have seen a similar fight among humans, as a senseless and criminal brawl resulting from "blind" sexual lust. So he looked with Homo Sapiens distaste at both animals and men when they behaved in a certain way. But he didn't ask himself *why* he felt the distaste. Had he done so he might have discovered that losing a habitat involves a certain recoil from the earlier "animal" state (in the case of monkeys the earlier pre-zoo state), and with this recoil comes disgust. His very use of the words "blind" and "automatic" and "conditioned", to indicate a lower or unwanted or disgusting status, shows how strong this recoil from the "wild" life of the past is, even after countless generations, even millions of years. The habitat, after all, doesn't walk away, so it presents a problem to the fugitive and always will.

Zuckerman seemed to see other animals as repulsive and degraded versions of men, who for this reason had boldly rejected biology for their own "evolution".

Of course, this is theology, not science at all. There is nothing wrong with theology. But if the theology is wrong?

* * *

Three years before his book came out C.R.Carpenter of John Hopkins University published a paper on the social life of howling monkeys which flat contradicted Zuckerman's findings. All a layman could do was compare the fieldwork of the two men and decide who was to be trusted. This is precisely what the playwright Robert Ardrey did in his book *African Genesis*, which was published in the 1960s.

First he pointed out that the magazine *The Scientific American* in its September 1960 number was still quoting Zuckerman as the last word on animal behavior, while no homage was paid to the African fieldwork that had been done no fewer than thirty years before Zuckerman's book appeared.

He implied that Zuckerman was unaware of this fieldwork—even that he discounted fieldwork altogether. In fact Zuckerman was as widely read in zoological and anatomical papers as any man alive. His view was simply that anatomically the animal you observe in a zoo is the same one you observe in the wild. He missed out altogether any changes in the mind and therefore the nervous system that happened in zoo conditions because these didn't come into anatomy.

Where he did differ from the fieldworker was in theological doctrine, not ability. His phrase "blind and automatic response" is loaded with disapproval. When a baboon answers another's call of alarm Zuckerman hears it as a simple reaction "to a stimulus", something very different from a responsible human reaction to a cry for help. Carpenter had no such theological hang-ups, if only because he observed animals in the wild. Which is to say that *his* theological doctrine (for we must all have one, as I shall show) didn't get in the way of his studies.

Baboons, Zuckerman said, would sometimes try to mate with a corpse. Again, this was "blind" response, indicating "ignorance of death". How he would place human necrophiliacs is a puzzle, because what necrophiliacs do is based squarely on awareness, not at all on ignorance, of the fact of death.

He saw all primate behavior as different from human in that there was little or no conscious choice behind it. All human behavior, he felt, springs from the unique circumstances of society, while animal behavior springs from, again, blind and automatic response. But he didn't explain to what extent human society creates similar blind responses, and whether what he saw as a blind response was in fact one. Free choice isn't visible in behavior seen from outside. He would have said that other animals don't think: they think now and then, within a particular context, but not in the human sense. This is true, but Zuckerman's words are just status talk, or what is called in logic an *argumentum ad hominem*—an appeal to your audience's emotions, not their reason.

He even denied a fellow-anatomist's suggestion that a baboon-mother who clings to a stillborn offspring until she decomposes, trying to lick it back to life, is expressing the maternal instinct. For Zuckerman the maternal instinct was a conscious human state of responsibility toward the young of which the baboon was incapable. The field of blind and automatic *human* response, which is thankfully vast (since neither society nor any transaction within it could take place without it) he disregarded altogether. Had he given it his attention he might have found that the human must construct blind response in himself *in order to learn anything at all*, so that his recall (of, say, a date in history) is as automatic as the raising of a cup to his lips. The zoo animal has to do precisely the same, but you can't see it from the way he scratches himself, any more than you can see Homo Sapiens from the way he scratches himself.

Describing a particular ape-mother in the zoo enclosure he said she didn't play with her baby and hardly ever held it, so that it had to cling to her fur. Sometimes she clasped the baby with one arm and hopped along on the other three. He put quotes round both "arm" and "leg" to make sure that these familiar human terms were being applied to the ape only by analogy. Since he knew nothing about the ape-mother's inherited methods of child-rearing, and seemed to care less, he implied there were none. That is, he assumed that the baboon had reached human levels of reflex-depletion—without tumbling to the common cause.

Again he was comparing monkeys to degenerated humans, and dismissing both. He was seeing humans minus laws and conscience—and calling them monkeys. He was recognizing dementia in the monkey enclosure but judged it to be a normal state of animality, thus getting within an ace of the truth about humans but theologically disallowing it.

Zuckerman was blinded by his own acute understanding. He knew, as no one else in his field did, that it was civilization and civilization alone that differentiates humans from animals, but he couldn't help attributing this to animal helplessness—precisely because it in fact indicated human helplessness!

Yet he was careful to avoid the word "civilization" because of its grandiose connotations. This was why he preferred the more detached "culture", which allowed him not to see that civilization was the product of religion, being its realization in daily community forms.

So his use of the word "culture" brought him no detachment from his own automated value-responses, which are as much part of human inheritance as grass-grinding teeth are in horses. His anatomical findings merely rationalized his disapproval. They had as little to do with "objective" or "scientific" knowledge as a baboon's salivations over a nut.

He saw that the human had turned his back on his animal past—that this was what defined a human—but he regarded it as a free choice like the schoolboy's wish to "do better".

* * *

Not that any scientist of his time, in his field or outside it, came forward to expose the theological overtones of his work. Nor would they today, for the very simple reason that the same theology is to be found in all the disciplines, disguised, sometimes enticingly and sometimes with crude whitewash strokes, but always there. Nor did Zuckerman deny intelligence to animals any more than any other scientist would. He also agreed that man enjoys "physical and mental kinship with other living organisms". He was aware that the primate frequently shows ingenuity comparable to that of humans. But nothing in the primate, he claimed, comes near to the intelligence that has created law, cities and constitutions.

The zebra could equally say that the human has never come near to anything like his stripes, especially as, for this very swift creature, these offer easy identification if you stray from the herd.

"Blindness in social relations" is a feature, Zuckerman says, of all monkey life. He finds baboons to be cowards. A threatening look or gesture from one male baboon sends other males scampering away.

9

His inference? That social response in the human puts him above his own immediate interests and is more likely to lead to courage. It is free choice again. But today, nearly a century after his work at the zoo, it isn't at once obvious that humans ever fly in the face of their own interests or rise above a state of fear and inner trembling if threatened by a superior, or omit to wheedle and even—let us say be bold and animalistic—to ass-crawl menially should that secure them an advantage. The "you're alone and you make your own world" that has superseded the world he lived in has made sure that this is so. Like the zoo baboons we are in a free-for-all now.

In a paper of 1937 he wrote, "It is perhaps in their demonstration of the ways in which human social behavior has renounced its biological background that studies of Old World apes and monkeys have greatest significance.'

Of course no one can "renounce" his biological past any more than he can decide not to defecate. Without reflexes, without automatic responses, he is lost, a forlorn and sickly creature whose immune systems have broken down.

What Zuckerman is really suggesting, not with his ideas so much as his whole approach to animals, is that the ability of humans to distance themselves from the habitat gives them the power to tell the truth about it, whereas other animals have no such power. We shall find that this theology, which was stated in its earliest written form in Greece two and a half millennia ago and given a resounding confirmation by Descartes more recently, features in all human minds, especially scientific ones.

Of course human "detachment" doesn't endow truth or light or anything of the kind. It yields knowledge, especially about how to navigate our way through strange habitats. But this isn't a definition of truth any more than a leopard's ability to outrun a roe deer is the truth. What we mean by this grandiose term is simply the knowledge we need for survival.

This Homo Sapiens publicity causes Zuckerman, and most other scientists (in fact he did it much less than most), to write papers in a special "I am not here" argot, bleakly shy on personal pronouns and rich in passive verbs. It helps one to convey the pathetic idea that at least *this* human has managed to supersede his biological past.

He calls man "monogamous" and "omnivorous". Well, monogamy might have held up, though only just, in the 1930s, but today it has an anthropological ring. "Omnivorous" means he can eat meat or be vegetarian, but, historically, it was only the self-styled aristocracy who were gluttonous meat eaters. The ancient Roman army survived, as we now know, on the Saracen corn we today call buckwheat. Until well into the twentieth century farming peoples in Austria and Prussia ate chicken or rabbit only on public holidays, while grains and vegetables were their staple diet.

The human's eating orientation changed on the whole *as he changed habitats*, so that it varied according to area, and changed with time inside those areas. But we are led to believe by Zuckerman that ethics is at work even here—by leaving or losing his original habitat man somehow floats above all habitats and so achieves the power to observe and witness all dispassionately. But of course any knowledge that the human has picked up is *specific to himself*, precisely as a nightingale's song is specific to the nightingale and a fish's absorption of oxygen through gills is specific to fish. You would think this was too simple even to state but the vast bulk of mankind will have none of it. It refuses to see that each animal's knowledge (like Mozart's "Magic Flute" to the human, and hunting stealth to the fox, and song to the nightingale) is valid solely for that animal, his specific genetic orientation.

The human's activity is "culturally conditioned", says Zuckerman, while the monkey with its harem is "without any vestige of cultural processes". What about Arabs and the Mormons? Are they without those processes because of the presence of the harem and its Christian equivalent?

But he doesn't include religion in "culture". On the contrary, he says that science or reason has "cleared the gods out of the sky". All the odder, then, that this very statement is from an ancient Christian doctrine which squarely declares that reason alone sheds light while animals live in darkness. How is it possible for him to argue against religion while offering a purely religious idea as his support? But here again he is joined by countless other self-styled scientists.

It takes but little thought to see that we have developed our rational and imaginative powers in precisely the same way as the giraffe has developed its neck, and for the same reasons: nourishment, survival, enjoyment and that peculiar exhilaration that goes with all animal prowess.

Our thought and imagination, our civilization and therefore our religions, are *animal manifestations*. It is so hard for even unreligious peoples to stomach this one, so deeply are we conditioned the other way.

The giraffe too might be inclined to believe that other creatures unable to reach the topmost branches of a nourishing tree are lagging behind in free choice: they are, after all, unable to access the choicest food of all. And as far as necks are concerned he is quite right. But he would hardly be right to claim that this was because he had rejected his biological background for something "higher". Or that he is therefore above everybody else. Or that he alone can see the truth. Other animals may not want to reach his heights. Baboons, for example. Gibbons love to swing to the heights but on branches.

Actually, the giraffe would be making a more scientific claim than Zuckerman does, being, in observable physical fact, probably the tallest mammal.

But other animals are apparently too busy to consider themselves wiser than other species, much less to adopt a moniker like Homo Sapiens.

If we self-glorifying humans were giraffes we would presumably designate our neck-development as The Ascent of the Giraffe, on the lines of a BBC television series in the 1950s called The Ascent of Man, which, still in the conquering spirit of World War Two, described animals as "a mere mark on the landscape".

TWO

Who Exactly Does Homo Think He Is?

How did Homo Sapiens get his name? In the mind of a Swedish botanist, Linné Linnaeus, otherwise known as Karl von Linné, who lived during one of Europe's many self-appointed ages of "enlightenment"—the eighteenth century—when Puritan scenarios were hatching the numberless revolutions of the nineteenth century, which in turn hatched the two massive "world" wars of the twentieth.

Linné listed plants and animals as genus and species. "Extinct" species of genus Homo were Homo Habilis and Homo Erectus, fictive predecessors of fictive Sapiens, the Wise or Modern One. How Homo could have been Homo without the mind of Homo, whatever his physical condition, Erectus or on all fours, was never explained because "mind" or "intellect" didn't come into the scientific disciplines as a determinant of what a species is—only teeth, bones and cranial measurements.

What modern Homo Sapiens was looking for in his search for himself was the fictive image he had of himself which Homo Habilis ("skilful") and Homo Erectus ("upright"), because of some trifling discrepancy of appearance, didn't fit.

This false persona, this self-chosen schizophrene, this floating absurdity that called itself rational and in perfect control of itself, considered that the White Man of Europe was what he was really looking for in bone-history, Homo Sapiens being entirely his invention anyway. So anyone whose brow stuck out too far or whose eyes were too close or who showed too much tooth or too snub (or squashed) a nose was disqualified.

Homo Sapiens has a long etymology dating back to ancient Greece. Here we are indebted to Aristotle. His word *eudaemonia* refers to a state of radiant satisfaction with life in which a human may be said to fit his own soul perfectly, such happiness being only possible in maturity or old age.

Just as then, so now—we feel we came on earth to do certain things, we have what we call goals, we strive through youth and middle age to realize these. But ours is a lay world, with religion pushed into the quaint area of "belief". Not so for the Greeks—they lived religion to the extent of not having a word for religion. It was simply all of life. So Aristotle, and for that matter any Greek, would simply not be able to conceive a state we now call "atheism".

The Greek world throbbed with God. Yet, and this was the most unexpected "yet" in the ancient Greek mind, *animals were a dark presence within this most radiant Homo Sapiens*. Yes, we must face the fact that Aristotle had more influence on our minds than any thinker before or after him. And he was certainly the first to give this Wise Man a name (for the moniker "Homo Sapiens" has certainly stuck*)*.

As to the word "philosophy" itself, it means simply "the love of wisdom", so by using it at all you are imputing to humans a particular kind of Homo whose existence has never been proved, just as the supposed un-wisdom of other animals has never been proved. Indeed other animals have shown, consistently, a much greater wisdom than humans have, which is revealed in the fact that they leave their habitats enhanced, not degraded.

Like all philosophers Aristotle stated what he thought, how he felt. But he never answered certain essential questions, such as how did animals, whom he considered to be, next to the human, so much trash, know how to leave their environments enhanced. For instance, simply the presence of horses in a waste, virtually dead area of country, will simply with their manure bring back the fauna and flora they are used to). Yet for our ancient Philosopher they were the nearest to (to put it in later Christian terms) Devils Incarnate, yet dreadfully and woefully alive and well in this radiant philosopher's body. Of course the damnable spot had to be suppressed at all costs and with untiring vigilance!

Scholars up to about 1860 were quite happy to say, with Aristotle, that the blueprint of perfection behind this upright primate Homo, with his small teeth and two legs instead of four, was a divine one. Few wondered why God should, first, have hoisted this creature up onto two long legs and, second, what divine significance lay in two long legs as opposed to four short ones. Even fewer wondered how it was that this lover of wisdom had lost all his fur, except for lank imitations on his head and round his chin, under his armpits and as a crown for his or her genitals.

It did seem (if insanely) clear, though, that the upright position demonstrated "release" from animal bondage to the earth. The human was unable to lick the earth with ease, or rub his nose in it, and certainly he refused to repeat this filthy deed by applying nose and sometimes tongue to, of all things, a fellow anus, even a lady's.

Yet Aristotle knew, as a matter of physical fact, what being initiated at a Greek temple meant in terms of "terror and pity". And he of course knew why in the ancient Greek theatres of his time (like the open theatre of Epidauros) this same terror and pity was enacted in its tragedies.

In my twenties I used to spend hours at that open-air theatre, looking from its highest stone seats across at the hills of Arakhnaion on the other side of the valley, with —on my immediate left— the forest dedicated since ancient times to Hippocrates, the god of medicine, its trees soughing and sighing like the ancient world returned.

I could measure the wisdom that Aristotle supposed to exist in the human as opposed to the animal, for I was living after not one but two world wars—with how many millions of humans dead?!

And we should remember that the ancient Greeks believed in war, and pursued wars with enthusiasm, on the grounds that wars were a legitimate way of "getting what you don't have and what someone else does have".

And then there is the fact that slaves numbered nearly half the ancient Greek population, as we know from the slave who rebelled, Spartacus, and who cried out "We are fifty thousand swords against fifty thousand swords!"

Now we modern "anthropologists" and "paleontologists" won't have anything to do with a God-designed human. Man is remarkable in his own right! And his remarkable personality testifies to the painstaking efforts over many millennia. Homo was patented in the Halls of Reason and the idea that Homo should need outside or divine assistance is preposterous. Man is simply, demonstrably, the best animal. He lost his strong teeth and his fur because of his general ability to cope with new situations. He extended the muscles of his body not with muscular effort but by replicating them in extended tools which worked first by fire, then by pulleys and cogs and the use of other animals, and later electricity.

But how do you substantiate all this by poring over bones? You can hardly ask them "Was it your intention to become a real Man?" Nevertheless bone-study has thrown up Homo Anthropologicus and Homo Paleontologicus as evidence of an early appearance of Homo Sapiens.

While a statement like "condensation takes place as a result of two temperatures" would never be thought self-glorifying in tone, the statement "a highly developed primate fossil" is really saying "You notice how inch by inch he grows into me?", which is breast-beating, not enquiry.

Solly Zuckerman would have none of it. He knew that the craze for tracing past Ape Men came from the eighteenth-century view of African tribes as a pre-historic yet still extant version of ourselves. That is, we were looking at live people who were a throwback to the first humans—enough to send shivers down any Homo Sapiens's sensitive spine.

Which reminds me of a book written in the 1930s by the artist Richard Wyndham called *The Gentle Savage*, in which he described the African tribe he'd just been living with for several months as far less predatory than his Chelsea friends.

THREE

From Sapiens To Saphead

The human has always congratulated himself on his own existence, always set himself aside from other creatures. And he has always improvised his way of life.

That is, he never belonged to a fixed or original habitat like other animals, i.e. to a habitat requiring no adaptation or improvisation on his part whatever, no thought, no planning, no aspiring. In fact he had to do all of these for the good and simple reason that he had lost his home, irrevocably.

He was all too terribly footloose and free.

And in this parlous state he must surely have noticed that other animals toiled not, neither did they spin, whereas *he* was cut off from this ease as surely as Adam and Eve were cut off from their own Garden of Eden. In fact, that is how the Eden stories came about (they being manifold, in many different versions worldwide): they all declare that his hard work, his thinking and his untold devising resulted from his having eaten of the apple (some say orange) of knowledge.

By the same token this apple or orange saved him. He went through a long process of adaptations and those more radical changes in his body that we call "mutations", namely daily adaptations which have become so familiar that they have passed into *automatic behavior* (we shall see later on how important automatic behavior is for human as for all animal performance).

Little wonder that he began to feel there was something very special about himself. And this perfectly valid feeling was only a stone's throw from believing, because of the sheer unsparing effort and ardor of his life, that he was the wisest creature there had ever been—even in the whole universe.

This is just how an Ape of Sorrows *must* think, for dear life.

* * *

Let us look at the men and women in the 1930s who were still claiming Homo to be Sapiens. What was their *actual* degree of wisdom, as displayed in their lives? Well, they had just finished the worst World War in history and were heading for another, much huger one. And they walked into both with entirely blind eyes, no more expecting them than they expected the end of the earth.

Certain people like George Bernard Shaw considered that the first one never really ended, that the 1920s and 1930s were but a ceasefire. And there were plenty of others in left-wing movements who not only knew a second one was coming up but demonstrated in the streets to get it started, their banner being The Struggle Against Fascism.

The "scientific" claim was that Man, not a few men, was Wise but how was it that the second war happened at a time when nobody wanted it, neither the Germans nor the British and French, whether they believed in one or not. How's that for free choice?

They had had enough of the frightfulness of war and knew that it only pulled the warring nations down and made the other non-combatant ones rich.

Now that is a very peculiar situation for wise people to find themselves in—namely that they walked back into the hell they had just come from, and on the same false grounds that the world would emerge from hell a better place. They went in for the usual ultimatums and solemn declarations of war as if they were in command of themselves and the situation. But they weren't, as the subsequent prolonged carnage always confirmed.

You would have to look hard in the animal world to find a parallel. Yet the idea behind this Sapiens business was to show that man was a master, the opposite of helpless, and that it was the animals who were the helpless victims of their own blind impulses and their acceptance of misfortune and disease without resistance.

This was why the Sapiens idea was being attacked in the Thirties as fast as it was being propagated. But attacks made no difference to it. Nor could they have done because Homo Sapiens was too deeply lodged in the Western mind, even in minds that consciously opposed it.

There was hardly a soul who didn't agree that man was the highest animal because the most intelligent, and that other animals were for his good rather than their own. When told that we resemble animals people were willing enough to agree. But this apparently new idea simply presented the old one in a new uniform. It said yes, we also are animals, namely savage and unreasonable, from time to time. Thus Homo was still Sapiens but he had this unconscious animal or libido to contend with.

Only today are we ready to suspect that this is a fraud. Having our backs to the wall we don't feel wise one little bit, so that we can acknowledge at last a certain wisdom in animals—if only because they don't go on murder sprees, or rampages dressed up as legitimate war, or institute frightful pogroms which we call "holocausts". Nonetheless we can't get rid of the idea that we act by free choice and that animals don't. This is because our lives (systems) are based on thought. What we overlook is that *our thinking is automatic* like that of all animals because it has to be—we would otherwise have to decide consciously to switch on the light every time we did so. Our automatic actions are necessarily the most of all our actions.

Our difficulty here lies in a certain fear that automation somehow invalidates thought. This fear is biological in origin, since deliberate thought was what won us all we have, or so we believe. Naturally we cling to our source of survival without examining how far, like all animals, we need automation and in fact base our lives on it like all other breathing forms.

Automation is the opposite of freedom for us but in fact it achieves freedom. We acknowledge that the freedom of a bird winging down over a vast valley is a pre-conditioned one. Yet the bird enjoys it as freedom. In everything we enjoy there is automated action, from swimming to making or listening to music or conversation while driving the car, such that at the end of our journey, especially if it is a daily one, we remember only the radio or the spouse's talk. Our driving was work—beware, Homo!—entirely automated.

Because of our biological background we are obsessed by the idea of our independence of mind and supposed high degree of consciousness but this idea withers under the smallest scrutiny.

The attacks on Rational Man in the Thirties never got home because they couldn't break this reluctance to see ourselves as automated. In fact they bolstered it further. Even Wilhelm Reich, who ridiculed Rational Man better than anyone else, never tackled the inherited thought-reflex which said that man's "dark" or "animal" side undermined him. On the contrary, he took that supposed "libido" as his pretext for exposing reason as a mere cover for it. After attributing "darkness" to animals we were meant to sublimate it out of ourselves or repress it or express it, without even a questioning glance at the starting premise. Which left reason where it had been at the start—a savior.

When Freud put forward the theory, by no means original, that the sexual motive was a dominant one in the human psyche it led almost no one to look into the nature of human reason itself. It *did* lead us to apply the theory to animals! So with perfect seriousness Solly Zuckerman could suggest that monkeys were motivated by sex while humans were motivated by culture, thus agreeing with Freud and rejecting him in the same breath.

His approach had nothing to do with "detached" thinking at all. It was simply the repetition of an inherited thought-reflex about animals as demons, just as the growing attack today on Freud's sexual themes is due not at all to thought but to the erosion of the sexual faculty, which of course does reduce the impact of "sublimation" and Freudian theory in general.

* * *

You might accept that humans could go through *one* shattering war and convince themselves that it was a temporary aberration from the norm (though four years of carnage is an awful lot even for human aberration). But to go through a *second* one provoked by a demented Nazi pogrom-based regime, namely a rehash of Homo Sapiens as the Nordic Soul, and for *another* four years of mass murder, well, it surely argued that something was seriously wrong somewhere.

Not only were those four years not examined for traces of dementia but at the end of it all Rational Man began assuring everybody that he was the author of the greatest civilization there had ever been—yes, the years from 1945 until almost 1985 resounded with such assurances! And, as if the millions of dead weren't enough, he went on not only to produce atomic weapons but, of all pitiable idiocies, to actually drop them on cities.

And *still* he retained an eighteenth-century picture of human life! What can we say of the Wisdom here?

We must never forget that Rational Man is required to be hyper-rational in his conduct of war, as he never is in peace. For one thing you can do a civilization-must-be-saved hype during a war: and war provides law and order at home such as never was in peacetime. Then, after the "peace" (what peace?) the mess of war is cleared up and the law-and-order make-believe resumed without a blush.

But now that law and order aren't a foregone conclusion anywhere we are more inclined to review our self portrait.

Our confidence in human wisdom capsizes under the weight of worldwide inflictions of every kind of human cruelty on whatever breathes.

We are even ready to consider the idea that our grandiose view of ourselves was just that—grandiosity, a simple feature of dementia. So it is that unfortunate people stare at the walls of mental institutions and see before them crowds of admiring ancient Romans and themselves as Caesar.

Our very independence—man's evolutionary trademark—exposed us to this. Too much independence of the habitat means ceasing to function therein, and this is a definition of madness.

The madman is free as no one else is. His connections have gone.

Solly Zuckerman wanted to show how dependent animals were, compared with humans. He quoted the case of the Californian sea lion. Its breeding season lasts from June 15 for a month. In late May the cows band together and early in June the adult bulls arrive, singly or in groups. As soon as the females have been served the bulls depart. The month-old society disperses. Once the sexual motive has been exhausted the crowd breaks up. This Zuckerman took to be the essential nature of all animal society, whether that society lasts a month or a lifetime. He regarded all animal associations without exception as a "reproductive organization". By contrast, the human with his culture could rise above the sex instinct, marshal and use it, so that a permanent and stable society could result.

Given present-day society this might look like black humor but it remains the basis of accepted scientific thinking on the subject. In anthropology and paleontology it shows up as the evolutionary idea. This says that man at some point in his biological history started becoming—even *tried* to become—human. He took a different turning from other animals. He became physically different. His standing upright was like a demonstration of his refusal to cower any longer under blind impulses. It was like someone saying "To hell with the old life, all that scratching and public sex and defecation!"

Instead of saying that the human is simply one type of primate differing from others only as the lemur differs from the gibbon, or the chimpanzee from the gorilla—and this would be the "scientific" analysis—the argument says that human *will* was involved. In a word, the human knew what he wanted to *become*.

This is why anthropologists and paleontologists are always on the look-out for primates who resemble us in cranial measurements, gait, posture, arm-length and tooth-size. The idea is to show just how this new animal Man was the result of a certain design which was gradually, remorselessly realized.

Earlier generations (up to about 1860) said that this design was divine. But as I said before, we speculative anthropologists and paleontologists, however, won't have anything to do with that: man is remarkable in his own right and the design is his alone, He patented it not in heaven but the Halls of Reason. That is, we developed "out" of an animal state and therefore need to find traces in our past of when Homo began.

Well, it has been a wonderful great puzzle looking into the origins of this Homo Non Biologicus. How do you find him in any biological description of him? You would have to ask an early Homo "Is it your *intention* to become a man like me?" to get a proper answer. Intentions simply don't show up in external behavior, let alone in corpses, least of all in fossilized remains of said corpses. So what exactly are Homo Anthropologicus and Homo Paleontologicus looking for?

There is one thing people can agree about, however—that man existed in some form, even with a small cranial capacity of 500 or 800 c.c., millions of years ago. Even if we can't decide what a man is we at least know that. The idea, you see, is that cranial capacity gradually "developed" over the millennia, though what this word "developed" means no one seems anxious to explain. After all, anything from garbage to cloudbursts may be said to develop. But in the case of the human primate *a moral evaluation is at work.*

Man "evolved" (another word-mine full of the gold of wistful assumption) into a creature that left all others behind in a mist of grunting ignorance.

These are surely not notions you can trumpet about if you simultaneously claim that science is a set of pure analytical propositions joined together by impeccably logical bridges. This is breast-beating again, not scientific.

Still, as long as you never define your terms—"ignorance", "blindness", "automatic behavior" etc—you can get away with an awful lot. Your cool analyses, dressed up in the language of scientific propriety, without active clauses and containing as many compound words of classical root as possible, can at least *suggest* what they can't openly declare. While my statement "Condensation takes place as a result of two temperatures" could never be thought an ethical judgment, an ethical *overtone* is always possible. So a reference to a "highly developed" primate-fossil could *seem* to be talking about cranial measurements, arm-length, molars etc (of no more significance than the bone you throw your dog) when it *actually* is about an ethical event. Translated into anthropological jingo-ese ("I don't want to fight but by jingo if I do!") the inference says "You see how inch by inch his molars etc grow into one of ours!"

Happily for Zuckerman, he scorned this kind of thing. He knew that the craze for finding anthropological ancestors or Ape Men came from the romantic interest in "primitive" or African tribes that started in the early nineteenth century. The paltry idea behind *that* said: if "primitive" peoples in Africa, Siberia or Australia look like earlier humans from whom we evolved, might it not follow that before them even more "primitive" forms existed, namely early apes from whom those "primitive" peoples, in turn, evolved?

Here self-congratulation achieves a sort of glow of ineffable idiocy. The word "primitive" means what it says—"prime" or "early". No more, no less. But its connotations today bestride our minds with received, conditioned and engagingly batty suggestions of moral turpitude and degeneracy. The "primitive" peoples are to us what early apes surely were to them, namely "behind". No wonder we clever fellows find cranial similarities between living bushmen and age-old fossil skulls. Nowadays, however, with the bushmen going to schools and watching television and lobbying their politicians you have to be careful how you present this.

The doctrine of progress, which also became fashionable as the disastrous nineteenth century thundered on, was a useful support for this biological revisionism. Coming as it did from the evangelical idea that life was a struggle from darkness to light, from evil to grace, it provided an easy framework for any number of highly evolved fairy tales. Just as history books are often a romance ("Athens was a blaze of light after the superstition and darkness of priest-ridden Egypt", "The Renaissance was a blaze of light after the superstition and darkness of the priest-ridden Middle Ages"), so anthropological, anatomical and biological studies became a lively source of illustration for the romance of Homo Sapiens.

Thus it is that the theory of evolution came to be propounded by men of highly evangelical temper first in France and then in England. It was this theory indeed that first created the interest in "primitive" peoples. The idea of one biological form being an early or simple version of a later complicated one which "evolved" out of it was a statement of evangelical values as neat as a nut. Applied to anthropology, it said that man had developed over aeons of time into his modern form, just as amphibians had developed out of fish, mammals out of reptiles.

We *all* seemed to be wanting to get somewhere, though only man really did get there.

Inevitably some people started asking when exactly man had begun his specific progress, distinct from other forms of animal life and his own "primitive" forms (perhaps in a cave—why not?). R. Briffault, of whose work Zuckerman approved, tried to describe how it happened. In almost incomprehensible scientific patois he wrote, "Language and conceptual thought, and the consequent introduction of a separate hereditary transmission, distinct from the physiological, constituted unprecedented conditions of evolution."

Rendered into lowly anecdotal speech this means something quite extraordinarily banal—that because of his culture (based on his power to conceive) and because of his articulate thoughts (language) man inherits a world quite different from that of other animals: whereas the animal is heir only to a *physiological* legacy (appetites, responses, reflexes and grunts) the human can expect to open his or her eyes at birth onto a human non-physiological world of infinite variety (corn flakes, airport lounges, nude shows).

Physiologically this is a can of old beans. What would a non-physiological brain be like? The primate brain has all it needs within it to become a human brain, otherwise humans wouldn't have happened, would they? The cerebral cortex and reticular activating system and the pituitary and thyroid and hypothalamus glands, and the nervous system linked to the brain and deployed along the spinal column, are all there in a primate. If not, why do biologists break open thousands of monkey skulls in order to discover the secrets of the human medulla? Why do they find in the animal such good laboratory material for testing our tricyclic antidepressants, our narcotic analgesics, our stimulants and antipsychotics and sedatives, not to say our perfumes?

In the nineteenth century—the Age of Grandiosity—there was a great upsurge of human pride. It was also the century of competition for imperial possessions, underpinned by all sorts of new wonders in the form of industrial clothes, trains, steamships, radio telegraph and ultimately gas and electricity. In Victorian Britain even the poor classes, once they had learned that the Industrial Spirit required you to scramble for money at any cost to decency or rectitude (these had to be left to the comfortable classes), got pugnaciously triumphal about it. No matter how low you sank in poverty and sickness (brought on by the moral ones above you) it was impossible not to be caught up in the excitement. And the excitement was real—poor people rushed to get their copies of the "penny dreadful" and, for women, *Tit-Bits*. Like the later Christmas "annual" for tiny children, called Tiger Tim, bursting with every kind of game and story, it roped everyone into a kind of classless society, which of course remained safely in the imagination.

And as always where there is vociferous optimism there was quaking pessimism underneath, requiring truculent opposite statements by means of which to hide itself. So the evangelical spirit became the modern political spirit, which began to resound with military phrases like "the forward march of civilization" and "breaking down the barriers of ignorance" which are still good fall-back phrases for the politician without a policy.

No nineteenth-century politician could do without the doctrine of "progress" and "development", or avoid the theme of better times evolving out of bad ones, any more than an American president today can get to the White House without saying that America is the greatest nation on the earth.

Jingoism, though considered an English imperial emotion of the last years of the nineteenth century, was in fact common throughout

Europe and North America as an extension of the Homo Sapiens routine into "we are more Sapiens than any previous Homo". Every nation that went into World War One did so with hot thoughts of conquest. The Austrian cavalry rode into battle on the Russian front in full parade regalia. Few understood in 1914 that over fifty years of progressively intense machine production must altogether change the nature of war such that it became a highly progressive destruction of the habitat, enough to bring Homo Sapiens down, together with the whole of the insapient animal kingdom, if push came to shove.

In England the evangelical (alias Puritan) movement was especially strong in the new industrial areas. The idea that man had "conquered the earth" was already well established. Hard work, unsparing moral self-examination and meticulous attention to duty in all things, from family life to the keeping of accounts, were considered paving stones to grace and happiness. The poor were allowed to improve themselves through work, and their low wages reflected the extent to which they fell short, morally, of the better classes—who determined the nature of that work, its whereabouts and the appalling living conditions that went with it. Just as men were superior to animals, so the rich were superior to the poor.

As we all know, this little philosophy, far from disappearing from the earth in a cloud of sapient scorn, is only now reaching its apotheosis.

Towns like Stoke-on-Trent lived in a thick roseate smoke cloud which seeped into the country lanes and darkened the streams. The Methodist churches were buzzing centers of evening and Sabbath activity, their councils consisting of important local men who advanced themselves socially by shows (by no means hypocritical) of moral rectitude. New wealth, the increasing availability of useful commodities that came not from a village hand but a factory bench, and warmly lighted shops and noisy streets and the invigorating ring of "brass" on bank counters gave the human a new dignity of which the baboon would no more be capable than it could stop itself scratching.

Evangelical ideas prevailed so oppressively that you had to watch out if you offended them, as the exiles Lord Byron and Percy Bysshe Shelley had occasion to feel back in the early nineteenth century. Shelley was abandoned by his family and class, and treated as a devil worshipper, for something he wrote in his teens in a fiercely anticlerical mood. All his work was privately printed and distributed. Not a London publisher would touch it. The role of poetry was very different from what it is today. The ideas it projected had a potent influence that was sometimes fearful to the growing echelons of respectable middle-class families newly rich from the degradation of the farm laboring class to sweated factory or mining hands. The issue of a new poem from Lord Byron would fill his London publisher's street with carriages and throngs of people anxious to buy. *The Corsair* sold fourteen thousand copies the first day. Verse sent shivers of rare pleasure down young spines. It created fashions of behavior. But as a form it yielded badly to evangelical themes of high moral worth as a reward for propriety and graft, which belonged to doggerel. Shelley, Byron, Keats, Blake, Coleridge, de Quincey and Wordsworth were like men taking a last look at a habitat about to be jettisoned.

* * *

The quaint theory of evolution (which treated nature as a free ambulatory area for the human idealist) mounted in the late nineteenth century ever higher on evangelical wings.

It was first stated in a clear manner by Chevalier de Lamarck. In his *Recherches sur L'organisation des Corps* (1800) he declared that all species derived from one another and that simple forms in nature tended to give rise to complex ones, single-cell organisms to complicated mammals. He was much influenced here by the earlier work of Georges de Buffon, a Burgundian naturalist brought up (like himself) by the Jesuits, and whose *Histoires Naturelles* had given the world the first clear hint of the theological notion that natural life has a *progressive* history, each detail of which is linked with every other.

Darwin a century later was well aware of these books and in any case his grandfather had similar high-flying ideas. The *Origin of Species* in 1859 and *The Descent of Man* (meaning not the opposite of Ascent, which would have made good sense, but "origin") eleven years later gave a somewhat new picture of nature in that they suggested *a struggle* between and within species. It was this struggle that was supposed to determine the evolution. Hitler worked it up as the very key to his regime ("Der Kampf").

It was another version of the evangelical doctrine that nature requires working on with will and purpose if survival is to be assured. Nature for Darwin was harsh and implacable. He referred to "victorious" forms when he came across biological traits that had survived, and "beaten" forms when traits died out. Not that he stated the theory of the "survival of the fittest" as dramatically as other biologists made it seem—notably T.H. Huxley, his assistant, and Herbert Spencer. His theory simply referred to the tendency in animal groups for the healthier ones in those groups (as well as healthier groups as a whole) to mate with similarly healthy partners (or groups) and thereby produce healthy and ample progeny capable of ousting rivals or predators.

Such an idea was excellent material for the optimism of the time and when it combined with the idea of progress—i.e. social life develops from good to better, from simple to complex, by dint of a struggle (preferably undertaken by other people)—it began a journey far beyond its simple Darwinian beginnings. The popular version now said that because man had survived against the greatest odds and was capable of altering and adapting almost any habitat to his needs, he could indeed be said to have realized at last his great biological design.

The name for this design is today orthogenesis ("straight-from-the-beginning"), meaning that, irrespective of outside influences, an organism directs itself toward a specific end. There are disadvantages to this idea since it can be extended to almost any activity. The massive wars of this century can be seen as the climax of an orthogenetic development from bows and arrows. Pollution of the atmosphere can be seen as an orthogenetic development from the first wood-smoke. In this way evolution can be seen as leading to the survival of the worst, and to an Advance, Ascent or Race toward utter doom. Having removed the habitat from the evolutionary equation, and substituted for it human will and predilection, the theory depends entirely on what you consider good and what bad, and not on realities at all.

The idea of progress is so deeply embedded in our perceptions that it no longer requires expression and therefore doesn't expose itself to our ridicule. It is in all plans. In fact "future" and "progress" are almost synonymous when we are looking forward to a change in our lives. As a result we can hardly conceive what it was like for people not to live on an internalized conveyor belt.

Darwin described some of the animals he observed as "ugly" or "stupid" in appearance. Scientifically of course he had no grounds for saying this, "ugly" and "stupid" being anecdotal epithets. But the words passed unnoticed because his ideas served to reinforce the view that man, in his special evolution, had made a spectacular advance into *another world* from which he could judge all nature.

The same went on in geological studies. When Casimir Picard at the beginning of the nineteenth century found some chipped stones and flints many thousands of years old he assumed that they were the relics of early or primitive man and that this man—to judge by the skeletons of elephants and hippopotami nearby of the same era—was a hunter.

In 1866 Edouard Lartet mapped out the first "pre-history". Here it is: before modern man (whose history is but a few thousand years old) there was another world, a rather chilling world at times, sometimes under vast glaciers, sometimes haunted by monstrously huge animals.

We've all swallowed *that* one. There probably isn't a schoolchild in the West unaware of that prehistoric chill—the awful loneliness of a world without a single modern human in it, let alone Mars bars.

Lartet also took over from Bucher de Perthes his theory of "stone" and "bronze" ages (the one a "development" from the other). But he divided the Stone Age (now endowed with capital letters, as if to say that the stone users knew what era they were living in) into the Age of the Cave Bear, the Age of the Elephant and Rhinoceros, the Reindeer Age and the Age of the Aurochs or Bison.

In the last century Marcellin Boule refined these stone ages into the "old-stone age", rendered in Greek as *paleo* ("old"), *lithic* ("stone"), the middle or *mesolithic* age and the new or *neolithic* age (plentiful shots of Greek rum-and-ginger to rose-tint the banality). The last period, that of polished stone during which agriculture and thus the first possibility of a decent cup of coffee came about, was "new" because (guess?) human ingenuity had taken "a giant leap forward".

What an awful gap of time it must have been before *we* appeared, a disgracefully barren time-hole in which there was no design for the sole and simple reason that the two-legged designer wasn't yet around. But consolingly human names with consolingly Greek or Latin roots did the job and reduced the chill of it considerably, for those icy pre-historical periods were a *preparation*, more pertinently a *creation* for the ultimate end of the first human copulation. The so-called Cambrian (or "Welsh") age came into being, based on evidence of marine life six hundred million years ago, leading through other ages to the Pleistocene, a mere six hundred thousand years ago when despite glaciers covering much of Europe and North America, man (according to some at least) made his First Appearance rather like a juvenile lead in provincial stock. At last he had a credit! It is a simple division for simple minds and since it covers so many millions of years it satisfies the lunatic's itch for ever more grandiose programs. We now find it hard not to see the appearance of the first jawless fish and then the superseding of amphibians by the reptiles and then the appearance of "primitive" horses and then, thirty million years after that, manlike apes, as a frame by frame success script.

Yes, even six hundred million years ago the design was there from which finally man, helped by the thoughtful withdrawal of the glaciers to the poles, came. From the simple to the complex, indeed—what a stirring story! Never were so many violins brought out as for this evolutionary soap.

When so much speculation and theory, armed with so little evidence, becomes the basis of a "science" (the word, by the way, means simply "knowledge") and this science is socially condoned and generously funded it is, of course, childishly easy to give an impression of seriousness without being so. You just have to keep your language abstract and lace it with Greek and Latin (that rum-and-ginger of the modern mind). You mention that you have instruments involving ultraviolet and infrared rays and that you are an expert in magnetic, microchemical or radioactive analysis. With these it almost doesn't matter *what* your premise is. We are blinded, all too truly, by science.

Here Zuckerman's skepticism comes in handy. Since he is looking for *anatomical* details he is less likely than paleontologists and anthropologists to find a design in every fossil (it was two anatomists, by the way, who exposed the fraud of the Piltdown Man in 1953).

There has rarely been agreement in those fields. Quarrels have accompanied just about every major fossil-find. Most French paleontologists refused to believe that the fragment of jawbone discovered by Boucher de Perthes in 1863 was genuine but they abruptly changed their tune when the English paleontologist Falconer said that the teeth found close by belonged to it. After which a team composed both of English and French paleontologists decided that it was genuine. Then an English digger who had worked with de Perthes for months said that de Perthes often bought old bones from workers which were in fact just that, old bones. An archaeologist called Evans then showed that the ancient tools had had their ancientness knocked into them quite recently. So the jaw was once more, and finally, a fake.

Several years before that, in 1856, the first "Neanderthal" skull caused tremendous excitement. Bone swellings on it indicated the disease called hypertrophic osteitis (which means precisely that—a bone swelling), though an Englishman said it was rickets. A German decided that it was neither, being a wound sustained in the Napoleonic wars by a Cossack. An English anatomist then gave the skull the name Homo Neanderthalensis and T.H. Huxley

(Darwin was more difficult to convince) called it the first "primitive" man, though as to whether this meant that the man belonged to an intermediary development between ape and modern man or was one of the first modern men wasn't clear. In the political climate of that time it would have been rather bold to make a direct connection between ape and man at all—people were inclined to take it personally.

Here paleontologists and their allies in anatomy and geology were in a cleft stick: they wished to say that man had made a resounding evolutionary victory, as compared with other animals, yet to do this they had in some degree to identify him with other animals, indeed to suggest he had once been one, or was still one. This brought them into battle with the Creationists, who held that the Bible was the only paleontological authority and that man had been created as he was now by an abrupt divine decision.

But even that battle was a fake because the two sides basically agreed with each other. Evolutionism and creationism were simply different schools in the same theology, which said that man was specially endowed and in advance of all other animals.

Ernest Häckel, like Darwin a naturalist (and incidentally one of his followers), published between 1870 and 1880 three volumes which suggested that all creatures had one origin in a microscopic organism which he called the "Moneron". Not that this organism existed. *He invented it.* In the same hypothetical mood he filled in some of the intermediary stages between one level of a species and another: he supplied an imaginary animal called the Pithecanthropus ("ape-man"), a name that stuck perhaps because it was long (the Peking Man is a pithecanthropus). Eugene Dubois, a Dutchman, actually went to the Dutch East Indies to find this non-existent creature. In 1890 he came across a lower jaw, in 1891 two teeth and the top of a cranium, and in 1893 a femur, all of which suggested strong similarities with the modern human, though it was an ape too (but then so was the human). His critics said that the femur couldn't belong to the cranium. Others said it was diseased anyway. Yet others—most of them French—said that it belonged to a giant gibbon.

Another bag of old bones from Chapelle-aux-Saints confirmed in 1908 the existence of a definite European creature with a large or Neanderthal head on a small body, walking erect with slightly bent legs, its cranium platycephalic ("flat-headed" for the anecdotal) and its forehead receding. This creature also had decidedly "animal" features, such as the high development of the visual region and relatively undeveloped frontal lobes. Clearly, this ape was an advanced creature, and perhaps an "early", even "first" man, but not as advanced as all that.

But what has happened to our evolutionary theory here? How can we talk of *undeveloped* lobes and the *decline* in olfactory and visual faculties as a feature of *developed* man? Where has the simple-to-complex rule gone, because clearly we have moved from complex to simple? The wings of evangelical doctrine have borne evolution so far into the upper air that it is now by sheer weight falling to the ground! But not to worry: since the decline happened in humans and humans are in advance of animals it could be considered a step forward. Better depleted than like *them*!

The paleontologist was never satisfied, it seemed. If he found an animal different from a human he called it an ape, and when it was similar he called it the "first" man. His premises simply didn't allow for the possibility that there was no development in a straight line, or along a chronological line, and that some of the other higher primates might have developed extremely cortical brain systems like man's in order to meet *similar requirements in their habitat*, and that these may have died out, been revived again, flourished again, not according to an inbuilt law of development but according to *changing physiological needs dictated by habitat.* And to pick about morbidly in the ruins of all these carcasses for signs of an imaginary creature is surely another sign that Homo Sapiens has long since lost whatever wisdom he picked up on the way.

When several examples of the Neanderthal man were available some were found to be "advanced" and some "backward", and of course it was assumed, according to the unexamined ethical premise underlying the whole investigation, that the "backward" must have been earlier and the "advanced" later. But this wasn't always so. Not that the premise was questioned. It simply fell into that let-out limbo favored by all scientific disciplines, "a mystery".

When we come to working out how intelligent the man-ape was by measuring the size of his cranium the subject becomes hilarious and we have to thank H.S. for at least not losing his sense of humor. It shows in fact a decided *regression* on the part of the modern human. A certain H.S. Neanderthalensis living about 150,000 years ago shows a cranial capacity from 1400 to 1600 c.c. Another example from Iraq dated 60,000 years ago shows a capacity of 1700 c.c. But the man honored with the highest paleolithic title, Homo Sapiens, from Cro-Magnon (20,000 years ago), is measured at 1580 c.c. And the average for man today is 1450 to 1500 c.c. So where is the "development"?

At once we hear (from Zuckerman among others) that cranial capacity isn't an infallible guide to intelligence! In that case why take it as a measure? It leaves the Peking Man of 700,000 years ago "behind" with 780 to 1225 c.c. and the earlier specimens from about a million years before that even further "behind" with a cranial capacity higher than the Peking Man's low. And how is it that the cranial fragment found at Vértesszöllös in Hungary, said to be as old as Peking Man, has a capacity of 1400 c.c.? And since cranial capacity is linked with the ability to make tools, and the finest tools belong to the so-called Maddalinian era (25,000 years ago), how is it that we find great cranial developments *earlier*?

But again, not to worry. Early man-like apes are "attempts" at becoming the modern man. The Neanderthal man is described as "still" simian in character, with features that are by inference "brutish". Or simian characteristics are said to "diminish". Or human ones "progressively" manifest.

What are "simian" as opposed to "human" characteristics? You can only reach such a division if your opening premise is that the human is distinct from the simian, but any outsider to both categories would place them firmly together, allowing for a difference of a tooth here and a foramen magnum there.

* * *

But now we come to really serious studies, undertaken by men and woman many of whom could still be alive. The Australopithecines (a bit of a mouthful for human teeth) were found in Africa by Raymond Dart and Robert Broom, who described as "behind" the man-ape fossils found in South-East Asia, and these latter as "behind" Neanderthal Man. But it is difficult to find what is behind this behind.

The Parapithecus found by Max Scholsser in 1910 in the form of a lower jaw, which displayed a dental form identical with the modern human and was dated between 35 and 45 million years ago, and Proconsul Africanus discovered by Mrs Leakey in 1948 on the island of Rusinga and dated about twenty million years ago, were both erect, fangless and dentally proper, with arms used not for walking or branch-swinging but activities independent of locomotion, as in the human.

We might conjecture from this that the primate world bifurcated into two departments, one leading to modern man and the other leading to those primates we call anthropoids (so-called because in their appearance and power to learn they resemble man), namely the gibbon, the chimpanzee, the orangutan and the gorilla. And we shall be further inclined to assume that where we find two examples of roughly the same kind of fossil-ape in places far flung from each other there has been a "migration", much as there would be in modern man.

These speculations overlook a simple physiological fact—that *adaptation is a constant and necessary feature of organisms*. All creatures whatever adapt moment by moment to changes within and without. The work done on immunology this century makes it impossible even for scientists to disregard this. Our bodies have been described as systems under constant bombardment by potential disease-sources but able by means of electrochemical self-adjustments to withstand them ("we get cancer three times a week and reject it"). Not a moment passes when a mutation isn't taking place. "Mutation" simply means change, so that when we speak of biological mutations we refer to changes in structure. When an ape develops a large cranial capacity and simultaneously loses some of its power to smell

36

or see keenly this is a structural adaptation, not a participation in somebody else's story-line.

Change is almost a definition of life. For instance, if we humans doggedly follow a fixed daily routine with no regard for leisure or play we soon find that we lose our taste for life. We need a change, which means that our adaptive mechanism has been under-stretched—a fact which seems to suggest that resilience in self-adaptation is *a mark of vitality*.

The theory of natural selection says that an animal which adapts well to its habitat survives, and the animal which doesn't is "beaten". The victor animal is structurally inherited by its children, those of the "beaten" aren't.

But the real story of adaptation is much kinder and blander than Darwin's account suggests. For instance, the body temperature of the female humming bird decreases while she is brooding. This means that she needs less food and therefore needn't take multiple flights from the nest in search of it, she needn't abandon her young. This is one "explanation". Another is that since she doesn't take those flights she eats less, and the body temperature declines as a result. But either way no *will* is involved, no *intention*. It is an autonomic process of self-adaptation and goes on without any drama or evangelical struggle.

The point I'm making in this recital of old wives' bony tales is that the inner (organism) and outer (nourishment) aspects of the habitat can't be separated in practice as they can in theory. Any change in the outer habitat will be matched by changes in the inner. The body's temperature *constantly* adjusts to temperatures outside. With the need for exertion the heart-rate, breathing, glandular activity will change. When we are terrified by a sudden event our breath will be drawn into the thoracic area in the form of a gasp, our eyes will dilate, our extremities stiffen and receive blood: these are all emergency responses which demonstrate the smooth state of unison within the habitat and thus our readiness to cope with the threat.

If you try to apply systems and tables and chronological lines to this story you will fail to see the most remarkable thing about organisms—their inexhaustible variety which derives from the power to adapt, and which reflects every change in the outer habitat, and the seeking of new habitats which stretches this power to change even more (here and here alone is where man came in).

Perhaps Australopithecus didn't need more than his relatively small allotment of cranial capacity for the habitat he had to adjust to. Perhaps the ape of over thirty million years ago whose teeth were those of a modern human was, far from being our "ancestor", simply adapting to dietary conditions similar to our own. Features of bodies come and go. They are displaced not by any development of the kind that produces a "more advanced" creature (whatever that might mean) but by new features which will deal with the habitat better. A cranial capacity of 1700 c.c. would have been useless for animals whose senses of sight and smell were so acute that no cortical activity could have supplied them with a comparable amount of information. And what about the relatively weak senses of sight and smell in the human today, and his loss of what are called specialized organs of defense—is this an "advance"? What animal would agree that to lose its powers was a sign of greater prowess and intelligence? Only, apparently, the human. And, like the giraffe and his long neck, he is right—for himself.

Man has simply developed faculties which make it possible for him to handle his habitat for his own purposes. But all animals do the same. And evidence is accumulating that *other animals do it better*.

* * *

The most grotesque theories abound to explain the origin of human traditions and habits. Cave dwellers "warred" with animals for possession of caves just because of some elephant bones alongside those of paleolithic man. Life "freed" itself two hundred million years from the aquatic habit. Mammals started their "second conquest" of the continents one hundred million years ago. The scratchings from bear claws on cave walls gave "primitive" man the idea of drawing and painting on those same walls. Evidence of burials in caves indicate a "cult of the dead" (though millions of elaborate burials by modern man presumably constitute no such cult). If animal skeletons are found in a grave they became a "food sacrifice", it being taken for granted that in all paleolithic life an animal was eaten and its bones simply left there (did they have no brooms?). Red ocher on skeletons is a symbol for blood. Some people were buried in the fetal position, and were tied up in that position, because everyone was afraid of death and didn't like the idea of a corpse moving! There was even a "skull cult"—fear of death is again the explanation, though in certain tribes today the skull, when used decoratively, is a healing or protective charm. The Sinanthropus (a former name for the Peking Man) devoured his own kind—because his skulls were always found broken, in the midst of other animal bones!

Since implements and reindeer skeletons were found in caves, and animals were drawn and painted on cave walls, the humans there must have been hunters, and, because hunting expeditions were also depicted on the walls, hunting must have been their pervasive and all-absorbing activity, which makes their wall-paintings magical in motive—designed to promote good hunts. Yet American Indian tribes hunted the buffalo and we know that they *identified* themselves with the animals they hunted, and respected and revered them, and a good hunt wasn't by any means the goal of their reverence. We also know that shamans and medicine men have traditionally dressed in animals' skins and adorned themselves with horns, tails, feathers etc. But since we are talking about an "early" stage of evolution we are obliged to attribute only crude motives or at best "magical" ones to it.

As for disease, paleolithic man knew nothing about it. When trepanned skulls were found, with signs of healing round the edges, the holes were attributed by Professor Pittard of Geneva and others to a primitive tradition of driving holes in people's heads to let the evil spirit out! A French doctor said that the lesions actually resulted from syphilis, though no one knows if syphilis existed in those times. Yet we do know that arm and leg fractures were mended efficiently in the same period, so why not allow trepanning as well?

Even as old wives' tales some of these theories are tall, like the one which suggests that man began to walk erect because he needed a pair of hands to develop bigger families with (the primate record for procreation is poor).

Another tells us that our ability to fall in love, like our alleged monogamy, was a "development" designed to make family life more secure and prolific. What about the sea horse, which chooses a single mate? Did it also choose the falling-in-love technique to make family life possible? What of the possibility that falling in love in our present sense has more to do with medieval troubadours than with life a million years ago? What of the fact that humans have again and again eschewed "falling in love" as a sound basis for marriage and family life? How was it possible in previous centuries to maintain large and secure aristocratic families on large estates under husbands and wives who a) rarely fell in love because their spouses were chosen for them, b) were regularly unfaithful and c) accepted the system because "family" never signified for them that exclusive sexual possession which was characteristic of the later industrial middle classes?

We say that during our "evolution" from lemurs (or tarsiers or gibbons) to man the brain increased in volume while the specialized organs of defense regressed. The higher primates are therefore called non-specialized. But why is non-specialization "higher"? How can we omit to see that the loss of sharp teeth and claws and speedy legs, and the erosion of sight and smell, are a simple physiological adaptation to needs? In what sense is the diminution of the human face in size (because of our reduced dependency on the faculties of sight, smell and hearing) a more complex development than a face of great size dedicated to a far more intense use of these faculties but called "brutish"? Is the poised position of modern man's head and the weight of his abdominal structure on the pelvis more "complex" or an "advance" on the physically sounder use of all four limbs for support?

Anyway, Mrs Leakey's Proconsul Man, a genus from the Miocene era twenty million years ago, *lacked* the specialized buttocks and ground-gripping feet which makes the erect position possible!

But it had a human feature—it looked through round windows of bone (the gorilla looks through rectangles). It had arms like ours, i.e. shorter than the legs. On the other hand, it lived partly on the ground, partly in trees. That is, it had a variety of characteristics designed for a similar variety in the habitat.

We also hear of a fossil-ape which combined the arboreal life of the squirrel with the need to hunt, hence its development of hands to cling with and snatch with (a human characteristic) and binocular vision to focus on distant victims (not a human characteristic). Since it didn't have to kill or forage with huge teeth the jaw was smaller, the teeth fewer than in most other apes—more human features. The feet "lost" their claws and developed gripping toes. So why can't we say here was a human? Who says that a human didn't swing in trees in one place and walk the forest floor in another? In Chicago or Windy City you need a thick overcoat in the winter but in Santa Monica you don't. Conversely, why should the primate we recognize as human (round eye-sockets, short arms and long legs, centralized buttocks etc) have been human in *our* sense? Is an animal which looks like a human necessarily human?

These are uncomfortable questions in paleontological circles because they point to one key question which has rarely been seriously broached, namely, what *is* a human? We can't say that he is just another primate because he isn't. But his differences don't lie in matters of eye socket and frontal lobe. The fact is that his independent thinking doesn't stick out like his nose (as compared with a gorilla's). Least of all can you find it in a fossil. So the whole bone-yard yardstick of trying to find humans in fossils is out of true. If bones could talk, of course, it would be different, because language indicates the mode and intensity of the thought. But language is like perceiving, it's something bones don't do. And the human primate was and is different from other primates *solely in his manner of perceiving*.

Man's frontal-lobe system and his tongue are highly developed. His *gyrus supramarginalis* (meaning "a fold above the edge") in the left inferior temporal lobe of the brain is unique, being connected with *speech and perception*, and this sharply differentiates him from the lemur, the gibbon and the gorilla. But this is only because of *the specific manner in which he has used his mind*. And the only way we can possibly trace his existence in the past is by asking questions about how he used his mind, and finding out how such a mind could have come about, and, since that mind is a strange and haunted one, what strange and haunting circumstances made it possible.

FOUR

God's Top Apes

Julian Huxley (Secretary of the London Zoo from 1935 to 1941) once said that only man can become something "new". No cat, he said, can change.

This is just more bone-yard talk. All you have to do is place a domestic cat beside a wild cat to realize that it has changed not only in the matter of its coat, its size, the nature of its claws and length and sturdiness of its legs, especially the hind ones, but also in expression, movement and above all attitude. Domestic cats also frequently need a change of scene and leave home for days or weeks or forever. If we call our cat "Tiger" it is in recognition both of the similarity to the wild form and the "evolution" that has taken place. It isn't that the domestic cat evolved as a better or more intelligent animal but that it simply adapted to a different habitat—the human one (an unenviable feat indeed).

The scale insects of California are another example of newness through adaptation. As early as 1914 they were proving resistant to the deadly hydrocyanic pesticides used in the citrus groves. It was found they had developed a way of suspending their respiratory systems for periods of as long as thirty minutes in order to allow the poison to evaporate in the air.

Huxley was referring to man's power of mind. This power lies in an ability to conceive. Via his conceptions man changes his life. But this power is by no means lacking in animals. On the contrary, when they are baffled by a change in the environment *they are obliged to conceive a new way of responding.* To suspend your respiration for long requires not only prolonged concentration but *deliberate planning.*

When an animal loses its desire to function it is because its know-how has broken down over a long period of time, and mutation-effects of a negative type can be expected, such as sickness, suicide, insanity. These may also provoke a new struggle for health. So calamity becomes an agent of change. It forces the animal's attention on new concepts of how to behave so as to build up new know-how.

Human dementia, as we see shall see, can provoke into being new techniques for the recovery of sanity. All the fairy tales about moral advance or biological "victory" have really been about the haunting question of *what man is.* When an animal loses certain of the reflexes and faculties which it once depended on it "forgets" vital information. The domesticated ape "forgets" how to take the sting out of a scorpion without being stung. The information about how to remove a sting now has to be sought consciously (Eugene Marais had to train his "tamed" primates to do this). It is at this point that the animal becomes confused as to *who it is.* Hunter or vegetarian, peaceful or violent? If it is a tree-climber and there are no trees in its new habitat it must walk on the ground and find its food there. If it is a ground animal and there are only trees it must learn to climb and swing and hang. All this creates confusion. So we shouldn't be surprised that there are scientific disciplines trying at extraordinary expense to find out who the human is, while never broaching the question itself.

Meat-eater, ex-hunter? Raymond Dart thought that baboons were carnivorous, hoping thereby to account for man's present meat-eating habits. DeVore and Hall's studies show that only about two percent of the baboon diet was flesh. And man's violence? Was he always like this? Dart wanted to show that predatory behavior in a large terrestrial primate is natural. In 1949 he argued that

Australopithecine Africanus had gone about armed. The use of weapons had thus preceded man, he said. This gave rise to theories about the "aggressive", even the "imperial" ape—from whom the human had learned his supposed love of violence.

Dart was also anxious to show that the ape fossil he found at Taungs, on the edge of the Kalahari desert, had made tools out of bones. So, in a shameless orgy of classical roots, he called its culture *osteodontokeratic*. S.L.Washburn came forward in the Sixties to corroborate this view. He and his associate Moore urged that the great apes eat with eagerness and relish (piccalilli? onion? olive?). The "imperial" theory thus got its support. It aimed to show that man derives his alleged aggressive and territorial instincts and carnivorous and tool-using and hunting habits from primate "ancestors". Wars, pogroms, massacres, terrorism and criminal assault involving millions of humans were now explained on the basis of the "dark animal" doctrine. Back to theology!

Robert Ardrey, the author of *African Genesis*, jumped into all this by declaring, in high-sounding prose appropriate to the warrior breed, that man was a naturally violent creature because of his— African genesis. He recalled how in Chicago as a youth he had gone (on Wednesday evenings) to the local Presbyterian church: while the adults were at song and prayer he and other youths met together in the basement, officially to decide on sports programs but actually, after a prayer and benediction, to turn out the lights and in total darkness hit each other over the head with chairs. If a boy was injured seriously he was escorted home. It was this Sunday-school class that, he believed, prepared him for African anthropology.

There are clearly snags about this. First, you can't prove that hunting and eating meat were signs of cruelty or even of an aggressive temperament. Second, the modern human's cruelty and aggressiveness seem to have intensified in highly sophisticated, well-fed societies in which no one hunts for his next meal (Chicago and Robert Ardrey being cases in point). Third, there have been in the past and there remain today remarkably peaceable and yielding human societies. Millions of Hindus were once dedicated, for millennia, to the idea of never harming plant or creature, and they never ate the latter, much less hunted it except under directions from mostly British sahibs. And there are even countless peaceful people, likewise dedicated to never harming man or beast, who nevertheless eat the latter with relish.

And then you can hardly say that aggressiveness of temperament was necessarily a mark of primitive peoples (i.e. those presumed, without evidence, to be nearer the apes than we are). There is also the ticklish fact that the vast majority of mankind was largely vegetarian until the late nineteenth century. Historically, regular daily meat-eating was brought in by the European noble classes well after medieval times, and it filtered down the social scale only slowly, so that even by the 1950s there were still rural families in parts of Prussia, Austria and Italy who ate flesh—usually goat, chicken or rabbit—only on holidays. And we are now told that the armies of ancient Rome fought and marched on a purely vegetarian diet.

And lastly there remains the fact that humans go to war reluctantly, and even in the thick of battle show a surprising lack of cruelty for its own sake. In the last world war, as in most previous wars, defeated populations were treated with respect by the forward troops but raped or disdained by the administrative echelons in the rear, who had seen no action.

The possibility arises, then, that human cruelty may be due to what has happened to the human brain *since* it ceased to be a typical primate brain, rather than to what it was before.

But Dart and his school had other arguments. The Taungs fossil skull, belonging to the period of the great glaciers six hundred thousand years ago, inclined them to the view that the environment must have been too arid for a vegetarian diet. Also there were bones of other animals on the site. And then the Taungs teeth resembled human teeth—small, thinly coated with enamel, their crowns inadequate for the supposed "grinding and munching" of the vegetarian!

There were three difficulties here: a) the great glaciers are thought to have spread largely over North America and Northwest Europe, so that South Africa might not have been arid at all; b) the bones of the other animals on the site might have been those of predators who had fed on the vegetarian Taungs creature; c) vegetarians do not munch or grind their food any more than anybody else, particularly if their diet consists not of grass but roots, berries and nut cutlets.

In the Forties, Dart found a new site in Northern Transvaal and began to speculate that one of the ape fossils there showed evidence of having used fire. So he gave this one the stirring name of Australopithecine Prometheus.

At another site Robert Broom found a completely different creature, which he called Paranthropus. It was big, thick-skulled and clumsy, though in all other respects it was like Dart's Australopithecus, which was small and agile. Paranthropus had a sloping forehead and crested skull like a gorilla, and heavy grinding molars different from the human and clearly designed for the "eternal chewing" (as Ardrey, clearly a fast-food meat-eater, calls it) of the vegetarian. And while Australopithecine teeth were as smooth as a leopard's, Paranthropus's were dented with sand (from roots). So Paranthropus was called Australopithecine Robustus, while Dart's earlier skull was renamed Australopithecus Africanus—the first vegetarian, the second carnivore.

There is a nasty paradox here. The meat-eater, by all current canons of virility, should have been the tougher, as he was presumed to be the rougher by the Aggressive School of anthropology in Chicago. But he wasn't. Indeed, the vegetarian was the robust one. Clearly there had to be an adjustment of premise here. So Ardrey said that, though robust, the vegetarian ape was, apart from being clumsy, "inoffensive" (presumably too much a sissy to develop into Chicago Man). So clearly, since no one could imagine Robustus beating fellow creatures on the head with chairs in the dark, Chicago Man came from Africanus who, little shrimp though he might have been, yet raged around with cudgels and ate chops.

What are the facts, aside from all this schoolboy yarning? When an animal roams far from its habitat, adjusting itself to new climates and new forms of nourishment, it inevitably experiences confusion as to what to eat. Humanity is able to survive on various diets—those that consist almost entirely of meat, those that have a little meat and those with no meat at all. The argument will of course arise as to what is "natural" but unfortunately the word "natural" implies a fixed and not a variable habitat.

When the habitat changes, an animal no longer receives inflexible messages as to what and how to eat. It will become a different creature to the degree of the habitat's changes. Those primates which swing on boughs or hang from them are not good runners. Gibbons and siamangs swing like pendula from branch to branch, so that their legs appear shrunken, their hands unusually long. When they reach the ground they are erect. The orangutan can grasp with both hands and feet. He stretches out all four limbs to grasp, pluck, eat. On the ground he goes on all fours, using the knuckles of the hands, and sometimes the fists. The gorilla is almost wholly on the ground—for roots, shoots, berries, so that while he is enormously strong he isn't speedy. Only the young gorilla will hang and play in trees. The adult is sedentary like the human and almost never runs. The gorilla too is a knuckle walker. The chimpanzee does a bit of everything—tree climbing, running, hanging, and he will sometimes hunt in groups and eat flesh, even that of a baboon or other monkey.

These are simply ways of adapting. You will find primates similar to the human in some or most respects. All apes are *potentially* erect. A certain type will flourish now, another later, according always to changes in habitat. Some say that apes flourished in the mild Miocene period because of the huge tropical forests, while the monkeys were less fortunate. After that the monkeys flourished better.

To wrap up this sequence of simian bone-picking, the competition in paleontology at the moment seems to be between the two-million-old fossilized skull called "1470" (its museum number), which made Richard Leakey famous, and the other newer claimants.

Solly Zuckerman forbade Leakey to show his fossil at a zoological celebration in London, just as years before (according to Raymond Dart) he saw to it that the Royal Society rejected one of Dart's monographs. Yet Zuckerman did accept "1470" as a man.

But what did he mean by "man"? If he meant modern man with his culture, of course 1470 wasn't that. He must have been a "primitive" edition of him. But how could you have a primitive edition of *a new way of thinking*? And why should there have been a "primitive" edition at all?

The answer is simple. It is that for all their vaunted objectivity paleontologists were incapable of monkey-wrenching certain ideas out of their own minds. One of these denied that man had existed a million, not to say two million years ago. That old fossil wasn't man in *our* sense, not *modern* man, not *us* because we only go back a few thousand years at most.

And this idea belongs to Christian theology, and a particular theology may be just as wrong as any other study of the divine. But if you use theology while having no use for it at all you are arguing from confusion.

All Western thought, including what we call "science", has been drawn from Christian theology, whether it likes it or not, as I shall show later in this book when I describe how medieval priests spoke proudly of the triumph of Christ in the form of self-propelled vehicles of the air and land and sea that would later come about.

FIVE

The Human Trick Of Self-Withdrawal

The more I went into these questions the more I realized that most people see the first appearance of man as a purely non-animal event just as they would have five hundred years ago. All the simian talk, the ape fossils and the fangs theories may just as well not have been aired for all the effect they had on our *perceptions*. And these perceptions continue seeing things through a theological doctrine that should never have been taken seriously to start with.

Not that I'm against theology as a basis for perception. I will go further and say that without theology no human perception is possible—that, in a word, theology is the manner in which all our perceptions come into being. Only there are theologies and theologies.

Now if science is adamant about one thing it is that it isn't theology. But I take this to be a kind of pet or tantrum due to having buckled under an unworkable theology for so long.

But before we get to the actual medieval theology which conditions our responses and perceptions we have to determine just how it is that the human transposes his thought-world into what he calls a real one.

First of all, he must render his thoughts unconscious. Then he sees *through* them. For instance, when he perceives other animals to be lower than himself, or when he perceives himself not to be an animal at all, it isn't that he is thinking anything consciously, much less subscribing to species-chauvinism. He is simply *perceiving* animals this way when he looks at them or thinks about them, and the theology that directs him to do so takes no account of whether he is a Christian or an atheist or anything in between. He may even be active in the animal-rights movement, he may disapprove of those of his perceptions which declare him superior to the very animal for which he feels compassion.

But getting rid of perceptions is altogether another matter. Once and for all we have to decide what makes a human *himself* and not a baboon or a gibbon. That he looks different isn't of much importance, and in any case he doesn't look all *that* different. At least, while he might look different to a fellow primate he wouldn't to a bat or a whale. He would be just another primate—decidedly odd-looking with variously colored sacks thrown over his furlessness, but still a primate. One thing would be clear to all. He must have come an awful long way to get to look like that.

In our "scientific" comparing of cranial measurements and eye sockets we overlook one quite obvious thing—that if we didn't think and perceive very differently from other primates we would be able to treat them as true brothers, and even cease to find their fur creepy unless dead. After all, we have everything necessary for a pleasant relationship, such as highly articulated front paws and potentially reliable tree-swinging limbs. We embrace in the same way and millions of us eat with our hands, e.g. scrupulously clean Indians.

It is simply no good looking at tools made of bone, bronze or stone and classifying them according to their age and degree of sophistication only to use them as a basis for working out our tiresome conflicts—as between whether we are carnivores or vegetarians, hunters or animal-worshippers, aggressors who bean each other with chairs in the dark or meditators.

We should be asking, What do these tools denote *mentally?* What do they say about human intelligence?

First of all, using tools is by no means exclusive to humans. Certain birds will use thorns to pierce wood. Primates other than man will use anything to hand at times to defend themselves. For tool-using is only an extension of inherited tools such as claws, beaks, arms, fins, sharp teeth etc.

But there is one thing about tools, especially the sophisticated ones that the Australopithecines are said to have used, which we mustn't overlook, and that is that creating them depended on an unusual ability to *think strategically.*

Again, strategic thinking is normal among animals. I've seen a tame rabbit at the Stockholm zoo nudge a turtle that had rolled onto its back into the upright position with its nose. The rabbit was clearly using a stratagem, whether it had been taught this or not.

When milk bottles were first left on London doorsteps the birds took little notice. As bottle caps became softer they began pecking them off and drinking the cream on top. An experienced cart horse will take corners into farm gateways with precision, never scraping the cart at the posts, and missing them by an almost identical fractional distance each time. And there are manifold stories of intelligence applied in emergencies by horses, wolves, chimpanzees. All these involve strategic thinking.

But this still falls short of *systematic* thinking such as the human goes in for. There *are* instances of system among animals but they are usually tied to an immediate event. A pride of lions will stalk prey systematically, heading off the prey at certain angles and speeds, in cooperation with each other. But in systematic thinking we are talking about plans devised *far from the event in which they will be realized*—far in both space and time.

It is here that a specifically human story begins, though we must be careful not to slip into evolutionary romance by suggesting that it was the post-primate human that "developed" it, or only one primate. The point of interest is not whether the apes who used tools of flint or stone or bone or bronze or iron were humans but the nature of the primate mind that devised those things.

Tools indicate that the biological tools with which an animal is already supplied—claws, swift legs, powerful teeth—are no longer enough. This in turn argues that the animal must be in trouble of some kind. Either his habitat has changed, perhaps in the form of more and stronger predators, or he is new to it, having abandoned his previous one. He now requires *a stratagem*, a cleverly conceived system in order to survive.

He has to *think things out* instead of simply using his legs, teeth, claws. In turn his need to think requires him to stop in his traces. He must *defer activity*.

In a word, designing a tool means shaping it to one's future, that is to one's imagined needs in another place and another time. But essentially it means that *the mind itself is now used as a tool*.

In other words the new tool (theory, plan) represents deferred action. It is put on hold. While thinking it out, the animal is immobile, concentrating not on a passing scent or distant sight or any other immediate event but an event which has not yet taken place.

Thus Zuckerman is quite wrong to say that animals respond only to immediate events, or are incapable of indirect responses like the human's. If that were so the human couldn't have made his tools. He would have inherited the wrong brain for doing so.

To invent systems an animal has to create a scene for itself in which it figures as one of its own characters. The other characters may be predators or prey, or they may be in a vegetable form as roots, berries, seeds. In the past this animal may have grasped stones or heavy boughs for the purpose of defense or digging. This was already a use of tools. But he is now making his own arrangements.

The bones found in caves belonging to Australopithecus Africanus were in some cases fashioned into sharp instruments. You could also say (as many paleontologists have) that these tools were fashioned by time, being simply the bones of other animals which had died on the same site. But the Australopithecus Robustus, on similar sites, used tools made out of lava deposit, not bones. And the nearest lava deposit was twenty-five miles from the site where presumably he lived.

Now to go elsewhere to find material with which to make your tools argues more than a simple stratagem. You must make a mental act of withdrawal not only from the habitat outside but from *your own pressing biological needs* to do things now with claws, teeth, legs.

In being required to put a brake on your appetites and energies you have to become a master of self-withdrawal. Out of this strangely alert state comes a plan, which may involve traveling some miles to seek out the right material for tools. There is a sense of secrecy in it, even conspiracy with the outside silent world.

Yes, the world has now become, for the first time, an *outside* world.

A peculiar contradiction is thereby set up. The more the Australopithecine achieves with his newfound faculty, passing from simple bone to lava tools, and then to bronze and later iron, the less accessible he is to other animals. The brain-faculty he now depends on makes him stand out clear and alone in the animal kingdom. His presence now causes concern among other animals.

Some say that the leopard, once it has eaten, will pass through a herd on which it habitually preys and signal the fact that it doesn't intend to hunt by displaying the white of its tail. Such signs and signals, shared like a language between species, no longer hold in the case of the new human or deferral animal. He is a stranger. He is obliged to divide up time mentally—he now has a past, present and future.

Having suppressed his own inherited commands (instincts) by a striking effort of will he can return to them only with difficulty. We must remember that he was *obliged* to throw them off in the interests of survival. The animal world now begins to see him as a threatening creature. He is even capable of viewing himself unfavorably, even of being disgusted by his own physiological processes. Such is the degree of his self-withdrawal.

Proconsul Man had a body much like ours. He wasn't however erect. His brain wasn't as big. His snout didn't protrude. He had long fighting teeth. But his arms were shorter than his legs, and he didn't use them to move along with. The paleontological story is that in the subsequent Pliocene era his teeth became weaker, he developed a snout and he became erect, and his brain grew slightly—that is, it grew while his other fighting and food-procuring faculties diminished.

In fact it grew *because* the other faculties diminished. *And tools, the fruit of thought, diminish the old faculties further.*

If the meat-eating Africanus was small compared with the vegetarian Robustus, and more agile, it may have been his very weakness that turned him into a carnivore and assailant of other animals.

In the Africanus, the Robustus and the modern human, namely the erect species, the large buttock and feet play a major role in balancing the body, while the classical ape uses his hands for locomotion and hanging. The human hand is highly articulated in comparison with that of the ape, and evidently this power of subtle articulation must have been present in the Australopithecines if they fashioned and manipulated tools. Here, in the hands, brain-agility is most easily recognized. We could even say that digital manipulation is a sign of highly alert mental function. Prowess in one part is triggered off by the weakness of another part.

But there is one aspect of the deferral or thinking animal that naturalists rarely touch on. He is now a *working* creature, whether in large degree or small. There is one thing about non-human animals which marks them off from us—they know of no strict dividing line between working and playing. The way the hawk descends to kill or the buck leaps or the lynx runs or the weaver bird builds its nest is so leisurely and seemingly so self-satisfying that it suggests play even when a kill is involved. In the case of humans survival means work, simply and purely because they use non-biological tools. Their withdrawal from the habitat grows even deeper. Its sources of pleasure dry up for them.

Unlike the human an animal follows its inherited course, inserting delightful individual variations into its play according to its personality. If it makes a nest it flies with unerring directness to the right tree or grass for its building materials, working with rapid movements which betoken a lack of mental surveillance. It does it "naturally", we say. But the human animal has to earn every inch of the way.

Here lies another striking contrast with other animals—the human's life is based on *fabrication*. He is forever devising with his mind. This constant fabrication is achieved not by means of inherited biological tools but by careful and sustained thought.

Other animals may live without a care for the future but *the future is the basis of human life*. Without his faculty for deferring, imagining and above all designing a future, man would have no abstract theory and therefore no systems, no cities erected from thousands of sketches, no theology, pomp or ceremonial worship, no holidays falling on certain days of the year, no drama or music or painting of imagined scenes, no dance steps, in a word nothing we describe as civilized.

Naturally we are awestruck by our power to conjure up so many sparkling imaginative worlds. We quickly convince ourselves that our subtle fabrications mark us out from the animal kingdom.

But the truth is that animals too are busy in fabrications of their own, though few of these are the result of deliberate thought. The termite, with its tunnels and chambers and deep-delving canals, and its systems of communication which we are unable to decode, is engaged in a collective fabrication as busily as we are. The manner in which the snow goose changes color until indistinguishable from the snow, its manner of sleeping with its head peeping invisibly out of the snowflakes impervious to Arctic gales, free from the predators which haunted it by summer, is a fabrication we are likely to scorn when we compare it with human cities. But this is only because we are blind to the marvel of living in the glare of snow and the hum of icy winds without trembling. No doubt the snow goose is blind to cities.

One species tends to look at another species for its own prowess since that is what it depends on. Looking for our own specific prowess of mind among other animals, we find it lacking in them. We say they lack intelligence because what we mean by intelligence is our prowess and none other. An animal's prowess is the most exhilarating thing it knows. So we look everywhere for the kind of prowess that can build from a few simple thoughts—Knossos, Heliopolis, the Arch of Ptesiphon.

This human prowess achieves all by *stopping and thinking*. We impose our designs on the habitat---temples, boulevards, cloisters and gardens, avenues leading to gleaming stone houses with pebbled walks, fountains, neatly shaped bushes, all from the imagination—by means of thinking about what isn't yet but could and might be.

This thing called civilization is a giant fabrication indeed and we are more likely to feel proud of ourselves than other animals because we supposedly did it without help from the habitat. After all, the tiger will hardly attribute his leap to his own ingenuity, or the zebra his stripes to industry, or the male ibex his splendid backward-curving horns to artistic insight.

For this reason it is difficult for us to view our fabrication as an *animal* activity.

But the power of the sea horse to change form and color at will is no less impressive a fabrication than Byzantium. Where does the independent judge exist who could decide between the ecstasies of *our* creation and those of the sea horse?

It is a discussion we shrug off with smiles. Or we argue that the seahorse is *obliged* to transform itself in the way it does. It is unable, we say, to alter the manner and procedure of its change, whereas we humans bring to our processes of change a conscious ingenuity. But here again we are judging things by our own special experience—because conscious thought is our life-saver. We have used conscious thought to produce wonders impervious to animal attack, storm, flood and wind. So weak were we once that nothing short of the globe would do for our collective survival. It was a triumphant survival of the weakest.

Our very instability caused us to become the arbiters of all animal life. Outer power combines with inner irresolution to make, as it always does, intolerance.

Wherever the human being appears there is *a sense of effort* lacking in the rest of the animal kingdom. Clearly, if we have to think things out instead of following reflexes "blindly" (our habitual use of this word in the context of reflexes shows where our fears lie) we do so because we are short of information. When a primate has lost the knack of recognizing the nuts and berries suitable to its digestive processes it must first devise and then commit to memory a system based on trial and error. This may not prove an adequate guide. When the human builds houses according to a thought-out system he risks the possibility that information which his *old* reflexes would have supplied is now limited. If he pours concrete over creeks and yielding sub-soils without regard for the forces within the earth-crust, his house will be subject to slipping and flooding, and earth-tremors will put it at risk. His system for building houses was *apparently* watertight but he left one thing out of account, the behavior of the habitat, about which *he is more ignorant than any other animal.*

This is quite a dilemma, one that haunts and bedevils all science. You can make your theories work but only for yourself. You can't say how the habitat will treat them. Today's triumph is tomorrow's disease. Ecology is simply the study of our desperately small degree of knowledge.

Periods of collapse like the present are caused by our information dwindling too far. This makes for more and more science, which is needed as a buttress against a falling building. The bigger the collapse the more grandiose the medical programs that result. But this in turn provokes studies far beyond medical ones—for instance, the gradual making of a new planet which will be a living one, instead of one groaning under the weight of its own refuse and poisons.

One of the effects of a poisoned world is that humans, and perhaps other species too, live far fewer years than they need. We are capable, as a simple measurement of our cellular capacity for self-renewal will show, of living for at least 120 years (the "Hayflick limit"), which today some cell-renewal students are putting at 140.

* * *

Being a thought-animal, the human has built up a whole new reality distinct from the habitat and all but independent of it, at least in appearance.

To do this he has had to turn his thoughts into *impulses as strong as animal ones.* These thoughts have to be put forward by people who have a big following. They have to be revered thoughts as their utterer is revered. In this way they are passed from the children to their children. They become so accepted that to question them seems absurd. It is now that *they pass into our perceptions.*

So our perceptions are made up of unconscious thoughts, which at once makes them very different from an animal's perceptions. They aren't better perceptions or truer perceptions. But they have to be that way because if there is to be a civilization some clear rules of conduct, as well as dreams and revered attitudes, must be inherited. It replaces the animal's natural inheritance, for which no buildings or original thoughts are necessary. Without thought-reflexes among humans there could be no agreement, no basis for any transaction whatever.

I shall examine some of these thought-reflexes in detail later. For the moment I just want to repeat that when these too erode people begin to perceive unreliably. This happens in periods of collapse, in fact it is the definition, the only possible one, of any "fall" or "decline". The fact that we can examine these thought-reflexes at all is due only to their erosion. Otherwise they would be too deeply fixed in perceptions to allow for conscious perusal. We can see them only when they weaken their hold on our daily conscious mind. Any attempt to examine them *before* erosion would bring us face to face with unanimous denunciation.

When thought-reflexes erode it is a grave matter because *reality is made out of perceptions.* So when our perceptions are wobbly it looks as if reality is less solid than it used to be. More and more people have fancies, depressions, hallucinations, thoughts of changing their lives suddenly, recklessly, which in the old reality they would never have dared or even thought to do.

Since our reality is based on thought-reflexes, clearly these have to be special. The people who utter them have to be authoritative so that assent is immediate and warm and unquestioning. It is the revered man's personality that is doing this.

I shall be examining some of these people later, together with the thought-reflexes that they brought into being.

When thought-reflexes erode, as they are doing this century in a spectacular manner, there is at first a remarkable sense of freedom. At last we've been given permission to live the lives we want rather than the lives we feel duty-bound or fear-bound to lead. Where, in the old world, the sex act was a quite difficult thing to arrive at, and evaded the efforts of most young people and even a lot of mature ones to achieve it, it is now on the open market. All of a sudden, it seems, we have the chance to decide not only about our own lives privately but all lives collectively. The hippie movement of the Sixties came about in the full flush of this marvelous sense of power—power not in the previous meaning of fear-oriented coercion but as warm assent.

But this freedom is only a phase before the break-up of the old society. Now only the police and the army seem to stand between ordinary people and those others who (also choosing their freedom) murder, terrorize, rape, pillage and vandalize. But the boundaries aren't at all defined, as between the "ordinary" people and "others". This is because the perceptions are breaking up. The censors, the guides no longer stand sentinel within. So no mutually exclusive sectors like "police", "government", "church", "class", "criminals" exist. Their being mixed and fused together is what gives rise to a scandal industry which almost rivals the crime one: who is next for the popularity guillotine?

Lost thought-reflexes mean lost information. In former periods when life was based on multiple small markets and the people could have static lives there was every chance of thought-reflexes being passed on from generation to generation just as if they were animal impulses. But this becomes impossible once the reflexes can no longer cope with realities. In the "fall" period there is an extraordinary degree of movement and no mode of conduct catches on for long. Everybody is trying "new" modes of dress, sex, crime, and there are *enfants terribles* by the million, trying to catch the public eye with something shocking (i.e. contrary to thought-reflex). It happened in Roman times. People began leaving the country en masse for the towns. The same happened in medieval times. In these periods it is the cities that argue out the new ideas that will be the basis of thought-reflexes in the future. The countryside loses its appeal except as a rest-place for the urban weary.

A new phase of civilization is in preparation at the very time when all seems to be lost. Lawlessness excites new law. Once the new civilization is in place there is an exodus from the urban areas because people now *perceive* in a manner that joins them together, and they pass this perception on wherever they are. It was said that a man could be a Roman thousands of miles from Rome on a mountain top, yet never have seen Rome.

In other words each period of crisis requires more thinking out to be done. The more serious the collapse, the more is necessary. It is in this light that we should see the scientific activities of the last two centuries, not in any "development", nor an access of intelligence, nor any kind of triumph whatever. When perceptions fail there have to be systems, and when they collapse to the point they have done, several times and each time worse, in the history of Christendom, they require ever more intricate systems.

This is how we should be regarding what engineers call the complex systems—food distribution, energy supply, communications, transport networks. Far from being a sign of "advance" (simple-to-complex), as grandiosity requires us to see all things human, they are a desperate shift to buttress a falling edifice.

Our lives involve complex systems with every breath we take. From the moment we switch off the alarm at the beginning of a day to the moment we switch off the last light at night we are using a system thought out step by step mostly by previous generations. We are so hemmed in by law (as to how to cross the road, drive, pay taxes, conduct ourselves on the street and even in the home) that we were clearly in need of order above all other things. Our systems are so complicated that we can't control their effects either on ourselves or the habitat, nor can we dismantle them. What is saving us is undoing us.

Essentially this means that our thought-systems become so complex that we cannot control them individually, indeed make any individual impression on them whatever. And the habitat reacts badly to these blind systems. So we are obliged to introduce yet more complicated systems in order to alleviate their effects on both the outer (species, plants, rivers, soils) habitat and the inner (blood, lymph, nervous and immune systems) habitat.

And the more of this thinking there is the weaker we become.

We are involved in thought to a degree that all by itself is a form of dementia. Driving a car in heavy traffic, getting a subway ticket from a machine and placing it in another machine to gain entrance to a platform, dialing a phone number or entering a plastic card in a bank-teller slot—the emphasis is ever more on alert thought. Combine this with the systematizing within ourselves which echoes the outer systems—to think out our "next step", to turn the most trivial outing into a project, every desire into a plan for the future, and it is a wonder that the distracted creature can sign his own name.

He looks back with pity on pre-systems people who produced the food they ate with their own hands. He has a far more intelligent system (i.e. more thought has been used on it) in which every single item of food that reaches him is imprisoned in a specially made box, pack, sealed envelope. His daily struggles to open these are a picture of what happens to a society when thought has to take over life in order to save it.

* * *

And it is all based on self-withdrawal. Just as it served the first man, differentiating him at once from other primates, so it serves him now in all the "stress" (our pretty name for hell) that his precarious sanity plunges him into with a regularity that makes his continued survival a miracle of tenacity.

There have been several great waves of self-withdrawal in our history. Our civilization has specialized in it with an amazing recklessness. The wave that had special effects on our present lives happened between the sixteenth and eighteenth centuries. Its first signs—in the sixteenth—were the first consensuses of population, statistics, the dissection of corpses for medical purposes, logarithms. Its climax came in the Age of Reason, as the eighteenth century is sometimes called, when laws for everything were invented—for supply and demand, for population increases, for prices, labor, for markets of this kind and that. All the ideas that produced the Industrial Revolution in Britain and the French Revolution in 1780 were argued out in that century.

An Age of Reason is *a crisis of inner-habitat erosion.* This is why that century was quickly followed by the violence of two revolutions. For cruelty and moralizing dementia these revolutions were a worthy forerunner of the Holocaust, namely the removal of the Jewish civilization from the face of Europe and enacted during this killer-century.

Eighteenth-century Utopias and Declarations of Rights and Constitutions and ardent proclamations of the infinite power of human reason produced not at all the promised era of peace but a nineteenth-century Europe so explosive in its competing ambitions that two world wars in the following century were hardly enough to cool their after-embers.

To repeat, when thinking-out becomes the basis of life it indicates that reflexes have depleted beyond a supportable level. This in turn requires further thinking-out as it erodes the reflexes even further. Vast populations come into being for whom the habitat is a vague background, more or less inanimate, of little relevance to human life, its millions of creatures (far outnumbering humans) invisible, a background that must however be preserved, that becomes a source of vague and troubling nostalgia, an idyll and Eden and paradise which when filmed has cloyingly sweet music synched over it, the more as it sinks beneath the weight of a million diseases which also cannot be seen but are vaguely, backgroundly called pollution.

Six

Popular Lore

All would be well if it was just a matter of not being able to get the stings out of scorpions or not sensing the approach of earthquakes and tornadoes or not being able to smell or see as finely as we could before. But the loss of reflexes goes much deeper than this, into an intimate field where the human may feel at a loss to know not only the right thing to do in certain situations but what he wants, what he feels, what he is.

In physiological terms it means ever fewer guidelines as to how to breathe "properly", choose the right food and digest it "properly", choose one's mate and have sex and give birth and rear children "properly", walk and sleep and think "properly". I put "properly" in quotes because once we forget what the "proper" way is we cease to believe there *is* a proper way. We even find that the word has ethical or repressive overtones.

Also in times like these we tend to become very adaptable. We have adapted ourselves somewhat to over-doses of radiation, to the hydrocarbons in the atmosphere, to additives in food. So where does "proper" come in?

It comes in precisely on that border where sanity ends and dementia begins. A function within the habitat can withstand so much withdrawal from it, but beyond that it ceases to be a function, can no longer distinguish outer from inner, birth from murder, anger from love.

Adapting to poisons and changes in the food-source is easy, because unconscious, compared with *changing perceptions*. The wolf which perceives colored ribbons as a barrier which he cannot even at the cost of life pass through will be shot by the hunter. It is its perception that hasn't adapted.

And in the case of humans perception is all. Change the colored ribbon—the perception—and he will pass through to freedom. But he can't.

It is because his thought-reflexes are so strong. After all, we meant them to be. They must become the equivalent of animal impulses. And undoing them is as difficult as teaching the hand *not* to recoil from hot water.

We need thought-reflexes as the animal needs impulses—to mate, mother the young, nourish itself. Like the animal we can't conduct life consciously. We need new reflexes all the time, to cope with new situations. When we learn to drive an automobile our actions must become automatic. Once habituated, we drive thirty miles to the next city without being aware of it, yet we drive safely. We only "wake up" to this afterwards. We are astonished at our power to act blindly and automatically, and yet with greater efficiency than at other more alert times.

Most of life is conducted this way. We can even listen to the radio while we drive. Reflexes allow us to do multiple things.

So when reflexes erode we are in a desperate position. When they erode too far we call that desperation madness: we are too withdrawn.

When we drive the car automatically we are perceiving *through thoughts we have learned*. Most thought-reflexes we learned in childhood. They came to us through the behavior of adults, mostly our parents. Conscious effort wasn't needed in order to learn them any more than it was needed while we were learning our mother tongue.

If perceptions were manufactured quickly, and quickly changed, we would find it very uncomfortable. There would be no reality and therefore no sanity. The more time perceptions take to form the more solid reality appears. The older our thought-reflexes are the surer we are about reality. Thoughts should be centuries, if possible millennia, old, however much they may be modified here and there in the course of time. Their job is to *explain* everything seen and heard so that our perceptions will come already packaged with details about the use and meaning of things.

When a civilization is very sure of itself so the perceptions are sure. When it isn't, as our civilization (now a global one) isn't, explanations are no longer packaged in sights and sounds. It therefore takes much longer for children to mature, even longer for them to make any sense out of things, longer still to apply the sense.

The key to this, in our present world (we call "the present" what has usually lasted at least fifty years), is *the collapse of literacy* to the point of crisis. Increasingly, over the past decades, the universities, including the venerable ones, from Oxford and Cambridge to Harvard and Hale, standards of erudition have had to be lowered so as to meet a lower level of understanding. It began to be said that the examination papers of, say, 1920 or 1950 or 1970, were required to address an ever lower level of understanding.

But the collapse of literacy means not that minds are failing to think but that thinking itself lacks any literate yardstick. Which in turn means that the human mind now draws its language and attitudes from journalism, not scholarship—from, in a word, the "media", namely the filter through which our view of life is passed. Whether we are talking about films, television or newspapers we are naming the new sources of understanding. That they are unreliable or grouped into factions or heavily weighed on the side of the income generated makes no difference whatever.

It is the effect on language that we should be looking at—chiefly at the fact that the age-old division of language into the written and the spoken part has split asunder. We are a long way now from the time when Marshall McLuhan published his ardent *The Gutenburg Galaxy* in which he described the revolution that the first printing presses in Europe brought about in the fifteenth century, when at last the written and the spoken parts of the language could meet and see each other.

Hitherto in medieval times, when a monk or priest said something memorable which the whole of Christendom should hear it was repeated by mouth but was inevitably altered or garbled during its journey. Or someone wrote it down on parchment but that too could be garbled. Now, with printing presses galore, all that was changed—a lively conversation across great distances could take place! Hundreds if not thousands were now "in the market" (yes, even that modern word might be used) for even garbled versions.

And the tragedy was that this union of Christian thought took place in the very century, the fifteenth century, when that thought, that one unquestioned centre and support of life, began if not to crumble, at least to split at the edges. Henry VIII of England was born at the end of that century and in not many years dealt the Church of Rome the most brutal and audacious blow it had ever received, namely the dissolution of her monasteries, and their sale for pitifully small sums. This was a protest indeed; not for nothing was it called Protestantism.

Today the written form of language merges with and is drawn from speech, while speech is drawn from the written, so that they drag each other down into cliché and anecdote.

The printed "book" or "study" or "essay" can now be in the language of a letter to a close relative, no longer a language coming from beyond the writer and received from "outside" (D.H. Lawrence used the words Holy Spirit to describe what the "born" writer was in thrall of—no concept *there* of a "mental property" jealously guarded).

Nevertheless, certain people, today as before, *must* be literate! Actors, government spokesmen, parliaments, congresses, the political parties that sustain them, must all willy-nilly rely for dear life on a literacy that has long since faded, yet will not give up the ghost.

It appears that to whatever degree illiteracy becomes the rule literacy remains the cornerstone of human life.

So we each carry about with us what I am going to call *popular lore*. It makes our language so different from what it was half a millennium ago as to be a new language, and its familiar pictures of life may be utterly unknown in two generations.

It is the same lore for everybody—the educated, the refined, the street people, the criminals, the leaders and the led. A few simple ideas govern this lore, and these rest firmly on other deeper ones locked in our perceptions, which are stout and irresistible after centuries of fortification.

The huge audiences worldwide in the 1930s for Hollywood films (showing to houses holding well over a thousand people, with several shows a day) are an example of how widespread popular lore can become with no effort at all. We can scorn the feeble stories and tinsel values and bodiless sex of those "flicks" as they were called in Britain but once in the cinema, close-packed in the dark, we sank into a childlike receptivity, irrespective of our frail opinions: the amplification of image and sound overcame our critical and imaginative parts. The screen became the most successful demagogue there ever was, and it still is.

This is why we call films a *popular* medium, and why that medium quickly abandoned the theatre and literature as its guides while, with a positive genius, keeping the old form of the theatre intact, with its high inaccessible proscenium arch, separated from the audience by an orchestral pit. The transition from theatre to film was therefore smooth, polite, unobtrusive.

This lore doesn't require a time-mandate. It opens its door to new ideas as easily as it rejects them. Films must be highly mobile: their "editing", namely their cuts from one take to another, must be so swift and exact that they pass unnoticed. It must forever be entertaining new ideas, however crude, and rejecting old ones, however valuable. In other words popular lore is our adapting unit. It tries to adjust to changes but in a safe and conservative manner. Films may be a mire of prejudice and fatuity but the editing side must be perfect.

The *popular lore* we all carry about with us is a language of half-formed dreams and attitudes scrambled from all kinds of sources including magic. Hollywood simply tapped into these.

It is why new thought is said to be "ahead of its time". This really means "ahead of popular lore": it digs into long-established perceptions. Hence the media's double role of projecting and bolstering old perceptions (consensus) while constantly puncturing them with controversial barbs (disturbance). The media create fear and pain as its stock play-material—the pain is what could potentially hurt us and the fear is that it is on its deadly way, though the "outspoken" or "provocative" side of media-language can't go too far because consensus (cash) would be lost.

Popular lore also follows our perceptions blindly. If crime becomes a daily and common occurrence popular lore will naturally fill up with crime and cruelty and a mean fascination for all disaster, explosion, maiming, mutilation, gang fights, war, bank robbery ending in a shoot-out, vendetta or ethnic massacre. Popular lore has no shames and goes hand in bloody hand with moralism of a most haughty kind.

Popular lore in times of collapse, as in imperial Rome, steams with gore and glowers cruelly at the fellow human. Nowadays it is easy for us to glimpse this in today's world. Traffic altercations are a good field for observation. A driver's raging mask directed toward another vehicle which has braked too hard or done a wrong turn or misunderstood an intersection symbolizes the carnage of this century, the burned and truncated children in our wars crying for parents who are dead. They symbolize the children who lack more than parents, lacking sight, sex, ears, legs to walk with, hands to touch.

The mask is Homo Demens who in that moment will kill whatever comes to hand.

But such a popular lore, dripping with the blood of innocents, is accepted by the nervous system with surprising ease. The angry mask falls the moment its owner steps away from his automobile for a meal or a rest. His perceptions save him. They tell him that whatever state of anger he might be in *during* the anger is of no effect on the "real" world to which he is just now returning. However many relentless stares and hardened hearts there might be, all is still well. Civilization is intact, nothing unusual has happened, life is a humdrum routine safely undertaken every day and not for a moment any cause for alarm.

The perception is a lie and a fraud but it stays the hand. Perceptions are always there to steady and reassure us because they are always anything from fifty to five hundred years behind the times.

It can't be avoided, this *supine complacency of the perceptions*. It is the price you pay for having to fabricate your reality instead of inheriting it. Perceptions take time to build and time to dismantle.

For instance, no amount of ecological data with their carbon-gas warnings can *wholly* penetrate our perceptions because locked within those perceptions is a concept of Mother Nature inexhaustible in her healthy nourishment. No matter what warnings we receive about the dire effect of sunlight, now it has lost its age-old filters, our *nervous systems* cannot believe that the warmth of the rays are unwholesome. Our thinking has given way to *what the skin is telling us,* out of its experiences for ages past, and telling us falsely.

When in 1992 two leaders of the Green movement committed suicide in Berlin it was possibly a desperate recognition of this fact.

A powerful idea put forward with authority will carry humanity with it very gradually, until it is a truism. Therefore our perceptions are filled with truisms rather than truth.

Our perceptions and thus our reality take no account of what their designers, e.g. the ancient Romans and Greeks and Egyptians and Minoans, felt in their spare time. Perceptions seize whatever is grist, blindly and greedily, here and now.

* * *

The word "reality" itself comes from the Latin *res*, meaning "a thing". A "thing" is in isolation from its surroundings. But this is already theory! Things are *never* in isolation. However, our minds have to perform the trick of untangling a web of entangled "things" in order to be able to manipulate them. And perceptions are based on our needs. A "house" is in isolation from the "street", from the "trees" and "shrubbery" surrounding it, from the "sky" above it, from the "smoke" that comes from its "chimney". Likewise a "room" in a house is in isolation from the house itself, and from the "corridors", and from the "people" in it. A "table" is isolated from the "carpet" and the "pictures" on the wall from the "cat" and the "couch".

In this way we select according to a need-gradient. Thus there is no one reality for all time or all humans or all species. Reality means "The way I need to arrange things".

Our minds select what they need to concentrate on for usefulness. This leads us into believing that our needs are the only ones in life. This is what the absurd idea "reality is fixed and independent of us" means. But we have to have it that way. We are obliged to live in illusion.

We also base our science on illusion, with consequent disastrous effects.

Our needs are locked inside our perceptions and we can't see them. So reality isn't *things* in the sense of static objects outside us but *impressions* we need in order to manage life.

In early childhood we were happy enough just with these impressions. Hiding or playing under the table we found no need to see the table as separate from anything else because nothing was separate from ourselves. An adult foot might stand out for us more than other things happening under the table but still we saw it only in terms of our comfort, not its use. We climbed trees, swung from their boughs, sat against their trunks, sheltered under them in rain, listened to the wind in them from our beds but still we didn't pick them out as isolated things. Everything was intimate to us, not useful. *To make something useful a certain withdrawal is required of us.*

Conversely, the desperate among us must seize on whatever comes to hand, otherwise they see no way forward for themselves. They may have shunned the small degree of "education" they have received (there are no laws against getting a bad mark, namely failing to get what the teacher is talking about). But they wish to make a mark simply because they can't. They live in a limbo of disregard from others, from what they are saying.

What they are craving is a new kind of fame. We must look into this important word (throughout all our Western civilizations). Both in ancient Greece and ancient Rome "fame" meant simply utterance or speech. It was pronounced the same in both civilizations, and of course "fame" in our sense is *being talked about on a great scale*. The dunce, as we used to call him, able to learn nothing from his teacher's bewildering soliloquies, feels the need to be talked about perhaps more than any of those "celebrities" whose names trip easily off the tongue. He wishes to be talked about at any cost—the punishment he might get is worth no longer living in impotence. The more you feel unnoticed the more you crave notice—the fame, the being talked about. You are caught in your murders or rapes or "unmotivated" attacks on people. You get life imprisonment. You are stood before judges and perhaps juries. Lawyers spoke for and against you. You have craved ancient "fame", namely many words spoken about you, and you got it.

* * *

If we look further into the word "reality" we find that its Latin root is in turn derived from the Indo-European *rai*, meaning "a piece of property or wealth". In other words it is something *we possess*. "Things" are our way of possessing and in our first years we don't need to possess, we are ministered to.

As adults we see a world marked out for us in terms of what we need to possess it for—trees for our wood, water to our mills, earth for plowing, vegetables and livestock for eating. We talk of metals and minerals, soils and rocks and fertile or waste land. Our very languages are languages of possession. Whatever civilization we belong to—whether it talks about Zeus or electricity, Icarus or airplanes—the reality we invent is a means of controlling a habitat always precarious for the human.

When Alice tells the Gnat in *Through the Looking Glass* that she knows the names of the insects in the woods he asks, "What's the use of their having names if they won't answer to them?", to which she replies, "No use to *them*, but it's useful to the people that name them, I suppose. If not, why do things have names at all?"

Names declare that things are different from our perception of them. They have a life of their own. In early childhood that isn't so. And in this respect the child mind is nearer the truth. Adult popular lore says, absurdly but pragmatically, "Our names are the only ones that could be given to things" and "The things we perceive are the only things there are" and "Both names and things are entirely independent of us, they go on while we aren't looking at them and even after our deaths", which is the purest non-sequitur.

Thus perceptions *always contain a misleading element*.

We make the easy mistake of believing that perceiving is a self-proving procedure ("if this is how I see and hear it this is how it is"). Little do we suspect that ideas can alter the way we feel sexual desire, how we embrace and approach the mate. They can alter the very sight and sound of things. For instance, the sound of planes arriving or parting can block rest for someone who leads a busy life but for someone else starved of company and fellowship it may console.

Of course we have heard from the psychologists that this is possible but as to actual *perceptions* becoming different, this is more difficult to grasp. The ideas (needs) in them were planted so long ago that we aren't aware of them any more.

In childhood we have to learn names and what the names signify because we must soon begin to use the world for our own purposes. Later we say that we "perceive" these things as a table or a book and it hardly seems possible that the table and book don't really exist separate from each other, and weren't born for our use.

Names are our means of controlling our habitat. We pity animals because they can't do this. As to the fact that they need our names as fish or worms need the giraffe's neck, it has little chance of penetrating to our thought-reflexes.

How much more difficult it is, then, for us to believe that our name-world consists of ideas that might be entirely false, indeed downright harmful and finally insane.

SEVEN

Knowledge Is A Pure Myth

We think we see things clearly, much more clearly than people in the past did. We think we can see the truth about things at last, and this truth is summarized and contained in science. We believe that people, say, a hundred or even two hundred years ago (our credit-allowance becomes less generous as we go back in time) did to some extent see things clearly like ourselves but only because they had science in its embryonic state (steam locomotion, machine looms).

As to the Middle Ages they were an impossible limbo of crudity and superstition and we don't feel they existed at all, or at least if they existed it was like animals and primitive peoples exist, in a half sort of way.

As to Greece and Rome, this is getting into school curriculum and few people go near that nowadays for the practical reason that it is irrelevant to the modern understanding of things.

About Egypt, well, we are entering a mummification world in which people thought they had to take goods to heaven with them (a mistake on two counts—the necessity of the goods and the existence of heaven).

Of course all of these peoples in their uncomfortable worlds (rewarded for their ignorance by high mortality rates) would have given their right eyes to be us and what is more they, notably the

Greeks and Romans, *tried* to be us but they only made it to the extent of mathematics, philosophy and things like that.

None of this bares examination and we know it. But it is the way we perceive it. And a *perception* requires neither evidence nor verisimilitude in order to persist in our mind.

For instance we go on accepting the names historians have given us for the dividing up of recent time into Dark Ages, Middle Ages, Rebirth (jacked up linguistically into "Renaissance") and "Modern" times without reflecting that there might be something seriously wrong with this revisionist scenario. In fact, once we look into it, we find it rather wondrous that any of the known facts about the last two millennia could ever have led to its formulation.

"Modern" means no more than *now*, in other words *us*. This same narcissism dominates the other names too. But again we mustn't be diverted by evidence, however demonstrable. Perceptions are made on the basis of doctrine, not evidence.

Bertrand Russell once said that the trouble with philosophers was that they got their ideas first and proved them afterwards, instead of working from the facts. But the fact *he* overlooked was that all science does the same, more especially as science arose from Logic, namely a property of philosophy. That an idea is called a fact solely on the basis not of facts at all but the doctrines that led to those "facts" would appear to most scientists as fancy, despite the fact that their hallowed Einstein put the truth neatly in his "first the theory, then the fact".

Bertrand Russell was unknowingly referring to experimental procedures that are the basis of "science". Now experiment involves a logical formula (philosophy again), namely Thesis + Antithesis = Synthesis. So if you are a doctor and define humans strictly in terms of their age (on the basis of the purely theological notion that everyone decays with age) you will simply feed this into your "researches" on the subject: you will use mice of great age as the Thesis of your experiment, then add the Antithesis of "hearty exercise" (which you will inflict on the mice and probably kill them) so that your Synthesis will naturally result in the "fact" that however much exercise you (mice) do in old age makes no difference to your destiny to decay with age. This "experiment" then ends with the proud expression "Quod Erat Demonstrandum", namely "Which was to be proved". But in fact you have cheated shamelessly.

It is a more than sobering thought that "science" (a word meaning simply "knowledge") is dedicated to these circular Which Was To Be Proved enterprises.

If we look into our division of the past into "ancient" and "medieval" and "modern" we shall find the very same peculiarity. We are on a moving belt of time, just as we are in our reckoning of time as past, present and future". The past is gone before you get into the present, which is gone into the past at once, leaving you staring bleakly into an even more ghostly future.

It is clearly ourselves we have to investigate if we are going to get any real idea of the past. It is just no good talking about the needs of past peoples as if our present needs were the only ones there ever were. It would be no use our taking a Mithraist attitude that the sun was God, and that all life flowed from it, and that all worship was due to it, if we were trying to determine relative speeds of light across a given surface. The one civilization will simply not permit the cross-use of its terms with another.

But we can't even cross to different phases of *our own* civilization! We perceive very differently from the people of Homer's time, less differently from Europeans two centuries ago, so Homer is impossible for us to imagine while Casanova and powdered wigs with fleas in them are easy. We perceive the dead as serious living people like ourselves only to the degree to which they resemble us.

It seems we have to ask ourselves what is this civilization that divides us so deeply from each other—not only the living from the dead but the living from the living?

* * *

The first thing I discovered when I asked this question was that all the civilizations we know about are known to us *by their religions.* We know of no civilization that was not preceded by a religion, *of*

76

which that civilization was the community. It wasn't a fact I set out to find or expected.

In fact as I looked further I found religion to be the cause not just of civilization *but every human activity there was.*

I knew the inherited "modern" attitude—Zuckerman's cliché that science had chased the gods out of the sky could be found in any tabloid as an inviolable thought-reflex safely supported by consensus.

Here the word "science" meant much the same as "modern". It seemed to say that while religion belongs to a person's private conscience, to which we owe respect, the facts of practical life are entirely scientific in nature, just as the knowledge provided by science is objective, while that of churches isn't.

And, similarly, when you looked into Zuckerman's "science" you found no analysis at all. All you heard from him were the bare details of a monkey brawl, badly and incompletely observed, just as it was incompetently managed by the zoo people. Aside from that all he spoke about were his own purely social feelings about animals, namely that they scratched and ate off the ground and had public sex and behaved disgustingly. Even when he talked about the diseases monkeys in the zoo are prone to he managed to make them sound socially deplorable, though they were exactly the same diseases as humans have.

His *style of approach* was scientific, his *style* was scientific, his *sentences* were scientific. But it was all social chit-chat. It had nothing to do with analysis at all. Not thought but prejudice, namely conditioned response, was behind it. And I suspected that this was the case with most of the so-called science we got. More, I discovered the roots of science not only in religion but the Christian one specifically. More even than that, I discovered those roots to lie in medieval thought, our own Christian medieval thought. I discovered that religion was always and everywhere the guiding motive, even when it invented atheism.

* * *

When the old Minoan world in Crete changed into the early Greek or Homeric world eight or so centuries before Christ, when the Homeric became the Athenian civilization centuries later, and when the Roman world turned into the Church of Rome it was always a religious change—from the Minoan earth-religion to the Homeric gods to Athenian rationalism to the new god called Christ. Each shift produced *a different way of life*, and the difference lay in the difference of the religion.

King Minos, Christ, Buddha, Moses, Mohammed—these were the names that divided one civilization from another, or one phase from another. These men were visionaries—spoken to by gods or angels in caves and meadows, and on mountains. Unlike the people round them they speak with authority. They have no doubts because of the nature of what they are told, what they receive from a source more reliable than human sources. This is the key to their authority and to the fact that others follow them. Their words are from another place, like words spoken at Delphi.

Not that this is the religion. A visionary or prophet or Lord simply enters your perceptions, turns them in peculiar ways so that you can't see life the way you saw it before. This is why we are always up in arms about sects. They take away our young just like that. The young are blind to our example and deaf to our words because they are seeing something they feel is better than dead truisms and clichés and safe socially condoned attitudes.

This is why the visions invariably seem an act of rebellion and are resisted by the State. It is why the first Christians were martyrs, and why their martyrdom in turn made converts. Something has thrown the perceptions on their backs. Rimbaud put it nicely—"One arrives at the unknown by means of a derangement of all the senses".

The fact is that we can't be made to change our lives by logical analysis or moral admonition. These leave our perceptions intact. In other words visions are disruptive forces. You can have too many of them. And this is where religion and churches come in. They recognize that *a stable life has to be made*, first of all for hundreds and thousands of people, eventually perhaps for millions. It is the church or the sect that teaches the community how best to live with the vision, incorporate and realize it in every waking act, the public and the intimate: this we call theology. But theology need not be written or even reasoned.

A vision comes with a clamor and urgency so overwhelming that it changes daily habits. But nothing short of this could produce civilizations so various. It is why the phases of a civilization are strikingly different one from another, for instance the Athenian phase of our civilization from the Christian one. One phase grows from another. Without an *earlier* vision no new one is possible. Christ the Jew was born in a Greek colony.

* * *

To my surprise this brought me full circle back to Zuckerman—and in measured agreement with him. It took an anatomist to see that an animal's anatomy isn't so very different from a human one, but that the differences in all *other* respects are vast. And those differences he called "culture", which he manages, being weak in history like most self-appointed scientists, to separate entirely from religion.

In the human *everything starts from the imagination*. William Blake called imagination "the divine body of man"—the one he survived with.

We have to put aside our grandiose prejudice that to use the word "civilization" we must deal only in hundreds and thousands, not millions of years. The idea was advocated mostly in Alexandria, where it was said that ancient Greece was a rehearsal for Christendom, and Plato a rehearsal for Christ, and therefore, by inference, that you couldn't go much further back in time if you wanted to make spiritual sense.

It is an idea too slight to examine but it burrowed so deep into our perceptions that to be told even today that there were flourishing civilizations millions of years ago (better than ours perhaps?) creates bafflement. Historical scholarship will have none of it.

But how do visions and theology, even fraudulent theology, come into modern practical life, especially as being practical is supposed to be the opposite of being visionary? What sort of vision is even remotely present at a board meeting, a biology congress, a finance committee's review of the company's cash flow into the pockets of a respected chairman? How on earth can the logic these men and women use, and the reasonable terms in which they think, and the practical matters they discuss, owe their origin to visions and inspirations?

Perhaps we shall find that the rationalism on which all this practicality depends owes its life to a vision, no less than Cretan civilization owed its life to King Minos's vision in the cave when he received the Laws, and Israel its life to Moses' vision of the Ten Commandments. Wherever you may look, even in the driest business speech, you will find the shadow of religion, however deeply forgotten on the board. And this doesn't mean religion in the accepted proselytizing sense but in the form of *the most detailed thought*. It means that no civilization, even the most practical or rationalist, can believe in its own world unless it came from an experience so awesome that *it was more important than life to those who received it.*

Less obvious is the fact that such experiences *determine what is to be taken as logical and ethical and truthful in any particular civilization.* While the animal at a very early age can pilot itself through the habitat, man must learn gradually, and from other human beings. In this sense he is always born formless—without a fixed reality to perceive. He must be *given* the reality, as it has already been decided on by other human beings. Man might indeed be called the visionary creature because without a vision of what life should be, or what life means, or how life should be lived, he cannot even form a society. Lacking so many of his old biological compulsions he is removed from the habitat whether he likes it or not and must therefore create *a secondary habitat* that so fills the air with its noise and color that he is swept off his feet from his earliest months and grows up to believe that this secondary thing is the "real" world, and even the only world, fixed for all time and completely independent of him.

It seems that the human can only stay in one reality a certain number of centuries. When it loses its hold on him, that is when his perceptions cease to convey it as unchanging and eternal, when he is no longer sure how he is going to behave or in what he is going to believe, only one thing will reunite him with others and that is a new reality which bursts on him like a truth that is both obvious and yet utterly original.

Whether we like it or not there is no experience we know of which can achieve this truth except what comes in a visionary form. Interests, needs, status, power—all willingly crumble before this new sense of belonging, this warmth that seizes everyone so that all suspicion and dread are suddenly gone.

When a new vision seizes hold of a people stories begin to be told and these we call myths. It is these stories on which our knowledge, namely our manner of satisfying our needs, is based. If these stories are set out in a thoughtful form we call them theology, but they still belong to myth. This is why myths have been called "somebody else's religion". We are never happy to admit that knowledge—in our particular case, science—is indebted to stories or theology for its form, but the fact remains that it is so.

Any thinking we do has to happen under certain rules. These have to be laid down, not only for each civilization but each phase too. Really a civilization is a vast zone of influence divided into many regions, and these change from time to time, and bring about changes in the whole. The main trunk of the civilization, whether Hellenic or Chinese, retains its general form, so that, today, East can be sharply distinguished from the West. In all cases the differences are due to the religion which launched each phase, even when the religion has long since been forgotten.

At this point we may extend our definition of civilization. Since it came about with the first human, that human *must have been a visionary*, otherwise he couldn't have magnetized other primates about him.

When scholars find no sense, particularly religious sense, in the Greek myths it is because our myth is different, not because we don't have myths too. One myth always excludes another in this way, which is why we create human history as the fragmented past, and the fragments are unable to gel. We prefer the idea that our knowledge, unlike "myth", never withers away, never ceases to be comprehensible, never loses its truth. But we feel this for a deeply practical reason—so that each separate phase of civilization will present *a "reality" that will have an entirely hypnotic hold on us.*

The Christian myth in particular is fiercely exclusive. When it was being built—in Alexandria, for instance—it banished the "old" or Greek myths and said they were untrue but accepted that, because of Plato, those myths nearly made it, being a grand rehearsal for Christendom.

So nowadays we have the idea, prevalent among advanced mathematicians, that the Greeks *nearly* made advanced mathematics but didn't quite have what it takes. That is, we are looking at the "old" myth with *our* myth, which means the old needs with *our* needs. So we make nonsense of the ancient world. We say that they didn't have a religion in the proper sense, meaning by this, "proper" Christianity.

We regard ourselves as "scientifically" equipped to look at other people's myths, which stops us recognizing our own. A proper search would show us that in science lies a late Christian myth so compelling that *it has been accepted as inviolable reality the whole world over.*

Our confidence that, on the contrary, science has been waiting in the wings to be discovered since the beginning of time is *part of that myth*, being derived from the central theme of Christian theology, namely that we (the Christians, now the world, whether we are "religious" or not) can see through and across other civilizations, can judge and compare and perceive truthfully all other and previous peoples, can tell the final truth about them and this truth represents *an absolute knowledge* which future generations will extend but never dethrone as an "explanation" of things.

Who would think that this was all worked out quietly and carefully in the medieval monasteries and universities? But it is there to be studied.

And who would have thought that the whole world would swallow it hook, line and sinker? Who would have thought that in the light of it millions of people would come to mean by the word "religion" the Christian religion they mostly don't believe in? But it happened and it is at least a homage to the fervent industry and prowess of mind of those theologians. They meant their ideas to be swallowed—they said they would be swallowed and they were.

The fervor was enough to overcome the Roman empire. Rome's household gods crumbled like a pack of cards before this extraordinary faith which said that *a god had, not long since, actually been alive.*

Our teachers have nearly always said that myth is what ancient or primitive societies believed in, while we modern people have shown them to be poppycock. For instance it is electricity that creates thunderstorms not Zeus. We even attribute to the Hellenic world a desire, and thus a pathetic failure to attain to our civilization—presumably to our aircraft and automobiles and instant light. As we shall see, the desire to travel fast and fly and illuminate cities at a touch belongs to our myth and none other, i.e. to Christianity and not to ancient Greece at all. Yet, such is the relation of one phase of a civilization to another that these deeply disparate societies couldn't have happened without each other.

* * *

When Christianity was declared official in Rome under the emperor Theodosius in the last years of the fourth century AD anyone found worshipping the old household gods could receive a heavy fine. These Roman gods were of course Greek ones with new names. A close link with Greek myth and thus Greek religion was retained. But Greeks and Romans began to be considered by Christianized Greeks and Romans as on *a low level of spiritual truth,* however commendable they might have been as rational teachers. Plato may have been the first "hero" but Christ was "the last true Son of God the world will ever see". Of course this can't be demonstrated but no myth can demonstrate its own truth. "Myth" here doesn't mean imaginary, for myth alone provides the yardstick of what is true and what is false. To demonstrate the presence of Zeus the Earth Shaker all the Aegean peoples had to do was to point to thunderbolts; to demonstrate the validity of atomic theory today all we have to do today is point to fission.

Myth is a civilization's personality and form—that by which it is recognized. One myth is vividly different from another—the Hindu Indian from the American Indian, the Persian from the Greek. No one myth can be called truer than another because a human can only absorb and understand the myth into which he is born. *All else he sees in terms of it*, making arbitration as between one myth and another impossible. He bases his logic on it, and his modes of gathering knowledge.

Our myth was formulated by Christian theology, taking elements from Greek, Jewish and Muslim thought. From our myth has come all our Western forms of knowledge, all science. And if some scientific disciplines strike us as crude (to judge by the state of the habitat) it is because the theologians behind it learned from their Greek, Jewish and Muslim mentors in a divided state of mind. They simultaneously discounted ancient Greece and Rome as pagan or infidel, the relics of an "ancient" world, and based their "new" world on them. The word "modern" simply means "now". Rather inevitably the expression "post-modern" came into being, meaning precisely nothing because you can't have a "post now": more precisely, the expression is a rehash of the Futuristic movement in Italian art at the beginning of the twentieth century.

Originally the word *mythos* meant genuine historical tales handed from one generation to the next. In late-Greek times these tales came to be written down. To us, by a remarkable process of reduction, the word "myth" means just about the opposite. In fact it implies that all civilizations except our own have labored under illusions from which we are free.

So we accept Euclid and of course Aristotle but we say of the Greek gods that they were an old belief-system that died away with time. We say that truth in the form of Euclidean geometry and Aristotelian ethics survived to become the basis of our rational grasp of reality but we miss out the fact that it survived for only one reason—that it was the one part of the Greek picture of life *the Christians didn't want to destroy.*

A myth has to *state* things, baldly and unequivocally, since it comes from one man's vision. It provides an agreed picture of life, determines how streets, market-places, government offices are to look. The lines of buildings, the clothes and gardens exactly express myth.

We only have to glance at our airports, highways, overhead cables and industrial sites to see what our myth is. They are the language of the religion that conceived them centuries ago, though the religion is now out of sight. Their lines are stark and grandiose, the thought behind them is analytical, and invariably close to them or infiltrating them is great squalor.

How different that world is from the world of the Gothic cathedral or the humped Romanesque church of early medieval times. In the same way these worlds too were strikingly different from the later Palladian and Renaissance styles, and both of these were very different from the much earlier Minoan or Egyptian styles.

We simply cannot divide ancient Greece from Egypt or either from Persia. Each variant of civilization indicates a different religion or the modification of an older one. But religion is never escaped. And if we are skeptical about its formative powers it is only because *our religion has produced this skepticism.*

If there is one thing about this modern myth of ours which sets it firmly aside from the others it is the fact that *it makes no reference to religion.* In mathematical law, in geometry, in the theory of sound waves or magnetic attraction, in thermodynamics, ballistics or geo-chronometry where can a mention of the meaning of death be found? where a mention of ecstasies? No invocations are heard, no fertility rites performed. No blessing of computer chips is felt to be necessary.

The hub of this myth is what we call *matter.* This is much like a Greek "universal", everywhere and yet nowhere, in everything but not in itself something we can perceive. In other words it is an idea, a thinker's tool, namely a made-up story. Matter is no less a story than anything else imagined.

But there is something about this tool which we are likely to miss if we don't examine it carefully. *It personifies alienation.* Matter is separate from us, it is eternal, it goes on after we die as it preceded our birth, it is fixed and unalterable and says nothing whatever to us. We could just as well be—matter.

If this is what Zuckerman meant when he said that science had chased the gods out of the sky he was right. Except that science did nothing of the kind. The Christian religion did—so effectively that even its One God eventually went too, except as a decorative thought after a long practical day.

Yes, even the origins of "matter" lie in theological history. As I shall show in detail later, Christian theologians were anxious to "empty the sky" and yet keep the Trinity. It was an impossible task. They handed "matter" over to the thinkers, and kept the Trinity to themselves. So of course we find no trace of religion in our myth!

Matter is really an absurdity, as any story is when we try to say that it is real. But this shouldn't worry us. Science can be based on an absurd idea so long as it works. If anyone doubts that particle theory is effective as a trick he should replay his nuclear explosion cassette. And what does "absurd" mean? Simply that it is a story and we can't perceive it. But you can't perceive any idea, any theory.

You are in trouble when you say that it *does* exist, that you *can* perceive it. And if you base a civilization on a false claim the results are—well, all we have to do is to look around.

The thing we should be noting here isn't how absurd science or matter are but the fact that they claim to *eschew the absurd.* Indeed they claim to be our only refuge from it, the first body of knowledge that we can call reliable and not a bowl of visionary tripe. Emotions don't come into science. Which makes my later examination of how science came into being—by what *highly emotional steps*—all the more pertinent.

Science makes no mention of religion *only because it was forbidden to.* Under the terms of the theological contract it had to stay strictly within matter, where there was no Trinity, no Christ, no imagination, nothing for the human heart whatever. After centuries of inheriting this theology we look up at the sky and perceive not the home of gods but a vast emptiness.

So the premises and hunches and deductions of science are a body of atheism for us. They describe a world to which the existence or otherwise of a God or gods is irrelevant. They find no evidence of such existence. And of course we take this as the truth about the universe. But science can't find evidence of anything we might remotely call religious or divine because it was intended not to. Even to search for it or surmise about it was rendered impossible by the terms of the matter-contract.

Atheism is a theological doctrine like any other. In the Middle Ages it was much expounded. It shocked people because, unlike "infidel" doctrines, it kept within the Christian framework. It said that there was no Creator, that God wasn't the Father and Christ wasn't the Son, even though they might worship Christ.

Atheism simply says that the world we perceive doesn't refer to any force beyond itself. Technology establishes the same: it offers no comment whatever, being a phenomenon that only has meaning in so far as we give it meaning by using it. In the same way a modern city offers no comment. It keeps away from the subject. Unlike the cities of every other civilization we know about, they are pure dwelling spaces.

So the theology of alienation won out, all too truly.

Atheism says that God doesn't exist quite as if somebody had ever said He did. But only atheists ever did, by suggesting that He didn't. No religion we know of suggests that any form of divinity exists in the usual sense of that word, namely as we exist. In fact "godly" existence is the very opposite, which is why it is called divine. It isn't subject to change, to death, and therefore has no form. Only things that exist have form. So atheism always starts from a misunderstanding of what religions say. Atheism talks about the world, religion talks about an experience. So the atheist doctrines have always missed religion because an experience, a vision was never considered to exist like a table does. Ask the hermit where he put his ecstasies, in what drawer, and he cannot tell you.

Buddhism is often described as atheist—but a religion just the same. It is the self, not God, that has created the world. Buddhism acknowledges no god to whom prayers may be directed, or on whose shoulders responsibility for demented human behavior may be heaped, or who can plunge us into an eternity of punishment.

Christian atheism, on the other hand, came from a misunderstanding of what religion is and this misunderstanding cut through Christian teaching and grew ever more quickly into power talk, existence talk, knowledge talk.

* * *

The Aegean peoples described their vision in terms of Pallas Athene and the Oracle and Persephone. And so it is with all pictures of life, whether we are talking of Angra Mainyu, the ancient Persian god of evil, or a mathematical equation. Their truth depends only on *what you wish to be demonstrated*.

We say today that thunderbolts demonstrate electricity, but there is no more truth in this idea than in the idea that thunderbolts demonstrate Zeus. "Electricity" and "Zeus" are simply names. We say "But we use electricity, it has transformed life all over the earth". What we are using is a force within the habitat. We "harness" it. Greeks called this Zeus. The force was the same. It may well be that the Egyptians also used electricity. If they did they didn't harness it for work or comfort. They had needs different from ours. Likewise electricity didn't fall within Greek needs. Zeus did.

The name Zeus had great power in the Minoan and Hellenic worlds, and electricity has in ours. Zeus worked for those worlds as the name electricity works for us. It is what we are trying to get out of life that makes the truth, not vice versa. We know the truth (about Zeus's thunderstorms or about electricity) solely on the basis of what we need. Zeus the Earth Shaker manifested what the Greeks needed, while brilliantly lighted cities manifest what we need.

All human needs refer to religion, as I shall show, but there are different religions, and different phases of the same religion, and it is these that produce civilizations that seem quite alien to one another. And sometimes a civilization is produced, like ours, which is actually *based* on the idea of being alien. In it the human stands alone and naked on his little portion of the moving belt of time, distant from nature, from all previous peoples, and yet, for himself, the only truly existing creature there ever was, the one who knows, and knows finally, and knows absolutely. Until he too is swallowed up, and a better story than the belt of time story visits the harried human mind.

* * *

A civilization produces *untouchable names*. Zeus was an untouchable name for the Greeks. "Electricity" is one for us. The names can't be dethroned. To say they don't exist is too ridiculous to consider, but of course they don't exist, being just names.

Our "scientific objectivity" simply refers to name-untouchability. A basic but ridiculous belief in our popular lore is that when theories work, i.e. when they make the habitat behave in a desired way, they are the truth about the habitat. You could equally claim that when two pots are banged together they make a sound and therefore the sound they make is the truth about pots. Saying that rubbing two stones together will produce fire isn't the truth about the stones or the fire, only your proposition.

What exactly are the needs behind all this Objectivity and Absolute Knowledge talk, this Final Explanation goal which has dominated the Western mind like a morbid compulsion for the last millennium?

EIGHT

Anything For A Change

It was unfortunate that Christianity should have happened in a period of dementia. But then this must always be the case when a new religion comes along, for the simple reason that the dementia has called that religion into being. A new phase of civilization is to be inaugurated.

When the perceptions blur and no longer give a sound picture of reality the haunted human mind goes on one of its self-withdrawal bends. It is time to change the reality but you have to be careful that the dementia doesn't taint you. Not only did Christianity not avoid this, it actually decided to take the self-withdrawal symptom and make it the basis of its program. Which means that the dementia became critical, threatening to become much more than ambulatory.

When the first Christians were trying to convert Rome people were watching fellow humans being mauled to death by animals or battered or cut to death *as a sport*. They even had bets on the outcome of these set-up conflicts, as we shall see. In other words we are talking of compulsions so blind that they must remind us of—the twentieth century.

There was everything in the Roman and even Greek world that the Christian would want to turn away from. But the most significant of his motives to reject at all costs the "ancient" world was the fact that he was born in it and shared its self-disgust and guilt and taste for dreams of grandeur. Alienation, working through disgust, breeds a desire for other places and other people and other selves. Even nature it would like to change because the alienated mind has never looked at nature with appreciation or any understanding at all of its secret languages, so the demented dream of other natures, other planets must needs take you over. And if alienation's friend paranoia is working on you too, sprouting enemies in the wind, a certain element of haste, even panic, will ensue. The "future" will become your most treasured term.

* * *

Right from the fourth century AD Christians argued that Christianity was *new*, a *departure* from the ancient world. The word "ancient" began to assume its present meaning, as in *ancien régime*, namely a worn-out state of affairs. The new régime will straighten it (and us) out.

The theme of renewal, revolution, reform goes through our civilization like an acute case of what psychiatrists used to call akathisia or the inability to sit down.

The first Christians were mostly Greeks and Romans awed and frightened by the old world, its temples and gods and stunning powers of thought, as it crumbled and struggled to retain its spell under emperors like Julian. The "ancient" world stirred revulsion in them and this was necessarily self-revulsion. They felt the competition not only of other sects equally fired, equally serious, but of "ancient" loyalties within themselves. It was the old story of thinking one way and perceiving another.

We use the word "backward" to describe anything from the state of somebody's mind to their degree of education. "Back" here means retrogressive—an earlier state of darkness and helpless groping. Partly this is disgust toward the "ancient" habits of the bath and banquet, and sexual excesses, not to say the blood-lust, and partly it is biological—the human looking back on a "dark" state of animality, before the brightness of his mind told him that he was God's favorite. This backward look existed very much in Greek thought too, and soon became a conviction that the mind was the human's only divine asset.

All changes, reforms are toward this end of *enlightenment*, namely a state of affairs brought about by means of information elicited by the mind. All wars, pogroms, ethnic massacres are for a better, cleaner world. All persecutions are a punishment of victims lost in the unthinkably repulsive filth of heretical, racial or political progeny. All murder is the disposal of unwanted, execrated being.

The phrase "up to date" conveys to what extent we favor *discarding the past*. This was a theological must in early Christian years because the past meant the "old" religion. At the same time we never really discard the past because our perceptions are made up of it. Christendom remained the classical world, through and through. It failed to remove Greek influence, except in the matter of dethroning the old gods, who were getting pretty tired anyway, and it failed not just because it perceived in the old Greek manner but because it needed Greek thought and civilization as the very basis and inspiration of its own. Unfortunately, because of these conflicts, it took Greek thought in a grudging manner which missed out the best of the Greek mind.

* * *

Even a hundred years ago most scholars were convinced that there had been no civilization in the Aegean world before Homer's time, that is before 3000 BC.

The work of the archaeologist Sir Arthur Evans made this look an egomanic idea. His 1900 reproductions of frescoes excavated at Knossos in Crete, showing court women chatting with each other at a public function at least two millennia before Homer's time, provoked a Parisian critic to exclaim "But these are Parisiennes!". Their styles of dress, even their gestures were a replica of those of the *belle epoque*. Their hair was frisé under a band over the forehead, falling down in long separate tresses which had strings of beads and jewels twisted round them. They wore puffed sleeves and flounced skirts with tight girdles. Their colors were bright blues and reds and yellows, with black and white stripes. They wore tight see-through blouses. In these frescoes they were seen in lively conversation, torn between their friends and the spectacle in front of them. Yet they were contemporaries of the ancient Egyptians.

An American college dictionary dated 1980 refers to this Minoan civilization as "pre-historic". And the Minoan religion is generally described as—note the primitive and magical overtone—an "earth religion".

The possibility that we were looking at *our own civilization* in these Cretan frescoes was still overlooked. Properly speaking the word "civilization" could only be applied to the Greeks, since it was their language and their thought that Christian theology was based on.

The Greeks themselves had no such exclusive tastes. They were in close touch with other civilizations, just as the Minoans were in contact with Egypt at the time of the Eighteenth Dynasty and maybe at other times.

The Minoan civilization may have been an offshoot from Egypt. King Minos descended into the labyrinthine birth-cave of Zeus (perhaps formerly an Egyptian god) at Psychro and emerged declaring that Zeus had spoken to him and shown him the Laws. As the Minoan world may have derived from Egypt, so the late Egypt may have owed its resurgence to events in the Aegean or Africa. There were great differences between the various phases of Egyptian civilization—between, say, the Old Kingdom (the period of the great pyramid builders) and the end of the Middle Empire when the country became so weak that it was ruled by Asiatic shepherd kings. After that came the New Empire and a period of expansion, and it is this expansion that may have spawned Minoa.

The ebb and flow of one civilization-phase in touch with another is a continual process which Christianity refused to acknowledge because of its ardent desire that Christ should overcome the world and *make all as new*.

Arthur Evans thought that the Minoan language—the written part he found specimens of—had gone through three phases: first the hieroglyphs (meaning literally "sacred carvings"), then a more flowing type of text he called Linear A, then a modified form called Linear B which was like an early form of Greek. We, conditioned by the progress-idea, are naturally inclined to see these changes as a "development" from the archaic to the modern, from the simple to the refined, and this is how many scholars do see them. We recognize the Athenian of, say, 500 BC as a fellow-rationalist but not the Minoan of 2000 BC, so we unconsciously opt for the idea that the early Minoan was in some way struggling "toward" the Athenian rationalist.

The Minoan religion has been called an earth religion because its myths referred to plants and rocks and animals as dynamic spiritual forces, and this helps us to see it as a "primitive" society on the lines laid down by Christian theology. At school we learn to contrast Athenian thought, that sudden "burst of light", with earlier dark Greek days of tyrant kings who were tribal in their justice. This is because Athens is the first place where we find the intellect being used as a means to enlightenment. That is, we can all imagine ourselves talking in a Socratic group. We may have enormous difficulty imagining ourselves as a late Victorian with a top hat but these dialectical excursions reported by Plato remind us of something we all do, whether we have heard of Plato or not.

Medieval Christianity adopted this discussion idea so fervently that it *became* a discussion—to such an extent that the Sorbonne was at times a vast bordello of rows, fisticuffs and murders provoked by dialectical issues. One could have foreseen as much in the 3rd century AD when the most brilliant Christian lecturer in Alexandria, Hypatia, was battered to death with tiles by Christian monks. It wasn't exactly an Athenian way of resolving an argument but then Socrates wasn't a divided person as the Christian was, with his Greek heart, Roman head and Jewish God.

The Christian wanted a clear, verbally explicit world which would at the same time acknowledge the impenetrable mystery of the Eucharist and the life of Jesus. And of course it couldn't work.

It put the intelligible against the mysterious and then said that the mysterious was responsible for the power to be intelligible. The idea was that Christianity, by blinding humans with the miracle of its newly acquired knowledge, would be shedding Christ's light directly, because he would be providing this knowledge as Hermes had provided it in the Greek world, and Mercury in the Roman.

It is difficult for us nowadays to realize what fervor and excitement went into medieval discussions. The Renaissance has eclipsed that world for us, by taking up all the room so to speak. We moderns recognize ourselves in the Renaissance, we see democracy, banks, overseas investment in the form of voyages to far lucrative places—and in comparison with this the medieval world, or rather our revised version of it, stands bleak and static in its "superstition" and "hidebound" orthodoxy.

Just like us, the medieval theologian recognized himself in the Athenian republic and eschewed all that went before. That earlier tribal world was indeed different. Families had administered their own law, as in the case of the formidable Locrian decree that required a king to send two of his daughters annually to a distant family for execution, to expiate some stain, and it went on for centuries. But the men who worked the system of justice in democratic Athens were far more corrupt than these tyrant kings, if the trial and execution of Socrates is anything to go by. Athenians got so rich (as early as the seventh century BC) that Herodotus, writing about the economic crisis of that century, during which whole classes collapsed, argued that it was the result not of seasonal economic fluctuations but *phythonos* or divine jealousy.

Much the same sort of crisis happened in "Renaissance" Florence, and divine jealousy came in the form of Savonarola, the abbot of the San Marco monastery who unflinchingly denounced works like Botticelli's Venus with its classical or "pagan" suggestions, although it was the great Lorenzo the Magnificent, Florence's governor since the age of twenty-one who had commissioned that picture.

Lorenzo was not simply a great diplomat for Florence—he kept the peace throughout Italy for a lifetime. Not a single event of importance failed to reach his attention. He was in everything

Italy's chosen diplomat. And he was a deeply devout man—devout before anything else, even duty. In the last months of his life he was assailed by remorse that he had devoted himself to power. And perhaps his remorse was exacerbated by Savonarola's dislike of the fact that under Lorenzo the city had become rich as never before. Also it seemed that Lorenzo was now happy at last not to lead—and even happier to die.

After his death the king of Naples said with great wisdom that Lorenzo had lived long enough to be worthy of immortality but not long enough for Italy.

And soon after his death Italy fell to pieces. The pope died too and the new pope was from the Borgia family. Italy was invaded by French armies and neither of Lorenzo's sons was placed, either by nature or power, for strong leadership.

Savonarola paid for his zeal by being burned at the stake. The reasons are obscure (and the story of his making demands for money ridiculous) but new popes could now and then find over-zealous prelates in need of a final lesson.

* * *

We always follow the thought-pattern laid down for us in the formative years of our civilization, and if ancient Athens or so-called "Renaissance" Florence are our two preferred historical reference points, then formative is how we will perceive them, long before we have applied thought to the subject.

It is the same with our vilification of the ineptly titled "medieval" period. It buzzed with talk. Manuscripts sped across Europe and the Mediterranean Basin like chain letters. And our historical claim is that the Middle Ages "stopped" because something we call the Renaissance started and Christendom "broke out" from the medieval restriction.

Yet in precisely the same way as in the thirteenth and fourteenth centuries *our* world buzzes with talk—and the same kind. There is the same frantic argumentation, disputation and ratiocination but it is now millions of books that are read, rather than hundreds in the parchment days. Our wars big and small are preceded and waged and followed by vast gaseous amounts of talk. All would be different if our talk was different, our obsessions different but, as I propose to show, they are not. And it is to the medieval period that we must look for *the chief conditioning ideas in our perceptions.*

The medieval world was fired by two quite opposite obsessions—to wait with patience for the Second Coming, and to make a new world that would be truly Christ's kingdom. It was a contradiction but really the opposites said the same thing: we needed to be elsewhere. Yet what excitement this sense of imminent travel created, as if the Kingdom was already here and angels, demons, miracles and visions were as close as the air itself. No wonder disputation took hold of the over-heated brain. Enlightenment would produce a new human, and all the world would be Christian.

We see the fruits of the enlightenment all round us—first in cypress disease, stagnant streams and later in city populations hawking and spitting under pollen counts ten times higher than the acceptable high. Did something go wrong?

NINE

Arguing Your Way To Heaven

When I went to Oxford I intended making history my specialty and took my first degree in it. But long before I got to the degree I tumbled to the fact that my papers weren't getting their messages through to my tutors. Clearly what they called history was different from what I called history. They urged me to attend to the *facts* and I couldn't explain to them (they weren't philosophers after all) that facts follow theory and their theory was a mess.

Their "Dark" and "Middle" and "Modern" ages were from my point of view a flagrant misappropriation of events but of course I was obliged to use them, which made any attempt to get to historians' first premises impossible.

The "dark" period (AD 500-1000) was said to have followed the "fall" of the Roman empire while the "middle" or medieval period spanned the next five hundred years (AD 1000-1500) until the Renaissance (rebirth of what?) introduced "modern" times.

I disagreed that a "dark" period had happened, feeling that it was only dark for the historians who needed it. Even the fall of the Roman Empire I was skeptical about since both Rome and her empire survived intact under the Christians, together with Roman habits of daily life, and the roads and the laws.

The Renaissance I found plain rubbish and attributed its existence to the need of historians to find evidence for "modern" times, which were said to have been kick-started into existence by this "rebirth".

It all sounded like the purest ideology.

A popular-lore rendering of this travesty would go as follows: once the superstitious, hide-bound, theologically hair-splitting medieval world faded, people started discovering America and opening up the world to trade and painting pictures and generally showing a great deal of imagination and vitality of the kind that the Church habitually thwarted, just as it thwarted people who wanted to borrow money (that Hitler was a great supporter of this tricky code should go without saying).

Leonardo da Vinci (1452-1519) was considered one of the great figures of the Rebirth. He dissected corpses, did sketches of mechanical devices, tried to produce a flying machine, designed engines of war and was always experimenting with new painting and bronze techniques which mostly failed (i.e. the frescoes flaked and the sculptures fell apart). Clearly he was looking for a new world everywhere (particularly in its explosive aspects). In other words he was a true "Renaissance Man", which means *an almost modern one*.

And nothing could be sillier.

Leonardo, far from feeling "The New Man" felt the very reverse—that he'd been born *too late*. Far from looking forward to a modern era he looked back to the medieval one. He considered that the most brilliant thinking had already been done, that the greatest discoveries of thought had already been made—yes, during the very "middle" or medieval period that is generally supposed to have been so hide-bound. He regarded his own period as one of *spent vitality*, not Rebirth at all. He compared his feelings to those of a man who arrives too late at the market and finds all the fresh articles gone. The great and daring ideas have already been articulated. Only inferior, over-handled goods remain.

As for the so-called Voyages of Discovery, leading to the discovery of the Americas, they were much more an act of desperation, a symptom of flagging faith than a new spirit. As for a Rebirth in painting, medieval work remained the marvel, while the "High" period was, in comparison, a baroque exercise. Leonardo lived at the beginning of the High period and accordingly had a sense of let-down.

In fact let-down seemed to be a usual experience of his time, especially when you had to deal with people in high places. Michelangelo, irascible at the best of times, once turned on Leonardo to sneer at his effort to cast the figure of a horse in bronze—it had fallen to pieces. Leonardo, described by the company he was with as "a man of fair presence, well-proportioned, gracefully endowed, and of fine aspect", stood blushing from his attack.

Michelangelo had many a reason to feel embittered. When the Pope received him in Bologna and ordered him to do a sculpture of himself in bronze, and to "cast it over and over again until you succeed", Michelangelo went ahead with the work but grumbled that after two years of labor he only had two half ducats left, and never received anything more.

Only the most foolish people "believed" in the Voyages of Discovery as leading to Paradise (which was first thought to be in India, then in America), just as the most foolish people, to judge by their conduct in other people's lands, undertook these voyages, while those who invested in the boats and sent them off from Venice or Spain were after the spoils.

The pop history continues: the Dark Ages were dark because they weren't yet illuminated by a glimmer of modern aspiration. The middle or medieval period, with its courts and universities that acknowledged Rome as their capital and spoke Rome's language, was only a bridge from the "Dark" to the Rebirth. It was the Rebirth's discovery of America (not yet into Ford motor production), and its invention of the banking system (the Chinese invented it), and its fragmentation of the "holy" empire into nations that warred with each other, and its trade routes, and its notion of perspective in painting, and its rejection of crude astronomical theories in favor of heliocentricity, that brought about the Intelligible World we know and feel at home in today.

We can trace this manic search for intelligibility, this cry from out of helpless dementia, like a red thread through the last two thousand years. Once extrapolated from the gossip of chronicles and official documents it stands out as a series of stages so compact and inevitably connected, each so logically and smoothly fitting in with the next, that an unseen planner might have been at work, biding his time (two millennia are hardly a long time for global conversion) in the quiet assurance that each subsequent generation of men would move the plan forward one more stage like sleepwalkers. And seeing to what extent our minds have been laid to sleep by it we must count it a success.

If "dark" meant poverty, ignorance, a backward agriculture and social chaos the Dark Ages weren't even shady. For Gregory of Tours, who actually lived in the Darkness, the problem was a quite opposite one. Far from being a destitute world, the one he describes in his *History of the Franks* is prosperous, and it is this prosperity he regards as the cause of the inner restlessness of his times.

"What do you not abound in?" he asked. "In homes delicacies increase immeasurably; in the storehouses wine, wheat and oil are in superabundance; in the treasuries gold and silver lie in heaps. You lack nothing: but not having peace, you lack the grace of God.'

We would hardly expect to find the same kind of Europe in the *Dark* time as in the *Middle* time, much less in the *Modern* time, but it was there. Orleans, Chartres, Rheims, Paris existed then as they did later. There were scholars, monasteries, royal courts and castles. The roads, largely of Roman origin, provided much the same network for travelers as they did a thousand years later.

The system of riding forward on fresh horses while stabling the tired ones prevailed then as it did in the Enlightened eighteenth century. The death of one's horse on the road was thought as calamitous in the fifth century AD as it was a millennium later.

Alcuin, the tutor of Charlemagne's son Pippin, in the eighth century, i.e. two hundred years before the Middle Ages were scheduled to begin, used the same method of disputation (by question and answer) as the later medieval cathedral schools.

The words written by Gregory above were echoed by John of Garland eight centuries later, just as they are repeated in various forms today. "The muses are silent, confounded, repelled, as if numbed by the sight of Medusa. Unless you are a money-maker, I say, you will be considered a fool, a pauper. The lucrative arts, such as law and medicine, are now in vogue, and only things which have a cash value are pursued."

In other words the Enlightenment that was promised and so fervently expounded as the Christian goal doesn't seem to have taken place. In whatever period you like to look at there is the same lamentation—that the present is a shattered vessel, the past wiser and golden. It is an inherited perception that derives from the dire theological error which said that *intelligibility would mean enlightenment.* The error is still with us, though horribly mauled by crime rates that have soared over the past two centuries of *increasing literacy.*

When we revise history into a chart with a line rising from low-intelligibility or "dark" times to fair-intelligibility, or "middle" times to full-intelligibility or "modern" times, we are surreptitiously saying that times got better, even while we may think they got worse. In this Data Age (to extend the name-dropping) we see the past as shy of data. Our world-wide electronic communications system argues such a high degree of human expertise some would say that Enlightenment is here, or rather back again. We know it isn't true but our perceptions aren't in the truth business.

* * *

The medieval monks felt that Christian teaching would be judged by a barbarian to be right and true because it unfolded a majestically calm and reassuring *intelligible world.* No more fear, insecurity, disordered emotions such as mark "declines" (the last years of the "old" Rome were still remembered with a chill in the blood).

It was really an imposing classical, Athenian idea. It was also the hidden theme of Socrates's discussions a millennium and a half before—that to *understand* was *to be enlightened in the spiritual sense.* Of all classical ideas this one sustained the Christian teaching in such a way that bit by bit it could lay hold of the minds of people in every corner of the Roman empire.

So the monks of the Dark Time, when the Christian monastery was often the sole reminder of religion for hundreds of miles around, were persuaded that all you had to show invading barbarians was that if life sometimes seemed unpredictable and chaotic to them it was because they lacked the key to understanding it, to *seeing its intelligible design.*

Here a civilizing process was in action. As a method of calming ambulatory dementia it was effective. If you could show life to have a hidden order the barbarian would perceive this order and after a time become ordered within. The barbarians of today would become the popes of tomorrow, and indeed this happened. We should remember here that in a "decline"—that hiatus between two phases of civilization—*we are all dispossessed.* Continuity is lost, and all sense of safety. The enthusiasms, the warmth and order of an earlier world—even fifty years earlier—are gone. The ardent discussions of those times are dead now. Death is cheap. A corpse is only one more casualty to that uncaring silence we all go to. Families, friendships, loyalty are seen to crumble as the desolation grows. It becomes a wonder how new-borns can breathe, let alone grow up, gathering their forlorn fragments of experience into something like an ordered whole.

And in this desolation a new phase begins, or rather in the desolation itself lies the commitment to find something else. Suddenly all is life again. Except that it might not happen. There is always something (for us nuclear spills or fission or increasing habitat disasters) that we feel may cause the end, such is the degree of our helplessness when in fact all the choices are in our hands—hands that are nevertheless powerless.

For the Christians it was the fear that never again would the world see the kind of order established by the old Rome, an order you had perceived in the language itself, not simply in the laws. Once we understand this we can see why the medieval period was so obsessed with intellectual systems. Order was so deeply craved, the sense of belonging was so missed that Hellenic learning was virtually plundered for the means of rescue.

As a means of taming restive Gauls and Visigoths intellectual systems couldn't be rivaled. They were a source of wonder to the goggling tribal mind, being easier to understand than the contradictory details of a living experience like the story of Christ.

The "barbarian" is simply a refugee from a previous civilization who is on the look-out for a new one. It is what makes him move into neighboring lands. So we have the invariable story of invasions that change the face of an empire—it happened to the Minoan world, to Greece and to Rome—so that the new phase should come about. Only the Christians, of all the sects competing for officialization in Rome, were capable of meeting this barbarian challenge, perhaps because they had strong barbarian disorders in themselves.

Classical learning became the basis of medieval education. It provided the only available guidelines as to how to behave oneself, how to think and how to govern. Greek and Latin set the logical rules. This, not ancient life itself, not the ancient gods or rites or banquets or baths, was what the Christian wanted. He asked for the Hellenic model but angrily rejected the Hellenes. He loved the golden serenity of Platonic discussion and vilified the messy lives of the gods (not that even this was original since Plato vilified it too).

A classical education was considered essential for medieval princes, gentlemen and scholars, a view that lasted well into the twentieth century. The purpose was to provide a social support for Christian values but in a Greek manner—by verbal, articulate and eminently intelligible means. Not only this—the Greek and to some extent the Roman was a model of behavior, thus a guarantee of sanity at a dangerous time.

But anything that suggested "mystery" in the Greek sense of the word, anything touching the closed secrets of initiatory sects and visions and states of ecstasy was as out as out can be, just as it is for us today.

The medieval scholar found it exciting to think up closed and complete systems with a beginning, middle and end. Historians call this "scholasticism" or "casuistry", as if it went on only in monasteries and universities, but the poor and illiterate were impressed and fascinated by it too.

When a medieval man had to argue something in court or chapter house, or prepare a new law, or compose a letter, he made sure that his words followed a precise system. Gradually the word "rhetoric" came to mean what it means for us today—an empty form of expression which is also stirring: even if what you say is baloney you are safe against exposure if you use key words deeply significant for popular lore ("advance", "breakthrough", "progress", "democracy", "evolution", "freedom", "scientific" are some of the red stop signs against the critical faculty today).

For the medieval mind nothing "simply" happened. Events could only be understood when connected with the great eternal truths such as *radix omnium malorum cupiditas* ("cupidity is the root of all evil"). Events had to be restructured into *an intellectual system*.

If a prince was to be exonerated for a crime (as in the case of the Duke of Burgundy's murder of the Duke of Orleans in 1408) an enormous document in the form of numbered arguments, with subdivisions for examples, was contrived out of Biblical texts and historical episodes so that the memory of what had actually been a squalid murder was now replaced in the mind with a thought-structure so authoritative and internally consistent that the murder itself could hardly be recalled.

Such a document (the 1408 one was so prized that it went on sale) not only closed the affair from the legal point of view but transformed a "mere" happening into something spiritually significant, even if entirely false.

This combination of the real event with "idealism" is as potent today. Media attention to the ecological crisis a few years ago was later docketed as a "media hype" as if the problems themselves had, because of the hype, walked away. It did more to kill the Green movement than public apathy by becoming a complete intellectual system, satisfying the desire to do something without anything being done. This is exactly how a system made medieval people feel. It wrapped up a situation nicely, for heaven to take care of.

Peasants unable to read or write were spellbound when confronted by such thought-structures. Mostly these were presented to them in the form of numberless proverbs which suited every conceivable human situation. When an event could be transposed in a proverbial or Biblical form it was felt to have changed into its *true state* so that something in the nature of a revelation had occurred. Lawsuits abounded in medieval life partly because people, including peasants, wished even their most voracious appetites to be enhanced and validated by a thought-structure, as the Duke of Burgundy wished his murder to be.

Today we hesitate to think of this structure-building as analysis, but analysis in some form it was. All analysis exhilarates. Some of Freud's patients said they left his room in a state of bliss. It doesn't matter if what we are analyzing is true or false. In fact, the analysis may be designed to conceal the truth, it may cite events that never happened, but it is analysis nonetheless. For the medieval mind analysis induced a sense of release and safety without reference to reality. In the same way our ecological worries have had their release.

Annual events, habits, traditions—of cooking, childbirth, study—were seen as parts of a system. Certain things were done and certain things were not. What was regularly done became imbued with an exciting spirit of permanence and mystery, as if part of nature, and divine nature at that. Footsteps in the dark, a bell, the closing of a door or the sound of a window latch in the dead of night provoked the mind to mysterious and thrilling suggestions. Today we only enjoy that sense of the sacredness of things and events in childhood, when cats, geraniums and log fires are big and fabulous.

Medieval people adored symbols, badges, shields, codes of honor, sayings and mottoes, heraldic designs in the same way as we do. Drama in their time became pantomime, even when serious (meaning moralistic). There was no concern in their drama for daily events, as in the earlier Greek or later Elizabethan plays. Events had to be revealed by analysis—actions judged as mortal or venial sin, as saintly or devilish, beatific or damnable.

They liked to see the saintly vindicated and the devilish punished precisely as we do in our soap operas, but they preferred the drama to be enacted not in terms of daily events but analytically, with the sins and perfections personified. In all things they looked for the excitement and reassurance of system rather than for haphazard and unexplained events, which were frightening for them until enhanced by the mind, again as it is for us today. We need the media to perform this daily function of mentalization for us.

One of our not so clever notions about the medieval era is that it was an "age of faith", and that people were always on their knees praying or burning witches or trying to exorcise a devil. The religious attitudes were very mixed. Princes were buried in the habits of friars, monasteries were respected because renunciation was a basic idea of the time, but friars were also ridiculed and abused, and frequently seen as blackguards. People did believe in witches and bad spirits and the power of the devil to interfere with the physical world to horrible effect but at the same time they were skeptical of these things. Certain priests did turn prayer and votary offerings and benedictions into magical formulae but others scorned it.

During the persecution of witches at Arras in 1461 almost no one, including the judges who passed the sentences, really believed that the women under accusation had ridden broomsticks through the night or that the Inquisitor who maintained that no one could be falsely accused of sorcery was other than mad (he did actually go mad). Yet the burnings and imprisonments in Arras went on. Finally the verdicts were officially annulled.

In medieval life one thing always implied something else. Nothing stood alone, or within boundaries of its own, for the good reason that everything was a sign from God.

In this sense alone were medieval times "faithful". But the "faith" was Greek, not Christian in the bell, book and candle sense. It was much nearer what we would call pantheism, a word invented by an eighteenth-century theologian to describe (with deliberately distasteful overtones) the discovery of God in *everything*.

Christian theology would have nothing to do with that. Giordano Bruno, far from being sanctified for saying the same, was burned to death for it in the Piazza di Spagna in Rome, during that fearful century the 1600s.

Yet it would have been absurd to tell a medieval person that an object was "just" a table or "just" a clock, as we say today. The very thought of things being "just" what they seemed was proof, from the medieval point of view, of a sterile and atheist if not diabolical state of mind. As we today would accuse the medieval mind of never observing objects in their "real" form, so the medieval mind would accuse us of never observing the life *behind* or *within* an object, that which brought it into being and gave it form and decided on its survival or otherwise. The medieval mind would find incredible our whole distrust of the word "divine" and our reduction of the words "spiritual" and "ethereal" to non-practical states, as if practical life could be anything but an aspect of divine life.

Medieval people simply didn't mean what we mean when we say "real". They were much closer to Plato's universals—the Idea of a thing present before the thing itself exists.

Colors for the medieval mind had a "real" (divine) significance (white for the virgin, red for martyrdom etc) just as the twelve months of the year indicated the twelve apostles, and different animals represented different sins—the lion was pride, a black dog envy (Roman women in the 1950s, especially if pregnant, were still crossing themselves when black dogs passed).

Everything that existed, every daily event as well as every object, referred to a heavenly or hellish reflection, and by itself signified nothing. This cast around life an amazing enchantment of which we today know little. Nothing could be touched, nothing witnessed or even imagined that wasn't without its divine thread, which gave it not simply meaning but joy combined with mystery, even though the operation was rather intellectual.

Fervor was formalized in prayer, mystical writings, sermons. It provided theologians and poets with endless opportunities for invention, as when Bonaventura in the thirteenth century described handicrafts as the Word transformed into physical action. The inventions could be tortuous and absurd. Theologians would construct a pyramid of parallels where hail maries and paternosters were shown to be equivalent to certain virtues and certain sins.

Our best historians of the period, even J. Huizinga in his *The Waning of the Middle Ages*, find it baffling and irritating that medieval thinkers refused to observe life first and heavenly hierarchies after, and that "life" didn't mean for them what it means for us, namely something *devoid* of the heavenly hierarchies.

Huizinga has to conclude that we are dealing here with a more "primitive" or "childlike" state of mind than our own, and he frequently quotes our "scientific" view of things which permits us to judge matter in a detached manner, unlike the more "superstitious" peoples of the Middle Ages. What he overlooked was that medieval systems were *the basis of science* and that our so-called scientific or detached view of things is characteristically medieval, and that it remains medieval today in all but terminology. In this, as I shall show, lies its tenacity as well as its weakness.

Medieval people didn't perceive our way—namely as if things were separate from what brought them into being. That would have been considered next to madness. The idea that we humans, unable to alter birth or death, could possibly *not* think continually about the world *before* and *after* would be for the medieval mind unthinkable.

If medieval theologians and friars were among us today we might find that far from acknowledging us as highly advanced thinking creatures they would see us as closed in a great sleep. A medieval theologian of quality would be able to confound most of us with a few moments of disputation. Our constantly reiterated "But it works", pointing at jet-fired space capsules, computer software and laser systems, would soon wear down, and we would be reminded of a remark by St Augustine, made long before the medieval era came into being, that everything that happens in this world can be performed by demons. And we would be obliged to think that one out (substitute "dementia" for "demon").

Here is what Huizinga says in his *The Waning of the Middle Ages*: "If the medieval mind wants to know the nature or the reason of a thing, it neither looks into it, to analyze its structure, nor behind it, to inquire into its origin, but looks up to heaven, where it shines as an idea."

The medieval mind *did* (more than we do) want to know the nature or composition of a thing and to analyze its structure and to inquire into its origin, but it would never have been satisfied to learn that the nature of water was H_2O or that the crust of the earth differed substantially from its hard core. These would have been considered definitions, not analysis.

Yet our science of definitions came from that same medieval mind, and was planned and given its strict boundary lines by that mind. Huizinga is simply seeing an earlier medieval mind from the point of view of a later medieval one.

Heaven and hell weren't simply felt to be close at hand (especially when the hand was about to commit a sin), they influenced every event. Thus, analyzing the structure of a thing and inquiring into its origin without mentioning heaven, which was the only reality apart from hell, would have been thought absurd to the utmost degree.

For this reason sins were enumerated and classified, together with punishments, which ranged from the recital of hail maries in groups of fifteen to eternal hell fire. There was really no such thing as a small sin because everything done by a human being was seen in the shadow of the eternal, it always involved the heavenly hierarchies.

For the medieval mind nothing that theory can say about water or wood or the planet deals with the *real* origin or nature or structure of things. For instance, Robert Grosseteste, who lived between about 1170 and 1253 and became Chancellor of Oxford University, developed his theory of light not as an analysis of light but as an effort to explain the action of the spirit on the body. His work was about how to get grace through the tireless seeking of light, yet he is seen today as one of the first "scientists". Half of his work has thus been lopped off, as we lop off the "myths" from the Athenians.

All we today call science would in medieval times have been considered simply descriptions of the *machinery* of objects, the way in which they work, not their origin or real structure or nature. Certain modern scientific calculations would have been appreciated but they would have been considered, surprisingly for us, abstract, namely a study of objects artificially extrapolated from their real conditions.

Yet the boundaries of what we now call science were laid down in medieval times. The Church *wanted only the machinery of objects examined.* And we have followed suit, except that the word "objects" has changed sense, it now being devoid of any suggestion of divinity or even life.

For the medieval mind a crushing divine power lay behind the "real" world, a blinding light. Its ecstatic and unbearably effulgent spaces could never be left out of consideration for a moment, being the origin of all events—so much that the smallest of thoughts sent waves of repercussion through the universe.

This doesn't mean that the medieval mind considered man's inner nature divine, or that everything was shot through with God, or was a manifestation of God, as in Eastern thought. It was *unfortunately* not so, as we shall see. God was considered very far from the world, hopelessly far from the human point of view. A human couldn't so much as touch the furthest outer periphery of divine being. Nevertheless a connection did exist—not a union but a connection, and it was this connection that transformed every aspect of life, and made every human act harmonize either with God's intentions or the devil's.

Here we can trace schizophrenia ambulating unsteadily through the cloisters. Inside you are rather pathetic, outside is heaven and hostility. You yearn to be in heaven but it repulses you. You yearn for an explanation. Wherever a color, flower, festive occasion, childbirth, battle, crime, emblem, candle, thorn, pasture, horseshoe offered a memory or association or legend or symbolic importance it was seized upon and an attempt was made to render it intelligible.

Never did so many people try to transform life into an Eden while seeing the world as Hell. Even death wasn't a release but an agonizing, unwilling journey into literally God knew what. The only hope lay in the Second Coming.

Your very renunciation of life was an attempt to transform it. The mania for systems was a yearning to make things so bright with understanding that not a thought or sigh would be left outside man's vast intellectual construction which would one day be complete. Like a Gothic cathedral it would leap away from earth to heaven but be solidly founded and balanced.

Their intelligible systems weren't ours but they still followed the rules of logic. Medieval descriptions of vast illuminated spaces were based on observation no less than our descriptions of the mechanics of acceleration in thermodynamics. The thing observed was different but the process of systemizing the findings was the same.

So far from the truth is our popular-lore picture of medieval life as a static or hidebound epoch (which it also was) that in comparison with it our present epoch is one of staid and unchallenged officialdom working by purely automatic processes toward chaos.

In many ways the medieval world *tried* to be static. It yearned for a society that would be an ineffable reflection of heaven. No community has striven so hard for an unchanging and secure way of life, which is why the medieval town, wherever we find it intact today, fits so quietly and humbly into the landscape, within stout walls, the houses avoiding the light in intimately narrow winding lanes designed to confound the stranger.

Nor has a society talked and argued so much about religion, for the good reason that it never attained the "faith" that historical theory finds in it—not for a moment. A state of inner anxiety is hardly faith. The medieval mind veered to and fro in its sudden changes of mood—from grief about the Crucifixion to joy in the thought of Christ's sweetness and birth. It could swing easily, precisely as our minds do. We take in a dozen television tragedies a night and promptly forget them. Like medieval people we accept restlessness as a condition of life.

There was hardly a moment of calm in medieval devoutness. People indulged in fasts and penances and sometimes flagellations and long praying vigils and all kinds of self-denying practices to show themselves cognizant of their unworthiness when compared with the endless firmaments of light and fragrance that constituted the Kingdom of Heaven.

The Church was never entirely happy about these things, even while it encouraged them. After all, popular enthusiasm expressed a morbid and nervous strain that might threaten social harmony (for which the Church was responsible).

Yet Church doctrines showed that same nervous disability. You were permitted to have ecstasies of a transcendent kind but were reminded that there was no such thing as transcendence, that God was so remote in His unthinkably immense power that you were lucky to have as much of His consideration as a grain of sand—and you only had this degree of it because Christ had mediated with Him for you.

You were given the promise of an everlasting experience of effulgent sweetness in the form of heaven but immediately after came the threat of eternal hell. At every point it seemed the human being was excluded from his own faith and must pass through so many tests and observances and varieties of self-abnegation to prove himself worthy of it that he could surely never rest for a moment, especially with the devil and every kind of minor demon close at his elbow to take advantage of an instant of forgetfulness.

Even in the most ardent quest you could be sure of nothing—the Church warned you that a vision you had had while fasting was possibly an hallucination and could indicate mere pride or self-deceit. Your tears might be false, your self-abnegation mechanical, performed in the hope of easy access to heaven.

Seeing that this official skepticism was applied even to saints like Catherine of Siena there was little chance of an ordinary person ever finding the golden mean, if such a mean existed. Even keeping a permanently low profile didn't work, for then you could be charged with a lack of zeal.

An "age of faith" was rendered out of the question by the nature of the faith itself. At every point this faith reflected the tempestuous changes in the medieval man's moods, his hesitations and terrors, his bursts of courage followed by contrition and brooding, his lack of belief that the good was either something he could claim or something he merited.

To cap it all he was reminded at all times that death awaited him, probably an agonizing one, since agony was then reckoned to be part of the dying process. In woodcuts, pictures, processions and

113

dramas he witnessed the Dance of Death where men's own corpses dragged them out of life, and the young, the good, the frail, the devout, the powerful and princely, the holy and the diabolical, the warrior and the virgin could all be claimed without redress at any moment.

Death (at other times described as a desirable state, since it brought one hopefully to the gates of heaven) was clearly implacable, remorseless, vengeful, even gleeful. It reminded you that life was fragile and tenuous, and that therefore you should apply your mind to death at all times. Some monks had sickening descriptions of hell read to them during meals.

No wonder intellectual systems were a balm. They had a strait-jacket function for manic tendencies.

TEN

The New World Makes Its Appearance—In The Head

If you need systems you are obviously looking for *a new world*. The present one isn't ordered enough for you.

But it was inner disorder that the first Christians were coping with, as always when a new sect is trying to extend its influence not among those who are naturally drawn to it, as in the case of those familiar with the Greek mysteries, but in the world at large. Simultaneously you are going to woo the society round you and reject it. You build up walls against it, and beckon people in at your gates.

The truth is that the "old" religion had collapsed in these people. That too is a prime difficulty with new sects. Much inner torment has precipitated you into the new religion. Your old life became unbearable, your old unhappiness and even your old forms of happiness were no longer worth staying alive for. You said you had no religion. Then you experienced for the first time ecstasy— someone inspired you, you got a sense of being eternal, you could at last make *happy* sense of your life. Something changed in you and you entered the sect in order to make the change permanent. As the best teachers told you, a new perception of life has to be protected like a young tree.

That you should wish to enact a certain revenge on the old religion is natural because you never in fact were one of its faithful. You only thought you were because you shared the habits of the faithful and went to the temple and watched the sacrifices and listened to auguries. You were never inside the religion. You were never initiated into its mysteries. And so you said that it had been no religion at all, only a lot of make-believe which no one with any sense can take seriously (just as millions talk about Christianity now). Indeed, you attribute your demons to that old religion and offer the world the new religion, the true religion, the true prophet and the true teaching, namely your own.

Restlessness to make a new and final world order entered Christian blood like a virus. There was a tremendous desire to think life out in new terms and make it all over again. Ancient life was seen as God's rehearsal for this.

We are still hard at it today. The ruined habitat stands as a testimony of our clumsy efforts in that direction. The wars of the nineteenth and twentieth centuries were all considered vehicles for starting-all-over-again. The "old" is still destroyed to make a world fit for heroes to live in or for democracy or freedom or ethnic purity or to bring down an unjust class or establish a suppressed one.

The word "ancient" was coined by early Christians to describe a world they wished to excise from human memory. The Hellenic gods and the Delphic oracle belonged to the discarded past while the future would see the dawn of a new human intelligence brought into being by Christ's visit to the earth. That was a very appealing idea to people familiar with Hermes Fleet of Foot—that a divine messenger should actually have come on the earth to teach. The way the Christians presented Christ's story to the world was classical from the start, which was perhaps not a good way of exorcising the classical man within the Christian.

As to ancient "images"—statues of Apollo and Persephone and Pallas Athene and so forth—they were not unconnected with devil-worship. The "image" of Our Lady was no such thing. This is the kind of double standard you have to expect of a sect in its early years, but the teaching was never discarded. In fact it has been adopted by the scholars and the learned down to this century.

It was a tall, political story but a whole civilization swallowed it.

Gregory, a bishop in Cappadoccia in the fourth century AD ("dark" ages), acknowledged Alexander the Great as an *ancient* hero but added that he was nothing compared with King Theodoric who was aware of the "true religion". A saint is a saint *inside*, he said, King Theodoric halts barbarian armies with *inner* truth, not the sword, and because the ancients worshipped "idols" they had known nothing about this. Attila the Hun was prevented from crushing the town of Orleans by the mere presence there of a certain Anianus, who exhorted the inhabitants to pray for the Lord's help and this came in the form of the king of the Goths and his army, who relieved the town.

This type of yarning went on from century to century until even modern Italian guidebooks to ancient monuments were doing it, with their reference to "pagans" and "heathens" when referring to classical worship.

* * *

The medieval idea was that Christ had introduced a new humanity which would by the force of its truth overtake the whole earth. This new world would radiate from Rome but surpass all earthly empires.

Rome would be the center not simply of possessions that stretched from Britain in the west to the Caspian Sea in the east, from the Elbe in the north to the Nile in the south, as the ancient empire had, but would rule a spiritual world-kingdom such as men had never dreamed of. Other faiths would wither before the obvious rightness of a new, divinely approved Knowledge, an Ultimate Certain and Complete Explanation of All Things.

This was a "new knowledge" and Oxford was one of its earliest centers. Robert Grosseteste, besides being Chancellor of the university, was also a Franciscan monk. He was fascinated by the Greek texts which the Arabs and Jews made available (there was a

Jewish community at Oxford, just as there were Sufis in Andalusia). His chief subject was optics because of his interest in light. He was also prominent in the movement to imbue Christian theology with Aristotelian principles, namely to turn it into "scientific" inquiry.

Before becoming Chancellor he studied theology in Paris (1209-1215) and gave special attention to the Book of Genesis. From this came his metaphysics of light. Matter couldn't actualize without light, he said. Light was the first form and could multiply itself indefinitely in any direction. It also behaved according to geometric rules so that no study of nature was possible without mathematics.

Like Pythagoras over a millennium and a half before, Grosseteste regarded light and dimension as a sort of spiritual language—they demonstrated that the world was the unfolding of a *divine* intelligence. Light was the divine source of life yet almost touchable—it blazed both outside and inside the mind. He connected it with the Trinity, the soul, grace. Following Plato, he saw light as the divine touch bestowed on the human body (to give it a soul) and on the world (to give it beauty). It had always existed but now, since the birth of Christ, the study of light had something momentous about it. Christ's light had shattered eons of the darkness of ignorance and helplessness, and *only Christian thinkers could complete the Hellenic effort*.

A new religion always gives the impression to its followers that it is the first revelation the world has witnessed. But that the new light, in the sense both of inner and outer light, had figured in the same way in the Hellenic mysteries or initiations was for Grosseteste not simply unthinkable but blasphemous. So it is that sects are easily tipped into excesses.

Oxford's lead in the study of fundamental mathematics a century later was due to Grosseteste's initiative but it was still a religious pursuit, not one designed to produce knowledge as an end in itself (i.e. "secular" knowledge).

For the medieval Christian the value of science or knowledge was its power to illuminate the world, which it would then transform into one perfect Christian state. Every scientific study at Oxford during the fourteenth century followed Grosseteste's example, whether in the matter of trigonometry (Richard of Wallingford) or physics (Richard Swineshead) or meteorology (William Merle). They were all designed to illuminate. Anything we might today call utilitarian was foreign to that.

Roger Bacon, another thirteenth-century Oxford scholar, spelled out the new-world theme clearly and passionately for the first time. Like Grosseteste a Franciscan, he too has often been called the first modern scientist. But this is only true in one sense—he propagated the notion that *science has an ethical and evolutionary role*, penetrating secrets and extending frontiers. In that sense, he was father of what has been called "pageant" science. From his time we may date the long process of glorification (really self-glorification) that has led to our believing that science is a name for the only truth.

It was precisely what the medieval theologian was after—knowledge that wouldn't touch on the religion. The child was science and never did a child eat up and commit to oblivion its parent in such a Promethean way—Prometheus having been a Titan used the fire from heaven for the benefit of the earth, for which Zeus chained him to a rock and organized a vulture to pick at his liver on a daily basis by giving him a new liver every day.

Bacon had a spot of prison when young, sentenced by his own order, and ended his life in a papal jail. But for the greater part of his career he enjoyed the friendship and admiration of Pope Clement IV, which meant that his work had the highest protection. His goal was to bring about a system of knowledge which would remove heresy from Christendom and make it possible to convert the world by force not of arms but incontrovertible truth.

Far from the Church persecuting this as dangerous for the Church's survival a number of popes were avid for it. Clement IV maintained special private contact with Bacon so that he could be kept informed of the latest scientific information. This often came from Franciscan missions in various parts of the world, especially in the East, and from Bacon's contacts with erudite Jews and Arabs in Toledo and Provençe (the Pope's birthplace). One of Bacon's suggestions, to which the Pope took kindly, was to do a survey of the whole world. He prepared a map as a step toward this and

Christopher Columbus later used it for one of his voyages, noting the Spain-Indies route it displayed.

Bacon called Clement his "angel pope" and addressed his treatises to him. He looked on him as the one man in Christendom able and willing to bring about a moral reform (the seed of later Protestantism) and by means of the "new" knowledge—pure because undeniable—which would eliminate any desire for heretical opinions.

He had little time for the Crusades because they were trying to do by force what could only be done by wisdom. Christianity had a chance—better than the use of the sword—to prove itself superior to all other theologies and doctrines as well as to the increasingly idolized Hellenic world (a nice statement of inner conflict, indeed).

Not that the best Christian scholars approached other faiths in a negative mood. They had lively discussions with Jews and Muslims. Simultaneously they felt that the only real faith was Christianity. And when their discussions with Jews and Muslims were discouraged, when Jews and Muslims were evicted from Spain by Ferdinand and Isabella, the story went out that the New Knowledge was Christianity's contribution to the world.

As Percy Bysshe Shelley said to his friend Edward John Trelawny, "All our knowledge comes from infidels". But our scholars and our learned swallowed the Church story, not Shelley's.

Bacon noted the corruption everywhere—at the Pope's elbow as in every university, every monastic order. He described the clergy as a body given over to venality. The universities were as full of ignorance as princely courts, he said—their discussions and treatises were intellectual and fruitless.

He feared that the New Knowledge would fall into the wrong hands and be used against the Church by those within it. His fear was shared. The people suspected were magicians, geomancers, sorcerers, alchemists.

He may well have been worried—magical aspirations became so deep a working element in science that today they are safely unconscious, and not a premise or prognosis shows their face.

At that time magic (especially necromancy) was used as much by the clergy as by princes. In 1318 Pope Boniface VIII even set up an inquiry into magical practices used by the Curia (Philip IV of France tried to cast a spell on Boniface), and he issued a Bull describing the use of sorcery and "pacts with the devil" as a widespread practice.

John of Ruperscissa, a devout fourteenth-century Franciscan, shared Bacon's fear. He argued that most of those who dabbled in chemistry and medicine (his own studies) were frauds. It wasn't that he was against alchemy (as opposed to chemistry) or cosmology (as opposed to mathematics) or astrology (as opposed to astronomy) but that he questioned the motives of most of those who studied them. To know how nature can be changed, he said, and how to do the changing, you have first to purify the mind.

Everyone wanted to change nature—impure people as well as pure, the orthodox and the heretical, the scholar and the knight. It was the Christian solution to life. Changing nature would be doing something for God. A New World, inner and outer, emanated naturally from Christ's teaching—a clean sweep in the temple as in the family.

From the Church's point of view a clean sweep was all very well as a slogan but it could be very unsettling. So it was both suspicious and happy about the "new" knowledge that was going to sweep the world. It feared the inspiring arguments while being won over by them.

But what harm could there be in studying the "marvelous coherences" of nature, as Giovanni de' Dondi called them in the fourteenth century, since they revealed a divine and perfect intelligence? Surely divine light would fall on the scientist's life and deepen his devotion?

Not that other scholars—or even de' Dondi himself—were sure about that. A conflict was at work—not a public one between Church authority and heretics but inside each man, whether pope, bishop or monk. Almost every thinker had faith in the new knowledge but foresaw dire trouble ahead. And looking at it as we do from the end of the second millennium they had good reason to.

In our entire acceptance of the "new" knowledge as gospel truth we say today that science divested itself of the "speculative" studies (astrology, cosmology, alchemy) by a process of knowledge "increasing" or even "progressing" or, to bring it down to vaudeville talk, "triumphing".

This was never the case. Medieval thinkers of the time, particularly if priests or friars, narrowed their studies to more and more matter-of-fact and practical themes *solely in order to avoid the suggestion that they were looking for special or divine powers.*

They were given very strict parameters for their studies. If science is a "secular" study today, if we now have "secular" knowledge, it is due to this intensely religious interdict.

It wasn't that anyone became *skeptical* about astrology or alchemy or magic. They feared them as challenges to Revealed Truth. It was their deep sense of *the effectiveness of magic* that led them to eschew it like the plague.

And then the Church was hardly wrong to look with suspicion at multitudes of occultists and magicians whose miracles might well expunge Christ's from human memory. Rather than have her scholars study a *divine* universe and meddle dangerously with its potent magical forces, the Church opted for *abstract studies*, especially the Greek one of mathematics. And a more abstract idea than "matter" you couldn't find, a real black cat in a blackout.

Today's "cold" science and her collective institutions, their research carefully demarcated by community rules ("first you publish a paper"), themselves austerely and augustly based on what, say, the pharmaceutical industry or the politicians or the defense departments need next, are the long-term outcome of Church *policy*, not at all Church *persecution.*

If the Church showed a lot of confusion and inconsistency in the way it indicted scholars it was because her scholars too were confused and inconsistent. It was the suspicion of magical or esoteric motives that brought saintly creatures like Giordano Bruno to the stake and brilliant if misguided talkers like Pico della Mirandola before the Inquisition. Even certain "cold" ideas fell foul of the Church (which didn't necessarily mean Rome, for papal circles were from time to time the more tolerant), just as today unusual ideas (mostly those not supported by the hugely subsidized chemical industry) fall foul of scientific authority.

The Church consisted of priests, scholars, friars and popes taking sides among themselves and frequently uncertain which way to go. They (including popes) were as afraid of incurring the charge of practicing magic as they were of others doing so successfully—not because they were any more superstitious than we are but because they were aware of the disruptive effects of what we now gingerly call psychic forces or occultism. They feared these could bring the Church to ruin and threaten law and order.

Even John of Ruperscissa, one of the mildest of scholars and the least tolerant of magic, ended in a papal gaol, having already spent quite a time in a Franciscan one. The Church was rocked by her own doubts. Her efforts to establish Church Law provoked more heresy. So many sects and schisms existed that it was a wonder the Church survived at all.

There was a particularly bad state of schism in the thirteenth century. St Francis of Assisi did much to repair this, chiefly by reminding people that the habitat and the creatures therein were alive and well. The sun was a brother and the moon a sister, not a concept called "matter" in a disputant's brain. It is said he learned his language of love in Provençe.

Orthodoxy was therefore always something of a Christian obsession. It was a necessary social safeguard in a too turbulent world. If the Church couldn't stomach heliocentric or Copernican ideas it was because of the *social* shock these delivered to men accustomed to seeing the earth as the apple of God's eye, served by a sun which revolved round it in the same way as men were served by horses as their means of transport.

Today the same kind of *social* considerations evoke scorn for scientific ideas which haven't received the imprimatur.

It wasn't the idea of the earth traveling servilely round the sun that appalled (it had been securely demonstrated long before the time of Christ) but how many useful perceptions it might disrupt.

Church thinkers saw that safe *reasonable* statements didn't rock the boat as much as apocalyptic or esoteric or visionary or magical ones, and that no strikingly new idea can quite avoid an apocalyptic ring. It is why Jung said that religion is a protection against the religious experience, which is far from reasonable.

About reasonable statements everyone can agree. We agree without fuss that an isosceles triangle has two equal sides. That isn't going to make people run through the streets crying heresy. We are hardly likely to base revolutions, even palace ones, on that kind of truth.

Giving life a reasonable (i.e. safe) explanation which in fact explains nothing at all, such as "Delay in the arrival of sound means that sound travels", is a far surer way of possessing the world than magical cart-and-pony shows with their flying brooms and crucifixes that fall off the wall and enemies who drop dead from spell-induced tumors. It was this that gave the Church more than a passing interest in advocating *human reason* as a specially endowed faculty unique in the animal kingdom.

Thus did intelligibility become a theological must. Thus was it decided that the universe (its center Rome) was fixed and unalterable. Not for nothing did the word *cristiano* mean for Italians, until very recently, "human" as opposed to "animal".

The most devastating thing about the Church's decision to create a non-religious knowledge was that it created—atheism. By producing a science which would be entirely about *appearances* the priests shot their own feet. The idea of "matter" was tantamount to saying that there was something independent of the human being and more lasting, yet it wasn't divine either. So it hung out there in a limbo. That was intended. And it was a clever idea. But if you start believing that this matter *exists*, is *real*, indeed all the life you see round you, you have clearly done away with God, not because you wanted to but because the Church had laid it down. You had found a dead and inert earth, and one day scientists would be divided between "vitalists" and "reductionists" for this reason. The day is with us now.

Naturally, wherever the Church extended its influence—in India, in Asia, in Africa, in the Americas—atheism eventually spread like, yes, magic.

It was surely what the Church wanted. If you expound a theory of matter that is to all intents and purposes dead, and if this becomes inherited knowledge, what else are you going to get but huge populations perceiving the world as dead? Our perceptions don't allow for niceties. They don't logic-chop. We inherit them with our milk and they are necessarily simple.

ELEVEN

The First Godly Principles
Of Godless Science

I never found much awareness of all *this* in the history books. Historians did notice that the Church of Rome's social hold on Europe declined from the fourteenth century on, when nation states came into being, but explanations tended to be ridiculous.

How on earth could an "age of faith" have led to an apparent collapse of faith? Some historians opted for a pop version of the progress-idea: medieval people got tired of waiting for the Second Coming and renouncing the flesh all the time; they wanted to be up and getting so they took to the sea and started borrowing money at high rates of interest and made profitable wars on each other.

And then there are the economic explanations. The Church's tight usury laws couldn't hold out against the Rebirth vitality that burst the seams of medieval sackcloth and flung the ashes to the wind in a final realization that Man (starring Leonardo da Vinci and Michelangelo) had his own kind of glory. There is even talk of a Rebirth Man (it sounds better if you say Renaissance Man) who could perform feats like leaping over a fellow R.M. without knocking the top of his head off, and other things like reciting the whole of *The Iliad* by heart. Better than cloister-shuffling in a cowl reciting hail maries to the click of a rosary?

This is why I crossed disciplines into theology. After all, my college had the best theological library in Oxford. But here I ran into the same trouble. The Theology had a special language with its inbuilt rules, just as every discipline had. Most of the other occupants of the library were future shepherds who would soon have village flocks and dioceses. They weren't looking for why the theology had happened, or even what theology was, much less whether it had existed in all civilizations, and in what manner the Christian version of it differed from the others.

Evidently this New Knowledge I was being educated into was a mighty edifice I wasn't intended to look into the foundations of or connect in any way to the habitat, which belonged to nature studies and biology and botany and anatomy, each of which had *their* inbuilt rules.

Yet one of my most all-round tutors was a priest. I envied his ability to sip at the honey wherever it offered itself, without tearing his brains out looking for a key which everyone said didn't exist. Had the New Knowledge never been made by human heads then, and fallible and frightened and perhaps mad ones at that?

My problem with theology was that *secular* history disappeared. All of a sudden there was no Black Death, no Frederick the Hohenstaufen or even Erasmus. The Rebirth had slipped out of sight and none of those fervent platonic discussions that went on at the Villa Medici came under the theological banner.

What I objected to wasn't that the secular stuff should have been in the theology but that there was no such thing as the secular! To this degree it *should* have been in the theology because theology was responsible for it. Or perhaps secular people only *supposed* they were free of religion, since after all religion had produced secular knowledge.

I was intrigued to know why it was that when a religion faltered, when the temples or sects or churches lost their influence, everything else went to hell. We mark all the "collapses" of civilization thus. Apparently humans are unable to live in what they perceive to be a dead universe for long. And the moment they start saying it is alive they have to state alive with *what*, and religion begins again, however defaced its previous images.

A phase of civilization ends when the old religion has become a system ever fewer people can give reasonable credence to. They will no longer, as in the case of Christianity, bother their heads with the intricate nature of the Trinity or the meaning of transubstantiation, though bitter wars were once fought about these things. A new religion (and thus a new phase) is always in some form a refurbishment of the old religion but it presents itself as *a religious experience*, fresh and ardent and requiring no more reasonable credence than falling in love does. At this stage there is no religion, only people who have fallen in love. A church, with all its tendencies to war and spite, has not yet begun to marshal and organize the new awareness.

So I returned to philosophy in the hope of discovering what changes in ideas had made it *seem* that life was secular. But no, philosophy was remote from both secular and theological areas, indeed from all animation whatever! It made me feel quite dead.

Since the philosophy people couldn't tell me anything about history I turned back to history, then back I went to theology again, like a man taking an endless walk in a street dead-ended both ends.

Each discipline was trying to claim status as a "pure" study. So if you stayed inside one of them you never knew what had brought it into being. If you tried to look at it from another discipline you got caught in *that* one. Each pointed to absolute and unshakable principles underlying all of them *and these didn't exist.*

Which was why I couldn't find them.

Each discipline from anthropology to aerodynamics simply threw definitions around for currently fashionable needs—comfort, commerce, war. This was my indignant impression.

I felt I would make a very big mistake if I tried to dig through what we called *facts* because these had been brought into existence by *thought* and this *thought* was now hidden within them.

Surely there existed somewhere a system on which the New Knowledge was based, or at least had deluded itself into believing that it was based on?

Then it was suddenly obvious to me. The books pointed it out, plainly, and for a long time my eye simply glossed over this heart of the matter. Neatly and explicitly it was laid out for me in that idol and untouchable of the Middle Ages, that fount of all medieval ideas, the almost god of the Christian universe—Aristotle.

* * *

If there was one thing no book about the Middle Ages could afford to miss out it was the importance of those singularly few but crucial texts by Aristotle which were all that were known of him at that time.

I had a bizarre thought—that a man living nearly two and a half millennia before me had given me those "giddy fits" of my childhood, and haunted my youth with the need to get to the bottom of them! But when I read his work I absolved him because it had been so deeply corrupted by his Christian disciples, and twisted to their uses, that I couldn't bear him any blame. At the same time I felt that he was responsible for that corruption taking place.

How on earth could a philosopher as trite as Aristotle have not only influenced Christianity but virtually become its guide?

In all medieval dispute he was the great arbitrator, the judge to whom everything intellectual not only could but must be referred. Here were people who wished to turn their backs on the world he had lived in (four centuries Before Christ) and considered that Christ had introduced a world far superior to his Greek one, yet his thought was virtually sacred to them!

Thus scorn the "pagan" world as much as they liked, Christians belonged to it because they were born in it. Rome inherited Hellenic ways of life, Christians inherited Rome's. How could you turn your back on your vast repertoire of daily habits, modes of address, gesture, in a word *your classical way of perceiving life*? It couldn't be done. If we modify our perceptions at all it can only be at the very edge. For unless we are able to share each other's perceptions, share them with each other, reality collapses.

Far from the New Religion revolutionizing or abolishing the "ancient" world, it was in fact, via Aristotle, squeezed uncomfortably into it—until it dominated the New Religion entirely! Once we discard all these revisionist terms like "ancient" and "classical" and "dark" and "medieval" and "modern" we have a chance to observe that this civilization we are actually in now has lasted with changes big and small *since early Minoan times.*

For one thing, the medieval idea that life can be rendered intelligible to us wasn't at all a medieval idea. Its first principles were set down by Aristotle in Book VI of his *Ethics*. Not that it was his intention to say the same as what medieval thinkers wanted him to say. He was far from being the rationalist he now seems. Having constructed "modern" rationalism on the basis of his ideas, we naturally take it for granted that he agreed with us, so we attack and defend him for what he never said.

He argued (*Ethics*, Book VI) that while we can't be sure that a thing continues to exist when it disappears from our view, knowledge (*episteme*) deals with *what must be so and cannot be otherwise*, and therefore it deals with *what is eternal.* It is therefore beyond a mere state of mind. It cannot either come into being or cease to be.

These are brave words. It puts the intelligibility doctrine in a nutshell. With no evidence, and only internal logic, it sets forth the idea that if you feel certain about something it *is* certain, thus overlooking the fact that certainty cannot be had outside the mind convinced of it.

Which means that, far from being eternal, it exists only *where that mind exists*, and only for as long as that mind exists. All knowledge must have a person knowing it. His knowing it is no proof at all of its existing independently of him.

But Aristotle was thinking of things you can't argue about. How can two and two make four now and five or six later? So it is eternal, math for all seasons, with or without a human mind thinking about it. But he omitted to add that even the things we can't argue about aren't eternal, only permanently convenient to us, and dependent on our convenience, a mere navigational tool. A human can only say that something is eternal for some immediate or practical end he has in mind. It is a mode of speech.

This eternal truth, he said, is found by a process of induction (i.e. by examining things), which process passes into another one, that of deduction (the finding of a law). If I observe that humans walk on two legs rather than on four and find no exception to this I can assert that they do so universally. If I then find a human who crawls on all fours habitually I can state that his act is an aberration from the law.

Clearly no religion could be quite happy with such propositions—namely that there exists an unimpeachable body of knowledge which makes no mention of God. All three Mediterranean religions—Judaism, Islam and Christianity—reacted unfavorably to this (seeming) Greek influence. But they all *fell under its sway*.

In the twelfth century, especially in Toledo, Jewish and Muslim scholars translated the notes or lectures of the Greek thinkers into Latin, and showed them to Christian scholars. Aristotle, like Plato, was one of the masters translated. From al-Farabi in the tenth century to Ibn Ruschd (known to Christians as "Averroes") in the twelfth, Arab translators presented a vein of rationalism which increasingly frightened the orthodox in all three religions, which is why the Arab and Jewish scholars who did the translating for their Spanish, French and Italian friends were invariably refugees from persecution in their own countries.

Aristotle's work is about truth that can be logically argued and deduced and demonstrated from particular instances to universal laws. It *isn't* about truth from revelation (a vision). In his system (in so far as there is one in his varied and sometimes tentative reflections) knowledge was a corpus of observations which might one day be complete.

But here too we must be careful not to turn his thought into ours: he held that wisdom itself was *revealed*—i.e. it happened irrespective of education or knowledge or even literacy. So he sharply differentiated wisdom from knowledge, which the Christian thinkers never did satisfactorily.

Church thinkers exploited Aristotle by declaring that only Christians (with Jewish and Muslim help presumably) were capable of compiling this new and complete knowledge of Aristotle's. Only in the light of Christ could his promise of a body of incontrovertible truth be fulfilled.

In this way you could retain your picture of "ancient" Greece as pagan and unenlightened while basing your life on it. As a result *our* lives are based on it. What is a "mystery" for today's research will be "unraveled" tomorrow. We know-alls will finally know all there is to be known.

It isn't easy for us today to realize what an immensely liberating force Aristotle's idea was—for ancient Romans as for Christians, Jews and Muslims. It offered the thrilling possibility of a world united in one divinely appointed order. And it was also liberating for heretics who felt that the divinely appointed order was in the wrong hands, and that the Church must be toppled to fulfill it. The New Knowledge idea had such a hypnotic hold on the Mediterranean mind that it caused both fear of heresy among the faithful and heresy itself.

For Aristotle, theology was a theoretical *science*. It took its place together with mathematics and "natural science" (science in our sense). For the Church this could be dangerous too—the thought that its doctrines might become the plaything of theorists.

But it happened. Rational proofs of the existence of God were in great demand and tended to be ten a penny. Of all confessions of whining doubt and failure that was the greatest, and it involved the greatest of the theologians, Thomas Aquinas included.

This is the way Aristotle argued: *nous* (common sense) provides us with *the first principles of science*. These are "given" (inherited) and cannot be argued about. For instance, volume, extension, density are simply properties of matter. Things have size, shape, motion—this no one can deny. If you talk about matter you must talk about these things. And these first principles are "invariables", he says. Everyone is going to agree about them. The "solid or empty", the "straight or crooked", the "square or rectangular", the "above or below", the "light or heavy", the "liquid or hard"—these are opposites we all agree about. They don't change, as two-and-two-make-four doesn't change.

There are three kinds of science for Aristotle—theoretical (mathematics, natural science and theology), practical (moral philosophy) and productive (commodities, art, drama). So what we today mean by "science" comes under the *theoretical* heading—as the study of nature. It meant all knowledge that required the rational faculty, including art and theology.

He described wisdom as "scientific knowledge plus intuition". He said that wise men (like Phidias or Polyclitus, who demonstrated wisdom through their sculpture) not only had knowledge of their subject but knowledge of first principles. An artist was a "productive" as opposed to a "theoretical" scientist. Science was nothing more nor less than knowledge.

We can see from this in what direction Christian theology corrupted his meaning. It established the study of nature as the only *certain* science, leaving all the other forms, even theology, uncertain.

Thus one pursuit swallowed all the others, claiming to be not only the sole arbiter and vehicle of truth but the only truly practical one. It quickly kicked away the ladder by which it had hoisted itself, namely Aristotle's principle that it was *a purely theoretical study*. Today we don't even know that the ladder existed. We have been deceived by sleight of hand and tricks of illusion into believing that science is the one study that deals with *real* life. And all we are speaking of is a loose collection of theoretical knowledge about anything.

A wise man in Aristotle's view needn't be wise at something or even good at anything. "The most finished form of knowledge" can be conveyed to a man directly, he said, without any recourse to reason. From our point of view this is just about the most unscientific remark that could be made. So his meaning was twisted, for theological purposes, to say that only knowledge arrived in the *opposite* manner, namely by the rational or analytical faculty, was valid.

Yet Aristotle was making an oblique reference to Hermes of the Winged Heel, the messenger bearing intelligence to humanity from the gods, and whose information came to the receiving mind directly, more often as an intuition than in a verbal or visual form.

The Christians used the *feeling* evoked by the Hermes tradition in that they called Christ the Son of God, and thus bearing intelligence from Him, but they still couldn't for the life of them understand that Aristotle was making a reference to a spiritual process in all beings. Since the Christians commandeered all spiritual processes for Christianity, it was natural that they shouldn't. And scholars have on the whole followed suit.

By what logical steps did Aristotle establish that the human mind was capable of a complete and finished knowledge? Well, he had one argument that supported all the others, and it is one we have inherited too. In fact, of all his arguments it is perhaps the most important one, and has been a virtual building brick of our civilization, if a fatally flawed one. It is the one argument of his which we have left uncorrupted (after all, it was so corrupt an argument in itself as to be foolproof against Christian misuse). Only now, as I said in my first chapters, is this argument slipping, crumbling and corroding in our perceptions. Which is why we can look at it analytically now.

Here it is, and very simple it seems (because it has been absorbed into our perceptions): *the human mind is distinct from the animal mind.*

It became the very basis of the rationalist position.

It was here that medieval thinkers most took Aristotle as their own. By doing so they could link his name to their doctrine of renunciation which said that only by abandoning the "animal" in himself could man attain to the pure mind which alone perceives the truth (two millennia after Aristotle it was trotted out again as the latest news by Descartes!).

This is the way Aristotle argued: he said (Book III, *Ethics)* that the pleasures of the soul must be distinguished from the pleasures of the body. Socrates, born eighty-five years before him, had similarly argued (in *Phaedo)* that the work of philosophy was to free the soul from the body. Thus the mind was man's only means of escape from a dark and helpless state, from both fear of pain and yearning for pleasure (i.e. the dreaded world of the "blind" reflexes).

Animals, said Aristotle, *lack this mind*. They lived in a dark state permanently, without hope of illumination. He added (Book X) that the happiness that came to humans from the act of reflection or meditation (as opposed to practical activities like politics or warfare) was due to *a divine element* lodged in them. So it looked as if this was the difference between animal and human—*the latter was divine*, at least in part, the animal not.

At once we see medieval theology's special interest in this argument. If divine really meant Christian, then the sail was set for that day when Rome would call humans *cristiani* to differentiate them not from Muslims or Jews but from animals.

* * *

Just as the intellect is divine compared with the whole man, Aristotle said, so *living* in the intellect is divine compared with *living* like an animal. It was the only way to "put on immortality". No animal could do such a thing.

Even here, though, the theologians did a little corruption job. They changed the meaning of the word "intellect". This was to aid and abet the making of a science that would have no revelation, no beyond-matter kind of truth at all. So "intellect" became cerebral in meaning, whereas Aristotle's word was nearer to what we today would call the meditative part of the human mind. Christian theology likewise became intellectual in nature, not a song of praise or a visionary statement. The "splitting of hairs" theology resulted from the new cerebral fad, a complete degeneration of Greek thought.

Aristotle distinguished between "higher" forms of biological life and "lower" forms, with the human as the highest (shades of evolution and fossil-mania). He argued that animals are like *crude humans*. They responded to smells because these gave them associations, not because of the pleasure of smelling, as in the human. A hound enjoyed the smell of hares because it wanted to eat them; the lowing of an ox is a pleasure to the lion because it intends to kill it. The lion could never take pleasure in the sight of a deer or goat, only in the fact that they will now or later make a good meal.

It is all pure Zuckerman stuff two and a half millennia before Zuckerman described the man-made monkey massacre at the London zoo. The Aristotelian monkey is capable only of appetite (digestive or sexual), never of society or even maternal feeling. How fast ideas travel among those preparing the last and final truth on the earth!

We feel, Aristotle said, that "touch" and "taste" are brutish because they are senses *shared by the animal*. Of these two senses touch is the more likely to excite our reproach because, being the most widely shared pleasure, it belongs to us not as men but to us *as animals*.

All this was music to Christian ears. It completed Aristotle's alienation program—withdrawal from the animal in order to be pure—by adding an element of disgust. It was responsible for the absurd reluctance to eat, make love or even sleep as "unspiritual" activities which culminated in the Puritan movement of the sixteenth century.

For Aristotle the "brutes" couldn't be described as being either temperate or licentious because, for them, the choice between the two values never arose. Since the animal had no power of choice it had no values to choose between (nowadays that looks like a good description of humans).

Aristotle wasn't fool enough, however, to regard humans as temperate. In fact he said that man could do more harm than animals because of his superior rational powers. He thus removed—for a whole civilization, had he but known it—the only yardstick of sanity for such a biologically intemperate species as the human one.

There is no doubt, he said, that rational powers are what make a man individual. Therefore a good man loves them more than anything else. A life "ruled by feeling" is inferior to a life "ruled by reason". The happiest life is that of the "intellect" because this is a divine faculty. *Man* isn't divine but the *intellect* is. So a human has a choice—between "thinking mortal thoughts" and "putting on immortality". If he chooses immortality it can only be through the exercise of his unique intelligence, of which the "brutes" know nothing. In other words he must think *beyond* his mortality.

The modern stage is set in Aristotle. "Feelings" are separate from "reason", "reason" is the seat of control. A man is succumbing to "the animal within" when he fails to use his powers of thought. "Feelings" and "physical pleasures" are seen to be in the animal camp, having quite arbitrarily been pre-parked there.

TWELVE

In The Crooked Steps Of The Master

The Englishman Roger Bacon absorbed his Aristotle like everyone else, and did his thirteenth-century bit to Christianize him. For this "first true scientist", as Bacon has been called since, a New World would come into being only when—wait for it!—*animal desires had been suppressed*. Only by renouncing life (the habitat) can life (the habitat) be changed.

He prophesied in detail the world we live in now. He even dreamed about it—foresaw self-propelling vehicles, machines that fly, ships that move under water. When machines come into the world they will banish magic, he said. Science will place all occult practices on the sidelines. Such remarks make him a prophet—but not, to *his* mind, one of gloom. He saw only glory ahead. Just as we do, through a deadly haze of pollution.

The fact that machines would place religion too on the side-lines together with all the other departments of Aristotelian knowledge—art, ethics, theology and hand-made commodities—wasn't foreseen by Bacon. He didn't get it that pretty well every serious human endeavor would tumble, along with magic, into a leisure-activity limbo.

What he also didn't foresee, though it was quite as obvious, was that *all religious experience, not just the Christian church*, would be placed on the sidelines. He thought the opposite—that science would remove all skeptical doubts, all heresy. Science would show the world what Christianity, through Christ, could perform, *and all the other religions would fall like awed ninepins before the effulgence of the only true religion.*

Other people were less blinded by the New World dream. Cecco d'Ascoli and Pietro d'Albano understood that the very nature of scientific thought, with its cultivation of a detached mind as a means to truth, was atheist in nature, and would produce exactly what it *has* produced, a "secular" (read atheist) world. An irony if ever there was one—that theology should with devout calculation work out exactly how to destroy faith worldwide, i.e. in other religions too.

Bacon's prediction was right in one respect—-that machines would carry round the world a message, namely that these were the *meraviglie* or marvels of Christian thought. Except that by the time they were realized, in the nineteenth and twentieth centuries, the word Christian had long since been replaced by "Western".

And the effect these gadgets and electrically operated kitchen aids that at the touch of a button washed and dried clothes and toasted and roasted food and relayed music and talk from afar, had was to make the religious past everywhere look simply incompetent, a world for dreamers.

* * *

A renowned, feared, reviled theologian, also of the thirteenth century, Siger of Brabant, did a better job in this direction even than Bacon. His great opponent was the chief disputant of the age, Thomas Aquinas. Yet they were far more alike than otherwise.

Siger was murdered in an Orvieto prison by a madman. It was the year, 1282, in which the Emperor Michael IV of Constantinople had all the Normans in Sicily murdered as a retaliation for his being excommunicated by Pope Martin IV. For an age purportedly united by faith it was awfully seamed. Almost everybody who was anybody was imprisoned, murdered, quizzed or spied on.

Siger was a rational *extremist*. Revelation—anything inspired or visionary—he quite explicitly put down. Scholars, he said, must ascend from truth to truth to build a rational knowledge so firm that "unreasonable" suggestions, such as that man was immortal or had a free will, or that the world had been "created", could be left to the superstitious mass of the people, who needed them. No reasonable mind would need to wrestle with these fantasies.

Since these "fantasies" were much of what the Church was daily propagating, a conflict was bound to occur, especially as Siger was exposing the holes in flawed Christian theology. Little wonder that a sigh of relief went up when news of his murder spread quickly across Europe.

Even Thomas Aquinas, seen as about the Church's best defendant, was frequently in trouble. A teaching ban was even imposed on him for a time. But he was allowed to return to his job in Paris to dispute with Siger publicly. His job was to undermine the so-called Averroists, of whom Siger was the chief. Giant must fight giant.

Averroes (or Ibn Rushd, the Islamic theologian) was similar to Avicenna and al-Farabi and al-Kindi and other Arab scholars before him in that he looked forward to the making of *a scientific world system which would have no reference to religion or revelation*. Naturally the orthodox of both Christendom and Islam saw Averroes and Siger as enemies, their doctrine as atheist. But as far as the effect on *our* lives is concerned Averroes and Siger won.

Not that the Averroists said that God could or should be left out of *all* accounts of life—only out of that area of certain and irrefutable knowledge on which future human enlightenment depended.

But what enlightenment could come from a non-divine area? Well, one that none of the foremost theologians foresaw—the Enlightenment of the eighteenth century which excluded religion altogether.

The debate between Aquinas and Siger was probably the most famous of all the dialectical word wars of the Middle Ages. Yet at the most crucial points of their arguments these two men seemed to be saying the same thing, quite as if the faith itself was showing the way inexorably to its own schism. The real conflict here was between Aristotle, or rather the corrupted version of him, and St Augustine. The Christianized Aristotle stood for reason, which he had never done, while St Augustine stood for revelation, which he had also never stood for. Siger seemed to represent the non-existent Aristotle while also arguing for the non-existent St Augustine, and Aquinas seemed to represent the latter while also arguing for the former. A marvelous if thoroughly useless debate was the result of this schizophrenic cosmology.

The two great figures, Aristotle and St Augustine, divided thought at this time not so much into two camps as two shades of thought that could never quite reconcile themselves to each other.

Very roughly, Aristotle stood for the power of the mind while Augustine stood for the power of the feelings, especially feelings of love. But both, with a schizophrenia that apparently spanned all the ages, saw the mind or spirit as in conflict with the flesh, and the "inner" life as in conflict with the "outer".

The Franciscans were more Augustinian than Aristotelian, but they too, especially the "spirituals", demanded the enlightenment of the world, its cleaning-up so to speak, through knowledge. Clearly Siger was more Aristotelian than Augustinian, while Thomas Aquinas tended to be an uncomfortable mixture (as who wouldn't be).

Aquinas too had read Averroes and Avicenna, as well as Jewish writings, with much fascination. Like Siger he trusted the intellect to find out all that there was to be known but, unlike him, he included God in the proposition. This was his argument: God is the fount of human intellect, being the first and perfect intellectual being, and this is why we humans are able to understand, in a limited manner, the world we live in; but we are also things of nature, therefore our intellects can be blind; to be blind of intellect means to be impure, i.e. unable to be good despite being originally good. It was an Aristotelian argument the tail of which turned into St Augustine. It argued that God was the fount of human intellect but added that we were "things of nature", thus neatly placing nature outside of God's power—a strange if not atheist thought.

Thus his dispute with Siger showed how brilliantly the two of them managed not to take two sides unless it was each other's.

* * *

In the last weeks of his life Aquinas told his secretary that his theological work meant nothing to him. He said that everything came to him in silence and solitude, in the form of revelations. Words and arguments were ridiculous. The two had nothing to do with each other. The truth was with him at last.

Yet he couldn't have said this publicly. To defend your "personal" vision was to excite the Church's distaste for hallucination. Besides, it would have opened the debate to all kinds of mad-cap fanatics and magicians who thought everything had been revealed to them. So intellect was *politically* a safer bet for the Church. Aquinas placed his bet on that side and became known as the greatest intellectual pillar of the Church, in fact the maker of a Church doctrine set out clearly for all to see, but even these ideas the Church managed to corrupt.

His position, or rather the corruption of his position by the Church, became the orthodox one: human reason cannot reason about God, about Whom the Church has said all that can be said; what reason *can* do is to think about nature, and it *should* do so, since by means of this thought human understanding will grow larger. So we are back to the "godless science" obsession, and the understandably passionate heresy and schism this invited.

In 1286, twelve years after Aquinas died, his *Summa Theologica* was adopted by the Dominicans ("the Lord's hounds") as their official doctrine. This order invented the Inquisition. Therefore it relied on a refined and meticulous use of the logical faculty. Of course inquisitors differed greatly from each other—some were "illiterate and avaricious" (the words of William of Ockham, a Spiritual Franciscan) while others were simply concerned to purge the troubled heretical mind of its alleged toxins.

The Spiritual Franciscans, namely the zealot wing of St Francis's order, set about reviling the Church as if it had no legitimate claim to the title "Christian" at all. Numbers of the Spirituals were forced to leave Avignon and take refuge in Germany and Bohemia—more and more of them urged separation from Rome. They linked up with other heretical groups.

"God" was more and more seen as distant from the human being. Duns Scotus, born in 1270, criticized even Aquinas for bringing God too close. We were at an immense distance from our knowledge of Him, he said. An infinite chasm divided scientific knowledge from faith, nature from the Trinity, ordinary philosophy from theology, the mortal from the divine. Aquinas had belittled the divine, he implied, and thereby undermined faith and worship. For Scotus *everything* was distant from the human, not only God but nature and his fellow creatures. Life was an extraordinary alienation, and the only real and lasting rescue from this was love.

Alienation was the hub of Scotus's work, which made him the one theologian who tried to confront human dementia and build a bridge over the chasm that divided man from his habitat and his own nature, and therefore, even more, from his God.

This was why he attached so much importance in his prayers and reflections to the Virgin Mary at a time when most prominent churchmen were cynical of the benefits of turning Her into a deity, let alone the Mother of God. Idol-worship was wagging its classical head, they said.

But Duns Scotus, like St Francis, was trying to draw tenderness into this doctrine-hardened faith, and to mitigate somewhat the anguish of the Crucifixion. Mary became a soft and intimate bridge to God, Who was now so far away. She, the Mother of God, tempered the forlornness of nature with her watchful concern and readiness to answer the prayers of the lonely and frail, and those who turned in fear from priestly judgment.

Here too Scotus understood something of *the biological predicament of the human*, his need to find a source of information the habitat no longer supplied him with, and which it supplied to all other animals.

In Scotus there is no real connection between the worshipper and God, or between the worshipper and the world round him. Man must create this connection with continual effort. If he wishes to understand the Trinity, only love will give him the understanding.

Here at last is a rejection of the enlightenment-by-intellect idea. For Scotus love and reason are simply separate faculties.

From earliest times Christians had argued and expounded. The Church Fathers had been fathers of argument. This was why Bacon, Aquinas, Siger, even Scotus, despite their creating distinctly different schools, perpetuated one and the same hidden code: *knowledge = non-divine*, unintentionally and unknowingly. Aquinas, at the end of his life, showed some wistful understanding of this.

A potent hidden code of this type is never isolated. It speeds over frontiers, languages, generations, magnetizing the most unlikely souls, falling like a shadow on different religions as if they were one and the same. Jewish and Muslim thinkers too fell under the enlightenment spell.

One thing we can be certain of. Those who succumbed to its grandiose appeal must have needed it. And since it has now engulfed the world people other than Christians must have needed it too.

Centuries after Duns Scotus the Puritan movement re-designed the male as a non-visionary, non-emotional, non-tender creature of principle, and the female as the serpent source of ignorance and temptation, thus finally shutting the door on the Marianists, as the protagonists of the Mother of God were called.

Like all doctrines Puritanism harked back to the Middle Ages (as all modern thought does too). No wonder great numbers of women joined the "heretical" movements, especially the Franciscan Spirituals, as a refuge from the "serpent" idea. St Francis and St Clare were living proofs of the divinity there might be between male and female. Today the Poor Clares in Assisi are still its living proof.

Of all the teachers in our civilization who taught by their presence, only St Francis in the twelfth and thirteen century personified in himself respect for all living creatures. They weren't simply equals but God's masterpiece. He called the sun Brother Sun and the moon Sister Moon. He brought everything close in this way. He wasn't a preacher. When he stripped himself naked in the streets of Assisi he was asking "Why should shame attach to nakedness? Do you not see how naked the animals are?"

It is why when you go today to his retreat in the hills you know he is still there. How can the ending of "life" mean the end unless you have given to life a crude definition as real—and thus the aftermath as unreal?

THIRTEEN

Climbing Mount Demens Without Tackle

It looks queerly as if Christianity was never based on Christ. Which may be why there were so many heretical movements which said just that.

St Francis's effort in thirteenth century Assisi to sing the habitat back into Christian consciousness, and to show that his Clare was his divine spouse, and the sun and the moon and the birds were "brothers and sisters", led only to more Roman officialization.

Yet this was his own wish. He pleaded for his little sect to be made a major monastic order and in doing so he of course opened the order to rebellion from within—that of the later Poor Clares, for instance, who in revulsion from male Franciscan cupidity, abandoned all possessions, while the Franciscan "Spirituals" abandoned the Church altogether.

The medieval world was so deeply bound to a non-Christian, Aristotle, as *the sole and final authority in all human thought*, and whose texts could settle any dispute, that successive popes tried to curb his absolute authority but had to give it up as a bad job.

The peculiar effect of this domination of Christian thought by an ancient Greek was that it distorted the Christian view of ancient Greece!

One of the most impertinent of the many Christian defamations of the ancient world, repeated over the centuries in schools and seminaries, was that it lacked true religion. The word used was "pagan". This was in fact a Roman word used to describe uncouth and superstitious people in country districts. And the insult was hauled by Christians into use on the ancient Romans and of course the ancient Greeks. They extended this inference of superstition to all the non-Christian religions except Judaism, which they needed if they were going to keep Christ.

Ancient Romans would have been astonished to hear that the tiny Christian sect in their midst would one day convince the world that ancient Romans had been skeptics and agnostics. Imperial Rome was considered *the center of religion* in the Mediterranean world and the first Christians or martyrs found in the Romans a people who very much knew what religion was! Strangely (to us) it was the Roman army that not only defended the old religion *but introduced Christianity.*

Precisely because of Rome's religious importance the martyrs found there first a largely scornful and later an eager reception. It was why Christian hermits in the Theban desert behind Alexandria came to Rome at the invitation of the ladies' salons. The Roman language itself—not to say the sense that Rome was the whole civilized world for those within its span—guaranteed the maximum attention for Christians. *Ubicunque lingua romana ibi Roma*— "wherever the Roman language is spoken there is Rome".

Rome, and certainly Greece before it, were in fact so meticulously religious that hardly a moment of the day wasn't dedicated to it. The word "religion" didn't exist in Greek because there was no need for it, it being all of life. It was the Romans who first coined the word— *religio* meaning simply "that which binds together".

Later Christians also suggested that ancient Greece worshipped gods who behaved more stupidly than humans. In fact as early as the fifth century BC the Greek Epicureans said that the idea of the gods being able to interfere in human life was extremely harmful and created much fear and distress—an example of "superstition", which in Latin meant "undue fear of the gods". Their impatience with the

147

old gods was a traditional *classical* attitude far older than Rome, let alone Christendom. Plato and Xenophanes, as well as the Stoics, ridiculed the idea of gods behaving like men at all. They found them often unjust, irrational. Plato tried to have references to bad godly behavior officially expunged from Homer's work.

This was why St Paul found the Athenians of his time "a most God-fearing people".

As for the "magical rites" Christians ascribed to Hellenic worship they played very little part in life after Homer's time and were in any case probably connected with Minoan ceremonies, which in turn had nothing to do with "magic" in the Christian theologian's bogey sense.

Nor were we Christians the first to talk about the dangers of magic. Magic has been called the practice of someone else's religion and this is where we should leave it, since whenever we look into the magic of religion (unless it is practiced under Christian auspices!) we shall find that it is spiritual in the manner that the Consecration of the Host is. I have heard the Cabbala described even by Jewish friends as a book of magic whereas the word itself meant that which was "received" or "given", and the book is in any case better described as a book of angels.

* * *

Paradoxically, the early Christians did a revisionist job on the ancient world with a relentlessness we should expect from people who belonged deeply to that world. We read, even from scholars, that the first banks to exist were in Christian Siena and Florence, and the first use of capital for dividends or interest in Christian Venice. Apart from the fact that both existed in China centuries before Christ they were present in Athens at the time of the Peloponnesian wars, and by the third century BC they were all over the Hellenic and Roman worlds. Under the Roman emperors, in the provinces as well, mortgages at four to ten percent were common and when the collateral was insufficient to match the loan the interest could be as high as forty-eight percent.

Long before the Middle Ages every attempt was made by Christians to expunge the world of Zeus and the temples of Isis from human memory. This in order to support the idea that civilization in the proper sense came into being with Christ and that Greece and Rome were at best useful cradles for His arrival.

The contrary is true—Christendom has if anything been in a prolonged decline since Roman days, especially *in the practice of its own religion.*

Our popular-lore idea today is that Christians gave monotheism or One God to the world, having received it from Judah, and that in contrast to this the "pagan gods" of Greece and Rome were worshipped as "images". On the contrary, it was the spread of Greek forms of worship during the Macedonian conquests and the so-called Roman Peace that *prepared the way* for the one God of both Jewish and Christian doctrine (and we should again remember that Christ was born in a Greek province).

Maximus, the Roman scholar, put it best when he wrote to St Augustine, "Which of us is so mad or blind as to deny the certain truth that there is one supreme God? By many titles do we invoke his virtues, which are spread throughout the universe, because we do not know his name. "God" is a name that all religions share".

In fact when the Christians of Rome suggested that their Supreme Being was the only one and that it could only be worshipped by Christians they were following a proud Roman tradition.

Far from the idea of One Supreme God being Judah's or Christendom's unique gift to the world it was a common Mediterranean inheritance. Porphyry, the neo-Platonist philosopher, once said that Apollo's oracles had asserted this "One Supreme Eternal Being" with every oracular utterance. Zeus in Greece and Jupiter in Rome had a status approaching that of the Supreme Being, though not consistently so. Even in this suggestion of a dual role Christianity followed suit. Christ as "the son of God" is if anything even more personal than the Zeus of the Roman Stoics (whom they called "That Which Cannot Be Named").

In ancient Egypt both gods and the One God were worshipped simultaneously (as the Holy Mother of God and the saints were worshipped by Christians simultaneously with God the Father). The Egyptian One God was nameless, incomprehensible and eternal. The word *neteru* meant gods, and these were differentiated from God just as the saints in Christian doctrine are.

In 1860 the Egyptologist de Rouge even described the Egyptian cosmogony as the same as the Christian one—a Supreme and self-existent Being, Almighty, the Creator of the world and of all living things, endower of the immortality of the soul and Divine Judge Who punished and rewarded.

The African peoples we used to call "primitive" held and still hold to the idea of One God, however many household or elemental gods they also recognize. The pygmies today call God Tore or Muri-Muri and have their Garden of Eden story. They say that their ancestors once stole the fire belonging to Tore and that for this crime their immortality was taken away and heaven on earth ceased.

Even before Rome existed there had been cults all over Italy whose gods controlled every aspect of life, but none of them was "idol-worshipping" or dedicated to magic in our sense. The religion of Numa was Rome's first state religion, named after Rome's second king. It involved neither images nor temples. Its ceremonies were carried out with great care, as later Roman ones were too. If a mistake was made in an invocation it was started from the beginning again. There were music and a simple dance.

Since the founders of Rome were Etruscans, it was natural that their religion should dominate. It included many different modes of worship in one—a mixture of Hellenic, oriental, Italic. It brought the Greek altar to the Italian peninsula.

As for the demonology which has sometimes been attributed to the classical world it figured much more in the Etruscan faith than it did in Greek or Roman forms. And though Romans studied under the Etruscans, learning the language of omens from them, their monotheism was quite unmoved by it. Apparently Rome didn't feel tempted to compromise her One God with an almost equally One Devil—which cannot altogether be said of Christianity.

In Rome, as in Greece, religion was the basis of state enactments, law, family life, education, thought. The idea that Christians came quivering with faith into an "unbelieving" Roman world is the opposite of the truth but, as Goebbels said, if you repeat a sufficiently outrageous lie often enough it will stick. In fact states of unbelief were much more a Christian than a Greek or Roman problem.

Christians were the first religious people ever to say that religion wasn't an utterly natural and given faculty which happened wherever a human felt wonder toward the habitat. They implied that the human could live without religion, that religion could fail to be wherever the human being was, that religion wasn't always and everywhere the worship of one force, however many divine fragments in the form of gods or saints or angels or spirits were also worshipped. And if the modern scholar writes about Greeks and Romans as if they were secular peoples and not obsessively religious it is because this is the only mode of thought he can understand. In fact the idea of secularity is itself *exclusively and entirely Christian in origin*.

The Christian calumny is in fact so far from the truth that daily life in Christendom at any period in its history pales before life in ancient Greece as a religious expression. The Greek calendar was a religious formula. The processions, competitions, dramas, music, sport, dancing were all extended rituals devoted to the state gods. Of course there was a difference between the old Minoan religion, with its "lady of the wild animals", its close connection to the seasons, to harvests and rainfalls, and the later Homeric gods of Olympus, which are the ones we usually associate with the ancient Greek world. But there was some continuity too. In both Greece and Rome the gods were agents of a divine power and since they were in human form they got things wrong in an earthly way—we shall see later why. When this power spoke it did so through the Oracle.

All religions need to personalize. Christian saints, who protect certain events or specialize in resolving certain human distresses, replace in a pale way the old gods—the Greek Hestia (goddess of the hearth), the Lares (protectors of the home), Persephone (corn goddess), Dionysius (wine and plant god). So it is with all religion: it fills the air with references to the habitat until the trees and rivers embody the gods, and household furniture belongs to them.

The notion of heaven and hell as an after-life was already present in Homer's work. The later Greek idea of the Elysian fields probably came from Minoan religion and was taken on by the Etruscans. There too the Christian story fell into a classical mould prepared for it by the devotion of others. The Gospel's "kingdom of heaven" was already understood.

Jews and Christians were seen in imperial Rome as *atheists*. Catullus described Christianity as a deadly superstition (i.e. "emotional religion"), its Communion was "cannibalism". He and other Romans regarded the Christian faith as crude and image-worshipping—precisely as the Christians regarded theirs.

The truth was that the civilization, whether in its Minoan, Mycenean, Greek, Roman or Christian phases, was a troubled one, increasingly unsure of itself, increasingly afraid of infidels, pagans, heathens, barbarians, heretics and above all fickle Providence. The dithering and mealy-mouthism of the medieval disputes can be detected at least eight hundred years before Christ was born.

So we mustn't exaggerate the certainty of the Greeks and Romans either, even though they did have techniques of initiation with which to achieve it. Techniques too can degenerate and be lost.

Anxiety wracks *The Odyssey* in the ancient world, as it does *The Divine Comedy* in Dante Alighieri's in the Middle Ages, as it does the works of Shakespeare in our times. This is why in all three cases *the narrating voice must be sweet,* it must shed the Holy Spirit on carnages and heartbreaks and lives led in self-illusion.

In all these the heroes are inexplicably struck down, they seek guidance, they quake with doubt, they find themselves punished when they expect to be honored and vice versa. The sacrifice of animals is supposed to assuage the ancient gods but only manages to increase human perplexity as to what life is all about. The early sculpted Greek head bears the same smile as the Egyptian head before it and the Etruscan head after it, but the *late* Greek head is mortified as if staring into hell, full of foreboding and wide eyes. What has happened since the days of King Minos, when the earth was close and the bull was used not for slaughter but somersaults?

This "ancient" world (it is really as modern as flu jabs) fitted uncomfortably into the habitat whose winds and stillnesses and sudden mists couldn't be trusted, whose gods behaved like lunatics with no regard for the human hearts that poured themselves out to them. What happened to break the Minoan spell? Or was that spasmodic too, a nostalgic invention of the world that succeeded the sacking of the palace at Knossos?

And what about Rome, Greece's child? Was she really as well-ordered as she meant to seem? Did the Roman really know with certainty how to behave on all occasions? The struggles for power, the sexual anxieties, the morbid cruelties—surely no mind capable of all this could be, of all things, sure of itself? And Rome's reasonable attitudes, foreshadowing our own, plus the reflective tone of Roman speech, the public dignity and high-flung rhetoric, the balanced marvels of the language itself—were they perhaps security systems to palliate the effects of a dire inner erosion of which the gross heartless spectacles of the Colosseum with their unthinkable display of humans fighting each other to the death or being mauled to death by animals *as a lively enjoyment for the audience* were the symptom?

Anyone who has lived in Rome for long and knows the "broken stones" and some of the history also knows that, just the same, religion was the key to her life—that the sense of eternity and self-sufficiency that pervades the city through all the thick and thin of sack and sewage, and modern traffic, must have been made out of human devotion, that Rome was the name of something unshakable of which the Romans themselves fell short and expected to fall short. The very composure of Roman speech itself seemed designed to end an inner torment, which task was gladly handed over to the Christians for mending.

* * *

When we look at the Hindu world for a comparison with our dead-habitat metaphysics we find that it offers an even more vivid picture of divine interference in human life than Greece or Rome, almost as if Greece and Rome were India's degenerate children. Hinduism has its Siva, dissolver and generator, its Indra the king of the gods and rain, its Brahma the creator and Vishnu the preserver, its Hanuman the monkey-headed god of physical strength, its Ganesh with the elephant head. Mother Kali with her many arms is the goddess of nature and she flies over human battlefields with screams of joy because all earthly experience is a veil of illusion. Here the imagination, fired by all kinds of radiant analogy, loves to play on manlike figures known not to exist but which capture in funny and terrible form those forces we are dealing with every day as logical and practical ones. Sacred to Siva is the blue jay because Siva, through compassion for us all, swallowed poison so that his throat is colored blue, like the bird's (Vishnu the preserver was in his belly to prevent the poison taking effect).

Until well into the twentieth century the Hindu's every habit was a ritual with a legend behind it—from the way to prepare and eat betel leaves to the habit among males of placing the so-called topknot or sacred lock of hair behind the ear when urinating. This union of the inner and outer habitat brought delightful stories into being. The tiny dark green bird with a black ring round its neck and a long beak, rather like a humming bird, is called the sun-bird in India because it is said to eat sunbeams. A plant with a small pink flower is called "God's adornment" (*hari shringar*). Coconuts were once broken in front of the image of Ganesh because of a sage who, after being defeated by Indra in a fight, decided to grow his soldiers on trees instead of waiting for them to be born. This alarmed the gods and they persuaded him to desist, which he did—but left the heads on the trees. So these coconuts are ritually broken open to show that the human mind can't make war on divine wisdom or really do anything very original.

For the true Hindu all life was sacred. He couldn't kill, not even a mosquito. He couldn't eat meat. He was tolerant of all animals though he preferred some, like the cow ("mother"), whereas the monkey with his black butt was called the "disgraced" monkey because of some offense against the gods. The Brahman caste was "the lips of God", the warrior caste "the arms", the tradesman-caste "the lions", the servant-caste "the feet".

Our Minoan-Graeco-Roman-Christian world has nothing to compare with such detailed ritualization of plants and animals, seasons and types of wind and storm, family hierarchy and meals and manners of sitting, standing, washing, touching.

By comparison, the world of *The Odyssey* is forlorn and brutal with its gross banquets and fatuous slaying of fellow-men and heifers to celebrate or invoke good fortune. From a world of chieftains who claim divine ancestry man looks out on the same incomprehensible and distant enemy-habitat.

Some people believe that Homer didn't exist and that both *The Odyssey* and *The Iliad* are, like the Bible, collections of verses from many hands (some bad links in the stories seem to support this). At present the status view is that Homer existed and was the author of *The Odyssey*, if not *The Iliad* as well (we are learning at last that if the Athenians revered a man called Homer then it is likely he existed).

The verses were carried from town to town orally and spoken at festivals. *The Odyssey* (about 12,000 verses) and *The Iliad* (15,000 verses) were in a mixture of Aeolic and Ionic Greek.

The Odyssey wasn't concerned with Troy and its siege as *The Iliad* was, being about one chieftain on his way *back* from Troy. The story starts ten years after the sack of that city. It is a voice from out of that unsettling world which we today know all too much about—a world that opens its eyes on the demise of one phase of civilization and the dawn of the next one.

Only Shakespeare magnetized anything like the same rapt attention from disparate peoples and epochs and classes as Homer, while yet adapting to every new generation and never losing pertinence to life. There were Shakespeare festivals as there were Homeric festivals. The same academic arguments bustle round each man. Was he real, was he more than one man, was Homer a tradition, was Shakespeare Lord Bacon or one of the other noblemen who wrote tragedies under false names, did Homer write *The Odyssey* but not *The Iliad*?

The idea that Homer or Shakespeare could have been simple or little-educated men without title, realm or much learning was always a bitter pill for rationalists to swallow because "inspiration" and "vision" tend to be the atheist's highly theological no-no.

But there is one big difference between the two. It lies in this fact of *The Odyssey* being a Bible. In Shakespeare's work religion is something scarcely glanced at in itself. Death, in the Shakespeare plays, far from opening a gate to the Elysian fields, is more typically described as an "eternal cold".

But let us look more closely into the meaning of this word "Bible". It clearly means sacred writings. But what happens if we deny their sacredness? Well, they can't be understood and can't provoke the intended emotions. But this was precisely what Christian thinkers wanted. Calling *The Odyssey* an epic was a way of saying that only the Old and New Testaments were authentically religious, while all other writings may be variously referred to as literature, essays, philosophy, criticism, namely everything that stands *outside* the sacred.

The story of Christ, a god who elected to incarnate as a human in order to bring divine information to the earth, was immensely appealing to peoples brought up on stories about Hermes, the divine messenger. But never once did Christians, though they might be Greeks, acknowledge that Hermes was divine in the manner Christ was.

In almost all religion there is this tendency to say that only certain behavior is religious, only certain places divine. This was quite impossible in ancient Greece *because no part of life could be conceived as outside religion.*

So, naturally, when we look for religion in ancient Greece (i.e. for our type of church-and-state arrangement) we find none. We see Homer as we see Shakespeare—as secular, namely devoted to "worldly" as opposed to "sacred" things, though this is a solely Christian schizophrenia.

But Shakespeare would have accepted the title "secular" because by his time the idea of human life being apart from religion (a quaint theological idea if there ever was one) had been accepted. Henry

VIII had by now seceded from Rome, and pushed secularization to a point where finally the religion could disappear out of life as what we now call "private conscience". For Shakespeare some learning belongs to the "carnal" area, some to the sacred, and the two classes shall never meet. The division was the very basis of medieval teaching.

Homer thought without hesitation in terms of the "deathless" ones, the gods whose play weaved in and out of human life. By Shakespeare's time that has quite changed. It is possible for some to be "godless".

So we have in Shakespeare anguish and terror, just the same as in Homer, but all sense of guidance, even of there being such a thing as guidance, has gone.

His plays were performed among dozens of others and probably attracted no more attention than the others did. If court approval is anything to go by he was probably judged inferior to Ben Jonson. He was neglected after his death, then worshipped and misunderstood. In the nineteenth century he was performed realistically, and cut, in productions that were forerunners of this century's "spectacles". And this ambiguity of reception is due to the lack of any framework of meaning familiar to his audiences, such as Homer and the Greek drama enjoyed century after century. The purgation through pity and terror that the Greek audiences expected from drama comes in Shakespeare as a style of speech—expressions so extraordinary that they surprise every time they are spoken, and supply that feeling of sweet detachment that hovers over all the action. The medieval world that thrilled with a sense of imminent light has gone, and the world that makes no sense of that kind of talk has taken its place, and poor Shakespeare hangs sometimes forlornly but always hopefully somewhere between.

His nickname "Sweet Will" captures his ability to observe all forms of behavior including the most demented in a style which bestows sanity, through the deft balance and rhythm of his lines, their choice of words that seem to come from a place far from humanity. Something like Homeric reverence was eventually extended to his name and generation after generation of secularized people began performing him and making him new and up to date each time, just as it was with Homer's verses.

In Homer the gods play the main role, in Shakespeare they act from a great distance on humans whose quest is muddled and erratic and who are largely unaware of any godly interference except when they go in for a sort of bland rhetoric ("we are but flies to the gods").

In *The Odyssey* all the best information and guidance comes from the gods, and the ability to attract this to oneself depends on having a "subtle" mind. In Shakespeare the human seeks restlessly to find the truth about the corrupt monarchy of which he is a part (Hamlet), cannot understand terrible misfortunes (Lear), plunges, blinded by desires and illusions, into disasters which he seems to have unconsciously designed for himself (Othello), tries to live in a new unguided Dionysiac abandon (Falstaff), innocently expects a world of inherited forms which are no longer there (Ophelia), conceives grandiose ambitions which lead to nightmare, remorse, suicide (Macbeth), schemes with a crippled, demoniac, nihilistic intelligence (Richard III).

The Odyssey looks for guidance and seems to know where, more or less, to find it, while the Elizabethan character has lost his moorings. The Homeric character at least knows that some guidance from the invisible world is possible, and that it only comes to those able to receive.

When, in *The Odyssey*, Penelope asks the singer at her dinner table not to sing a certain melancholy song because it reminds her of Odysseus, her lost husband for whom she pines, she is reproached by her son Telemachus. He says, "The singer isn't responsible for his own songs—neither the order in which he sings them nor their content". These are in the hands of the "deathless" ones, the gods, he says.

We must remember here that no Hellenic poet or minstrel would start on an epic or song without invoking the Muses, which meant seeking information *by means of concentration* (the nearest word we have for this is "prayer"). His material, like his style, was *given* to him. There was nothing creative, for the Greek, in art, only a state of receptivity. It was more remembered than created. "We have only hearsay and not knowledge, while you gods see all things," says *The Iliad*. It was therefore a matter of contacting the gods and maybe attracting the attention of Hermes, the divine information-bearer.

This was why Democritus said that poetry was sung with the *holy* breath. Our word "inspiration" (from the Latin "to breathe in") expresses it exactly, and probably comes from the use of the breath in the Greek sects to excite visions and states of ecstasy or fear.

This is the first time in his life that Telemachus speaks this way. He seems to have surprised himself. He certainly surprised everyone else present. He has never spoken with authority about such things—or with authority at all. People have the feeling that he doesn't take after his heroic father. His change is brought about by the goddess of wisdom, Pallas Athene. She needs him to search for his father. So she gives him courage. She even makes him bold enough to dismiss his unwanted dinner guests—spongers who are always hanging round the palace in the hope of marrying his mother. Telemachus tells them that if they don't get out he will call on "the deathless ones" to help, Zeus in particular. Antinous, one of the guests, observes that it must be the gods who have given him the gall to say this as he certainly doesn't have the gall himself.

In *The Odyssey*, as in the Greek drama, power comes from the invisible, from beyond death, beyond the habitat.

It is again Pallas Athene who gives Telemachus the courage, next day, to call a meeting of the elders. It is the first meeting they've had since Odysseus left. One of the elders says that it must have been engineered by Zeus, since Telemachus was hardly capable of it, which also means that Telemachus must now be favored by the gods.

The elders urge Telemachus to tell his mother to leave her house sometimes. For four years she has been a recluse and refused suitors (they assume, wishfully, that Odysseus is dead). Telemachus replies that this would put the "dark powers" against him, and his mother would call on the Furies to torment him.

Here Zeus himself interrupts the meeting. He sends two eagles down to fly over the elders. Halitherses, a master of bird omens, tells the assembly that this omen is particularly bad news for anyone trying to marry Penelope since it means that Odysseus is on his way back home. Eurymachus scorns this and says that on the contrary Odysseus is dead—but he shows by his arrogant manner, Homer says, that he is out of touch with the "invisible". He speaks *from himself*, Homer says, and that means without guidance or information from the ones beyond death who know, and are the only ones to know.

Telemachus decides to look for his lost father and prays to Pallas Athene to prevent his mother's suitors from stopping him. At once Pallas Athene enters his father's old friend Mentor, who was also at the meeting. Mentor goes down to the seashore with Telemachus to prepare boats for his voyage, discussing arrangements with him. But Telemachus knows it is really Pallas Athene, not Mentor, speaking to him. So we realize he has a "subtle" mind. He can recognize the presence of a god. It is the difference between a "hero" and a "gross-minded" mortal.

The suitors are too drowsy from wine to hinder Telemachus's preparations—again the work of Pallas Athene, who got them drunk. And when Noemon, son of Phronius, allows Telemachus to borrow his ship it is she who puts him into a cooperative frame of mind. She tells Telemachus that *some* of what he will say in his conversation with Nestor at his first port of call, Pylos, will come to him unaided, but *some* will come from the gods. Much depends on Telemachus's powers of diplomacy if he is to elicit reliable information about his father's whereabouts, so Pallas Athene feels he has to be forewarned.

Mentor goes with Telemachus on the first lap of his journey. Homer sometimes calls him Mentor and sometimes Pallas Athene. When Mentor receives the libation cup from their hosts at their first port of call it is Pallas Athene who *actually* receives it.

Thus the gods go in and out of men—unpredictably and often without their knowledge. When Telemachus is dismayed by Nestor's account of the siege of Troy and begins to feel uncertain that his father is still alive (whatever the gods may say about it) he is mildly rebuked by Pallas Athene (through Mentor). In his reply he is still pessimistic—we feel he has lost touch with the invisible for a moment. It is his fatal weakness. He wants to hear human, not divine, advice, and so his voyage will not proceed easily.

Though Mentor is now in Pylos he is still being seen on the streets of Ithaca. This is part of Pallas Athene's plan to confuse the minds of the elders so that, seeing Mentor as usual, they will be less ready to assume that Telemachus has gone off in search of his father (whose return they fear). Being out of touch with the invisible they are blind and Pallas Athene wishes to keep them blind for a little time yet.

Like Shakespeare's men and women, Homer's plunge themselves further into the demented pit by their actions, and it is only a few, the "subtle" ones, who escape this downward flight. But there is one aspect of Homer which is absent in Shakespeare. His story is about *a quest*, and the verses themselves form a quest. So deeply did the idea of quest seize and transform (continually) our civilization from its Greek beginnings that we call a quest an "odyssey". This is a special heroic quest which overcomes untold obstacles.

The habitat in Homer is wild, often a blind revengeful enemy, its furies of wind and wave a challenge to the quest which depends on *sustained concentration* through the upheavals of climate and season, as well as those caused wilfully by the gods. Here the human's *biological predicament* is put in a nutshell. He stands facing a strange and alienated habitat with only his own resources, his tenuous contact with the invisible and the silent, and his entire reliance on concentration for his survival.

So the verses, whenever they were repeated, acted as a reminder of the predicament while promising a rescue from it. That was the religious emotion which the festivals and of course ancient drama were designed to evoke.

It is what made *The Odyssey* a Bible, partly. For the rest, verses were an account in veiled terms of what happened in an initiation in one of the Greek sects, just as the later Greek drama was too. As far as I know scholars have never given an account of either of these things, perhaps because the "epic" nature of Ulysses stands in the way of their recognizing religion.

For the Homeric quest for the lost father, with its terrors and hopes, its doubts and unexpected setbacks just when the prize is within grasp, was a replica in heroic form, stage by stage, of an initiation, which enacts all these things in silence and immobility.

FOURTEEN

Throwing The Pagan Out With The Bath Water

One thing I do hope, if we ever achieve a new phase of civilization—is that we drop the monk's calendular torture of making the ancient Greeks reckon their lives backwards, viz. that Aristotle died (322) sixty-two years before his birth (384), while Socrates was born (470) seventy-one years after his death (399). If ever a people had to perceive life through a narrow and petulant doctrine we are surely that people.

The BC calendar was the unfortunate brainwave of a sixth-century theologian in Rome called, if we are to believe tradition, Dionysios Exiguus. *Exiguus* means "small" or "scanty".

If we did abandon this calendar we would have to start history somewhere, hopefully without theological revisions, and I would put this start thirty million years ago. There is no less logic in saying that civilized men and women lived thirty million years ago than there is for saying that ants did. When we see ants frozen within amber from all those years back we don't hesitate to assume that they were precisely the same ants that are to be seen today. They look the same. And if humans had been frozen in amber at the same period they would no doubt look the same too.

But we have somewhat grandiose attitudes on the subject of time. It had to be squeezed down to include as little as possible of any other civilization than the Christian empire of Rome, with certain time-allowances—e.g. for the Jews because we took their Bible from them, and for ancient Greece because we took almost everything else from them, and, thirdly, to a much lesser extent, Egypt, since it was mentioned in the Bible as actually existing. Apart from those allowances you can say that civilization started a few centuries before Christ, with Egypt trailing its satchel in the dirt of pre-history along with Minoa.

All remarkably callow, we may say, but we mustn't be hard on a sect which had to struggle for dominion as every other sect before and since has had to. A sect comes into being with the purpose of creating a community apart from the rest of the world, as a shield from the madness of that world. It makes an attempt, however botched, to substitute the sanity that lies within. In this sense all sects are *embryo civilizations*, and the scorn they receive and hand out, like the brisk competition between them, is a measure of how aware the sect is of just this.

A sect's way to the top isn't easy because the sect has little training in slipping into the seats of power. Mistakes are made, based on panic fear of being swamped by the madness outside, and we shouldn't wonder that the Christians wanted to produce a doctrine as hard and fixed as military directives, more especially as in the Rome of that time it was the army who not only defended a faith but, as in the case of the Christian gospel, adopted it.

Then there is the fact that every sect appears mad to the outside world. Its behavior is different, its rules are openly defiant of established law and since sanity means for most people whatever law has established, few are in doubt that sect-members are nuts. You must therefore, as a sect, prove that you personify what the outsiders pine for—honest dealing and integrity and the power to suffer any degree of persecution, unto death. If anything, it was the Christian martyrs who, by showing that they cared nothing for survival, swept Christ into the picture as very possibly the true Savior.

There are so many pitfalls for a sect. The madness it flees from may also engulf it. Tampering with visions and trance-like states and revelations is dangerous. Unless the right knowledge has been passed on to you, even in the matter of the simplest dietary-fast program or breathing system, you will easily get megalomania in the leader or blind docility in the follower.

So you get sect leaders who store arms, order group-suicides, claim all the women for themselves, speak not with the tongues of angels but demons. But even here we have to tread carefully. The group-suicide is an earnest of the devotion in a little community, its preference for its truth over life (something not even an established religion can do without). One can judge little from the outside.

The adage "all wars are caused by religion" isn't so far from the truth, despite the fact that in the twentieth century there were worse wars than ever before. Not that this stops the motives being of religious progeny. No war is ever fought without enlightenment or rebirth goals, even when it is nakedly property-seeking. The two big wars of the twentieth century were an orgy of such goals, while ethnic wars are fought under blatantly religious banners.

All sects are based on a secret. It is this that creates both the fierce ardor within and the fierce enmity without. We today have a particularly superstitious approach to sects. Are they into sex orgies? black masses? voodoo? spells? corruption of the young? This is because any successful sect, like the Christian one itself, immediately imposes a hidden ban on other ones and by means of centuries of contumely may *gradually enter this ban into our perceptions.*

We can see how far this has gone in our automatic acceptance of the Christian revision of history as the story of one civilization only, with other minor "pre-historic" or "pagan" manifestations serving as domestics. Whether we like it or not this has been swallowed by scholarship and is only now, with the demise of the civilization, open to examination.

But here again we must tread carefully. As a vision or a conviction there is nothing wrong with the *la civilisation c'est moi* attitude. It is only saying "Christ will bring you life for the first time so what do you want with other so-called faiths?" A sect's truth comes "from out of the blue". And, like a myth (meaning something to do with the gods), it cannot be really challenged.

* * *

Naturally, if a sect like the Christian one attains so much power, and influences the whole world, its interdictions are going to carry weight. So when it describes the Homeric verses as an epic or heroic poem it can rely on funds of social elbow to win support.

So it never gets at the secret behind *The Odyssey*, namely that a sect is speaking, and a sect—even if socially accepted—must speak in an alternative language, precisely as Christ urged his disciples to speak in parables.

Secrecy pervades *The Odyssey*. Telemachus tells no one that a goddess has entered his father Ulysses's friend Mentor invisibly and is using him as a mouthpiece for her advice. He doesn't even discuss it with Mentor himself. Perhaps Mentor doesn't know. Also Athene enters Mentor only in his relation with Telemachus. Otherwise he remains as he always was. Any claim by Telemachus that "Pallas Athene has spoken to me" would have singled him out as a man of un-subtle mind and therefore worthless to guide.

This is the point about the secrecy of a sect. You don't talk to others about what they won't understand. Only when they undergo the sect's initiation will they reach the sub-text. All therapies apply the same logic. You must try them to see if they work.

The Odyssey and the Greek drama are parables too. But we must subtract from the word "parables" (a word de-classed in our secular period) its moral uplift implication. Far from being concerned with ethics, *The Odyssey*—like the Greek drama—was a step-by-step account of an odyssey or quest on the part of the hero for what turns out to be a death journey. The underworld is there in Book XI. The dead talk to Odysseus, as they do to Dante Alighieri millennia later. It is their knowledge that Ulysses carries back to his wife and son. Plays and verses were largely for people who hadn't undertaken that journey and perhaps never would. The "secret" was conveyed in the form of an unbreakable code. The pity and terror evoked were an echo of what happened in the mysteries.

In *The Odyssey* it is the *secret* part of the mind that the gods occupy or possess when they wish to give help. The word *ate* in *The Odyssey* means a state of inner confusion which may lead a person to do or say rash things. It manifests in drunkenness. But it comes from the gods. A man is temporarily "beyond himself" when he murders, insults, assaults and afterwards feels he isn't responsible for what he did. Homer's men always consider themselves free of blame when *ate* is upon them.

This is a precise reference to human dementia. It assails even the hero, the subtle-of-mind, and withdraws his responsibility; he is, as we say now, temporarily incompetent. The *secret* part of his mind isn't under social control. People outside a sect who hate and revile its members will kill or maim the leaders, try to bring them down in the public eye, the more so if the attacker is a jealously guarded control agency (a government, for instance).

The Greek mysteries or sects were equipped with techniques which could tap certain information felt not to be accessible to outsiders. So on the one hand you could be plunged by the gods into *ate* or you could, through the secret information, become as a god yourself, that is, achieve sanity.

Ate is what makes Oedipus a blind young man, long before his actual blindness. He is haughty with the oracle, disregards plain warnings and unknowingly, i.e. without competence, marries his own mother. When he blinds himself his worldly sight is no longer necessary because he is now endowed with the *secret light*. We have a peculiar idea of the implacable nature of fate in the ancient Greek tragedies but "fate" for them is really hermetic law, which has the power to turn the frightful into joy. Oedipus's blindness isn't self-punishment so much as the natural unwinding of events from a blind beginning—the crowning rescue from a demented course of action, and thus arrival at sanity.

The Greek gods were simply images of those dynamic and sometimes dreadful forces we have to deal with in life. Love was Aphrodite and Eros, song and drama were the Muses, the prophetic gift was Apollo, ritual ecstasies were Dionysos. Again the subject is human biological predicament, which is why these forces were called by Socrates types of *madness*. This madness has to be "turned", otherwise it won't become song or prophecy. And this was where the secret came in—it was the key that turned the lock.

Socrates devoted his life to this act of *turning* and described in detail what it was. When the *turning* had been done a light broke, human madness became radiant, it involved an odyssey or journey through darkness (non-understanding) which could be frightening, which is why it is called the death or underworld journey. This same method of turning a disciple or client is used in a thousand different ways without religion connotation. Jacques Lacan the analyst habitually "turned his client round" so that he could face his past from the opposite end, so to speak, and thus see it for the first time.

The "kundalini" journey of Hatha Yoga, in being the turning of sexual energy, is nearer the Greek mysteries than any analysis could be. It requires breath control, long hours of concentration, but care must be taken not to disorder the mind. That is, it must always be remembered that "yoga" means balance. All such methods involve risks, which the teacher is depended on to prevent. These risks must always be there because human dementia is actually being utilized to turn into its opposite. The terror that accompanies one stage of some initiations, like the moment of tragedy in the Greek play, is really alienation taken beyond the point of the bearable.

The mysteries were being talked about as late as the first century AD. Plutarch said that being initiated was "like dying, with all its terrors", and then "a light came to meet you and pure meadows received you, and songs and dance and divine apparitions".

* * *

All initiation, in whatever part of the world and whatever its modes, is the same. The one-time sexual or "left-handed" tantra ("yielding") of some Indian temples was echoed in the Dionysiac sect where the "master" carried a phallic column and there was a wand or "thyrsis" twined with vine leaves or, some say, mistletoe.

It was the "nothing in excess" doctrine of Delphi, to which the Christian sect belonged. Traditionally Christians have favored sexual sublimation and have been scathing about the use of sexuality in a sect, which is why the media today is too.

Presenting sexuality and by inference the womb as filthy, the Christians preached that your talk of sexual ecstasies was so much hypocritical cover for this filth. So today we perceive a clear distinction between what we call "spiritual" conduct (devoid of sex) and "carnal" conduct (devoid of religious or mystical content). That is, we perceive the matter *precisely in the terms of Christian theology*.

Yet the Christians also believed in the sublimation technique used in some initiations, while castigating initiation as such. Sublimation of sexual energies could *also* lead to ecstasies, but they weren't sexual in nature. So we must beware of hitting the Christians too hard for trying to breach the sensitive borders of our free-sex-for-all world. The fact is that both sexual indulgence and sexual prohibition can, when used as techniques, produce the desired result.

The disgust and venom of the early Christians on the subject of sexual love came about because they knew nothing about initiation in its overall role. They took an outsider's view and adopted techniques with the most arrogant recklessness. They took pot shots in the dark and they mostly didn't work. You couldn't just stop sex and expect results. You had to be trained, and therefore an experienced master with a special discipline was necessary. The simplest dietary fast requires this. Again and again the desert hermit, monk or churchman stumbled through a haphazard program of self-imposed misogyny, and plunged into a proportionate yearning for sex in any shape or form. One hermit received daily and sometimes hour-long visits from an imaginary black girl. She sat on his knee and did frightful things. He even had a name for this naughty little bitch. That sex murderers and cannibalists came from all this is hardly surprising.

Like any other initiatory technique sublimation leads easily to madness when undertaken without guidance, just as sexual abandon and every other "mysterious" form does. But Christians played with madness like pyromaniacs with fire—until a whole civilization burned down.

The results of botched sublimation-training are dire indeed because the sex the trainee recoils from is only one aspect of a general recoil from "animality", including of course the personal functions. Nearly all acts of killing can be explained by a pervasive self-disgust. It was strong enough in ancient Rome but in Christianity it achieved a millennial heyday. If now the Pope appeals for clemency toward children, toward those in the womb, it is late in the day. First the old perceptions have to be dismantled, before a new spontaneous compassion is released.

* * *

This seems to be leading us to the idea that the Christians never had an initiation or mystery. *But it was impossible to avoid one.* The earliest usually happened in babyhood—baptism by water. Undoubtedly under its master St John it was an effective "turning" ceremony. But, intent on eschewing anything comparable to Greek practices, the Christians allowed even baptism to become a symbolic and ritualist act.

Yet this lack of any secret was what made them refreshing in the Roman world. No Dionysiac excesses here, no processions in the night, no terrors or journeys into the underworld, no secrets that sealed the lips of initiates ("mysteries" = *musterion* = "sealed lips", from which we have derived our degenerated expression "hermetically sealed"). All you needed to do as a Christian was to close your eyes and see yourself as belonging henceforth to Christ in all things, wholly and utterly: the Mediator came to you in the silence of your mind, in whatever situation, at the brink of whatever disaster. He plucked you, at once, from the disaster. You only had to yield and the results were miraculous. At first thousands, and then millions found this to be the case.

It inclined Christians all the more to scorn the mysteries, without realizing that what they had found was a—mystery. They insisted that any form of *physiological* initiation belonged to that large field of superstitious activity which the Roman characterized as pagan. When I was a choir boy and fasted on Good Friday while singing in church most of the day the hunger had no more connection for me with *how* I was singing than a headache.

Even St Francis looked back on his ascetic excesses (his exposures to zero temperatures on Mount Averna, for instance) and understood that they achieved the opposite of the desired effect. In the mysteries there were certain laws which, if disregarded, could lead back to distress, even madness. And excess was one breach of those laws.

FIFTEEN

The Original Architect

The name is Socrates. As far as Plato knew he belonged to no sect. Yet he was a master and had followers. Also he had a quite remarkable power to change their perceptions. He simply talked. An initiation occurred without his followers being aware of it. No "pity and terror" as in the Eleusinian mysteries. All Socrates did was ask questions, and the man who answered went on his own journey of discovery.

The medieval monks, working through our educational systems (now worldwide), have given us a typically hilarious picture of this man. He is supposed to have been the "philosopher" who pulled the wool of ignorance from the eyes of the Athenian young. He was ugly but adored.

The real story is much more pertinent. Like Christ, Socrates was executed for his ideas and like Christ he could have avoided the death sentence by fleeing the city. In Athens at his time an influential man (as he was) about to be charged with sensitive public offenses might, if he could lay his hands on the money and had the right friends, escape to Thessaly or Crete, where he would no longer cause political embarrassment.

On the contrary, he stayed put, and everything he said at his trial could only rile the jury. Like Christ in Israel he was seen as a public enemy, though unlike Christ he was well-known in high places, making him at once both more vulnerable and more able to maneuver a reprieve.

Even after the jury declared him guilty he could have prevented the death sentence by accepting banishment. Instead, he went out of his way to tell the court that he had no intention of leaving. Even after the sentence he could have accepted his friends' offer to spirit him out of prison but he firmly turned the suggestion down.

Renunciation was the key to his ideas, as it was to Christ's. Almost certainly he was never initiated by a sect, though as certainly he knew something about the death journey. Yet he presented to Athens a precise religious program which his accusers took to be a questioning of established religion, just as Christ's accusers took *his* to be.

When, 339 years before the birth of Christ, three Athenian gentlemen brought a public action against him for corrupting young minds and producing traitors like Alcibiades they were thinking not of his ideas (of which, as he pointed out in court, they knew nothing) but his manner of presenting them—with a serene authority which made official authority look poor indeed. He exposed effortlessly and without arguing. Naturally he attracted a lot of intelligent people, especially young ones.

The charge of corrupting the Athenian youth is usually taken to be the principal one by scholars (on the basis of our notion that Greek philosophy was a secular pursuit) but the much graver part of the action brought by Lycon, Meletus and Anytus lay in their claim that Socrates was an atheist.

In this too he resembled Christ. The two crucifixions shared the same theme—*chosen death* for ideas emanating from divine guidance. Socrates told his jury that he was determined to persist in his teaching even if they reprieved him. He said he was unable to do otherwise, being divinely directed. His speech was as little a defense and as much of a silent defiance as Christ's was. It created an uproar among the jury of over five hundred men—so much that only he, the accused, was able to bring them to order.

Quite apart from his ideas it was his claim (and, with this, his aura) of divine authority that earned him the charge of atheism, though everyone knew that he had never disavowed the state gods and the religious forms of his time, just as Christ had always advocated obedience to the laws of Israel.

It really is remarkable how we can read Plato's account of his various conversations but miss the one key fact about him—that he was guided, that his work was a service he had to complete even at the cost of his own life, that death in any case was no punishment for a man who had long ago renounced life. Instead, we insist that this is the first rational (meaning secular) discussion we have heard in the ancient world, that *this* was the Greek enlightenment. So we brush over his repeated assertions of respect for the state gods as if he were simply abiding by a social form.

This first blindness of ours prevents us from seeing what an unusual idea it was to *talk and reason* his way along the death journey, not moving from his seat. It stands out as a different sort of heroism from any other Greek variety. His problem was that of any master of initiation, how to achieve that identification with death in his audience necessary for the journey to the light.

Christ entered a world already formed by Socrates. The kind of renunciation we attribute to Christ (the renunciation of sex, ambition, comfort, the animal nature etc) was in fact advocated by Socrates, *not Christ at all*. Christ made no mention of sexual continence except to say that there are those who give up sex and those who can't. As for animals, he saw them in the same yielding and sympathetic fashion. Nor is it possible to find in his words much interest in making life intelligible at all costs. Least of all did he single out the reasoning faculty as of special value for the disciple. It was Socrates who required the mind to make life intelligible. Christ asked for no such thing and this is why it has always been hard to recognize Christ in our civilization.

The moment we examine Socrates's thought we find our own intelligibility doctrine laid down clearly for the first time, in passionate terms. Above all we recognize *the rejection of the habitat* which became a key attitude in our own civilization.

No such thing is present in Christ's teaching. But tragically the civilization in his name inherited it.

One of Socrates's most important claims was that the real thinker ("philosopher") *despised his own body* and tried at all costs to become independent of it. Philosophy was a religious quest. You reached the truth by means of pure reason and pure intellect, and these were the fruits of inner purity, which in turn was attained only after a long struggle to *avoid the senses in every manner possible*. No man could think clearly while his mind was concentrated on sexual desire or food. In an impure state he could only think impurely. Only the soul could perceive truth. The body contaminated truth, being imperfect, changeable and finite. The soul was perfect, constant and infinite. Pleasures, sickness and pain hindered the soul from acquiring mastery over the body, just as ridiculous fictions and fancies—by which most people's minds are entirely possessed from birth to death—continually distracted us from the act of true thought.

For Socrates wars and revolutions were part of this same process: arising from the body and its desires they gave us no time for reflection. Death meant freedom from the body—but we had to seize our freedom before death if we wished to enter that state in a proper manner.

It is perfectly clear from his every word that he is an hermetic master, and knows he is. Hermes, the bringer of divine intelligence which endows the receiver with authority, only touches men if certain methods are applied. But the hermetic process in Socrates is extraordinarily original: he says that everyone can, *at any time* and without anything more than the will to do so, tap into the hermetic source.

Rebirth (liberation from the death-conditioned perceptions) was present in his thought but as a *rational* acquisition, a product of thinking. His initiation—open handed, clear for all to see—was the opposite of the "sealed lips" which characterized the mysteries. Had those mysteries, even the one at Eleusis which initiated the great Athenians, been as open handed they too would have fallen foul of the state. Socrates like Christ offered himself as the redeemer. The similarities between the two grow on examination.

For Socrates philosophy was a continual *preparation for death*. This is why, he said, the philosopher was regarded by most people as half-dead—i.e. he gave no more attention to his body than was necessary for bare survival. By maintaining himself in this apparent half death, he ensured the readiness of his soul when the time came to enter heaven and meet his peers in perfect equality. Heaven was open only to those who followed the philosopher's road, while those who dedicated themselves to desire hovered after death round the cemeteries as ghosts, longing for what they had left behind until they were re-absorbed into life in another birth, the quality of which was determined by the quality of their previous life. Here was the Indian idea of a *karma* inherited from one's previous life which is gradually shed through successive deaths until *the state of the philosopher* is finally reached.

Of course this is no philosophy in the scholarship sense, namely a secular wondering about reality with no more effect on the perceptions than a crossword puzzle. His is designedly hermetic.

And all as wide-awake rational discussion! No wonder the state took alarm. Would he abolish the gods, the sacrifices, the altars, the processions with one of his dreadful leading questions? Was he producing a generation of young revolutionaries who would abandon work and family to become "half-dead"?

How scholars could have seen all this as *secular* philosophy is a mighty puzzle even when we take into consideration their theological conditioning. I mean, Socrates actually laid it down, as every guru of oriental doctrine does, that there are certain binding laws which cannot be reasoned about—they are "given" experience, and the cycle of deaths is such an experience. And this is *rationalism*? Apart from the fact that his famous dialectical system was designed to elicit given knowledge entirely independent of the reasoning faculty!

Some of the best and the worst of Eastern ideas are present in Socrates. The popular Eastern notion that if you fail to shed your *karma* in this life you are in danger of returning to the "animal state" in the next birth was lodged in his mind as it is in the minds of the crudest Indian teachers today. Animals, he said, show the depths to which a human being can fall. People who have been gluttonous, selfish or drunkards are likely to turn into donkeys (for Socrates donkeys are "perverse"). Irresponsible or lawless people may become wolves, hawks or kites. Those who have been merely good law-abiding citizens, leading controlled lives without dishonesty but also without illumination, will more likely become bees, ants etc, namely creatures who never pause from industry.

The seed of Aristotle's thought on the subject of animals is here laid, and it is a message which the medieval world could comfortably receive as a basic tenet. Man was a religious, not a biological animal, and had been created as such.

Socrates rejected most other oriental ideas. Quite alien to him was the Indian *bakhta* notion that once a man has purified his mind (taken the death journey) he may return to a full earthly life and enjoy his appetites again. The idea that sex may be resumed with the same ecstatic pleasure as worship was for Socrates as repugnant as it was centuries later for the Puritans, who carried his renunciation into the most intimate details of daily life.

That sex figured in at least one of the mysteries was certainly known to Socrates. Whether the origin of our repugnance toward the idea of sex as a religious or hermetic function lies in him or the later Christian suspicion of all sexuality is anybody's guess, but behind our repugnance is the notion that biological = non-spiritual, which may have more of a Manichee or Persian root. What is certain is the fact that from about the third to the seventh century after Christ this attitude showed up in all the Mediterranean religions in some form.

Again there is nothing we know of in Christ which suggests that *any* love is out of place in a religion.

Socrates was a far more ascetic prophet than Christ. It was more from Socrates than Christ that Christendom inherited its sackcloth and ashes and, therefore, its sexual obsessions, partly because it misunderstood him or saw him through half-moon Manichee spectacles. When Socrates talked of the philosopher as being "half dead" he meant that he was distracted from the colors of this life by the brighter, indeed blinding colors of the next life, which had no Persian flavor at all.

The early Christians inherited the reincarnation doctrine, or rather they perceived it as a natural truth. But their doctrine balked at it. Reincarnation meant that you were free to renounce life in increments over maybe hundreds of lives—a kind of steadily diluting *dolce vita*—which wouldn't do at all for bishops anxious for all the punitive control they could get. So reincarnation was out of the Christian system.

Ecumenical (meaning "universal") councils could decide that sort of thing. The first Council ever, in the company of the first Christian emperor, Constantine, decided that Arius of Alexander was wrong to say that Jesus wasn't divine, only very special. He had to be entirely divine, a requirement that cost many an Arian his head. Thus one ridiculous argument compounded another—ridiculous because both reduced divinity to status, where it solidly remains today.

It seemed that Christian policy had to sound authoritative on all things but it arrived at its authority by discussion! Nothing "given" here. It was the Socratic mystery without the master. So a doctrine at variance with practice was inevitable. When it came to the renunciation of sex there was no doubt about the doctrine but only a few outrageous people looking for sanctification were expected to abide by it. Hence the Italian tradition of priests living with their "sisters" who never looked like a blood relation.

In this way the hermetic sublimation school was allowed to echo degenerately down the centuries until it became a purely rational term meaning a defense mechanism that diverts rude animal energies into social forms.

* * *

On the day of Socrates's execution, while he and his friends waited for the arrival at sunset of the man whose job it was to administer the poison, he began putting forward his views about the human soul and, more emphatically than usual, he rejected the senses and desires.

Since *chosen death* was the completest act of renunciation he naturally wished on this day to make renunciation his crowning argument, fulfilling it with his own death.

In the space of a few hours he had to convince his friends, who were still ready to organize his escape, that in death he would prove his claim that the soul survives and comes to know heaven.

He described with great feeling the earth and the heavens as they *really* were could we but see them—brighter and more glorious than anything in life, perfect as no earthly vegetation was, a landscape of such radiance that our ordinary vision would be shattered by it. Only in death could our real eyes open.

There would thus be *more* of our present reality after death, only a perfect version of it. He compared us to creatures at the bottom of the sea who believe that the surface of the water is the sky. We live in "the hollows" and are unable to see beyond. Only death, once we have liberated ourselves from the cycle of births, releases us into the true reality, compared with which earthly life is a distilled dream.

He told his friends he believed in "something like" a sifting process that took place after death. The good were separated from the wicked, those who acknowledged the existence of the soul were separated from those who remained sunk in the body. The wicked were obliged to live desolately in the dark subterranean hollow of the Tartarus with its swirling waters and winds, some for ever, some for limited periods, according to their crimes, while the good passed upward out of the dark regions to the pure surface where they lived without bodies for ever. Those who had led middling lives were guided to a lake called Acheron where they underwent purification.

He argued, on this his last day, in clearly expounded stages. Anyone who studies his remarks will recognize where the logic-chopping and obsessive systems-building of the medieval schoolmen came from. He talked about forms and opposite forms, of forms being exclusive of each other while not being opposite (such as Oddness and Evenness). It is strangely intellectual for a last discussion on earth. But nothing can stop Socrates trying to make life intelligible, namely a rehearsal for a reality after death too overwhelmingly radiant for anyone who hadn't been through a second birth in life, a new perception.

He is fervently convinced that man is the only creature in nature to be equipped with the faculty of understanding (meaning capacity for rebirth). Man can see to the very edge of death. The soul that gives him this understanding is carried forward into death, purified of the body at last. Its powers of analysis must be used to calm the terrified heart, which inclines the mind to fall into the popular belief that the soul is extinguished with the body.

How far Socrates is from logic-chopping and analysis in *our* sense. "The mind" means so much more than the faculty of calculation for him that it is difficult for us to grasp that he could enter death armed with that alone and yet enter it so passionately. For Socrates "mind" is what we would call spirit, only its vehicle is *thought*. Thought alone opens the door to heaven for a human being, gives him the power to detach himself from the things that stop him going willingly through that door. Thought rescued the mind from its binding and blinding perceptions.

Like Christ's his actual physical presence was felt for many generations after his death. It blew a terrific wind through the Mediterranean world, so much that Christians were unable to conceive life in any other terms, even Christ's.

In that last death debate two of his friends, Cebes and Simmias, are unconvinced by his description of life after death and put their objections to him. Take a musical instrument, Simmias says. It may be compared with the human body in that it is visible and earthly and mortal. While alive it emits delightful, indeed divine sounds. But when it is destroyed music can no longer be played on it.

How can Socrates say therefore that because the human body has its divine attributes during life those attributes survive its destruction? The others were struck by this argument and felt deflated.

Socrates has his answer. He points out that a musical instrument is *all* body, therefore it can never survive beyond death. Alone it could never produce music. It depends on human hands, human breath, it must be played. Human imagination is really what produces its music. And this is what lives after death—the soul, not the musical instrument it brought to life, nor even the music.

Gradually Socrates restores confidence among his listeners, though not all doubts are quieted. It was his unalterable serenity and composure that convinced. He *was* his thought. He didn't believe, he knew. It was evident in every breath he took, including, most of all, his last one.

His death was the triumph no jury could steal, just as it was with Christ.

SIXTEEN

Smothering The Fire Of Love

He triumphed not only over the jury but Christ too. He wouldn't have appreciated his triumph over a jury of Athenians who lived in "fictions and fantasies". How much less would he have appreciated a triumph over any prophet, least of all Christ.

But without him I doubt whether the Christian sect would have got beyond its martyrdom stage. The "cannibalist" and "atheist" labels would have stuck and the Romans would have gone on to Mithraism.

Not that Socrates was acknowledged as the Master, the true teacher of Christian civilization. Had his influence been a consciously chosen one all might have been well. But it came in, as so many classical things came into our civilization, under disguise. You couldn't after all revile the "ancient" world and be seen actually to base your new religion on it, which in effect meant *inheriting the "old" religion in a vastly changed and unrecognizable form*. You had to do a lot of construction work on the past.

Anyone who wishes to lift the veil a little on early Christian thought can see the Master easily. I wonder that the construction work wasn't seen through right away, let alone left intact for nearly two millennia, as it has been. Socrates came in under Plato. That was the disguise. We are allowed Plato. It is after all Plato telling us about Socrates. Without him we would have none of the dialogues. And Plato is a philosopher. He wasn't executed. He didn't annoy heads of state or turn the heads of the young. So he could be taken as a bright intellectual light from within the "ancient" darkness. This didn't involve actually denying that Plato was a religious man or that he presented a divine cosmology. Only that cosmology didn't have Christ in it. So it was kind of empty. It was waiting, in its perfection, for Christ to happen. It almost predicted Christ, almost gave birth to him and it certainly nourished the human mind in preparation for him.

So Plato was the first Hero, Christ the second and complete one. This was the heart of the so-called neo-platonism which was so formative for Christian theology. It flourished in Alexandria, the home of what was said to be the biggest and finest sacred library in existence, burned to a cinder in a typical brawl so that any written account of the mysteries conveniently disappeared from view for all time.

The neo-platonists offered Socrates safely encapsulated in Plato—Socrates without his mission, in case it overshadow or compete with Christ's, without his passion in the sense of agony and martyrdom, for the same reason, without his defiance of the jury, for the same reason, without his indifference to the death sentence, for the same reason, without his citation of divine guidance, for the same reason, without his crucifixion by poison, for the same reason.

The Master seemed to step into Western civilization as he did into a discussion with his followers, simply asking questions as it were in passing, with what is traditionally called "Socratic irony".

* * *

So Christianity became Greek. This was why it appealed to the peoples of the Roman empire, that willing and awe-struck child of Greece.

It isn't really true that the "old" religion was losing its hold in the first centuries after the birth of Christ. It was only changing. The Isis cult had a vast following from Persia right across Europe as far as York in England. And the way Christianity turned out was living proof of its continuing hold. Even the Isis mystery it tried to incorporate in the form of Mary Mother of God, and this did have a softening effect on the doctrinal tendency to vituperation. To this degree the "old" Hellenic religion changed into Christianity.

Constantine, the first Christian emperor, was a Hellene. He established himself in Constantinople, "the second Rome". He had two reasons for this. First, he was convinced that the Christians couldn't be beaten (Diocletian had tried with the so-called Great Persecution but had failed). Secondly, he needed to stand out sharply from the four previous emperors who had ruled the Empire simultaneously and badly, and the Christian cause was a usefully clean one.

I am putting aside Constantine's vision of the Cross and the word *Hoc Vinces* written over it just before his battle with the emperor Maxentius. One never knows how much of what he said could be believed (his wife and his son would have been negative in verdict had they lived to tell the tale).

Christianity was established by means of some surprising tricks. Constantine sent his mother Helena to Jerusalem and she came back with what would nowadays be a truck load of relics. She found them on Calvary (having first found Calvary), and they included the cross and those of the two thieves, and the crown of thorns (intact after three centuries) and the soldier's spear and even the sponge! If we think the CIA has pulled some fast ones the emperor Constantine was a streak of lightning, and unlike the CIA he was never exposed from within. The relics probably did more to stabilize the empire and de-stabilize his enemy emperors than a decade of bread and circuses in the old days.

Constantine recognized in the Christian *his own Hellenic mode of worship*. In earlier days, as Caesar of the West, he himself had been regarded as a descendant of Apollo, and to that degree divine. So he was able to understand how a god could incarnate for a time as a human. He also understood why the Christians refused divinity to anyone but Christ, including himself. It was through Christ alone that they had the power of absolution. Being emperor of

Christendom he was therefore absolved of his partiality for cutting throats.

He set about making Constantinople a Greek city that would be a monument to the old civilization and the "philosophy". And the fact that Byzantium lasted nearly twelve hundred years is evidence of a perfect marriage. You now had rationalism and religion in a genuinely liberating doctrine. It was *the freedom* that appealed to Constantine. The Christians said that if you have a mind to think with, and if you think about Christ, you are free be you slave, woman or criminal (the three tended to get equated). And Socrates was behind this freedom.

* * *

We must put aside any thought that rationalism was a *cold* thing then as it is now. It was Hellenic and simply meant *the use of the mind as a means of initiation*. Otherwise it would have influenced no one, remaining simply a dialectical style.

Socratic rationalism said that you didn't have to undergo sensory deprivation, fasting, special breathing in order to reach that trance-like state in which divine information could be received. It required *only an act of thought*, and this was what Christians offered in place of the mysteries. That key was the Socratic contribution.

Rationalism could never have come about *rationalistically*. Even hard-nosed and double-blind tested statements require *inspired beginnings* no more based on observation or deduction or wide-awake analysis than the Book of Revelations.

Also Socrates came packaged with renunciation. He laid it down that you have to have a clear and detached mind—detached from animality or the senses—if you want liberation from the death-haunted ego. Once it got into Christian hands this Greek renunciation became a ridiculous all-or-nothing quest, probably because all sects start by being extremist. Marriage was condoned only as a safety valve for unworthy desires. Monks and nuns were preferable to husbands and wives.

It wasn't good news for a civilization that asked to be the greatest ever, indeed the only one ever. Pulling long faces at copulation, even legalized copulation for the creation of monks and nuns, wasn't a hopeful sign.

* * *

Richard Rolle, a fourteenth-century mystic, had an opposite (or perhaps antidotal) message. He said that only *the fire of love* could breathe life into emptiness. Love was a "raging sun". He once passed his hand across his chest to see if he was really on fire, so tremendous was this force that unbalanced the mind and made the Form and Idea of Athenian philosophy totter.

But Form and Idea claimed the Christian heart. Rolle's message that the universe had actually grown, sprouted, flowered from love, that love still worked all its parts, that love could actually be perceived to be working in every movement in the universe, in every change of light, wasn't in the *classical* tradition at all. It was what the Christian tradition *should* have been, was *meant* to be by the one man missed out of it!

In early Christian minds sex wasn't far from bowel-elimination in status. So it was unthinkable that Christ should have had a natural, sex-produced birth. This too fitted in the classical tradition. Plato, Pythagoras, Alexander the Great were all considered gods in their lifetime. Their mothers had given birth to them without an act of sex, as a result of divine command.

Kings and robber barons had also professed this status. Just as Constantine was descended from Apollo, so Diocletian was from Jupiter and Maximian from Hercules. Divine status was even claimed by a Christian mystic (Simon Magnus).

Of course, if you suggest that birth is a calamity and biological functions evil you are a stone's throw from making bitter assertions about women. They become "serpents" *because they have wombs*. They use their serpentine wisdom in the form of wiles, temptations, artful manipulations, in an effort to drag Pure Mind into the service of vile animal functions. Women are biological (i.e. close to the habitat by virtue of their reproductive powers) and therefore their attainment to Pure Mind is all but impossible.

This view was generously Christianized by Tertullian, Cyprian, Jerome, Ambrose. The beguiling mystery of Isis or the divine mother was stamped out in anger (the Mary cult came much later). Jerome (third century AD) argued that a woman could only achieve spiritual status if she ceased being a woman. Ambrose said that for a female to lose her virginity to a man was "to defile the work of the Creator". A girl who fasted and diminished her sexual appeal and curtailed her menstruations was already shedding some of that monstrous guilt which, derived from Eve, lay naturally on her shoulders.

Jerome's only justification for marriage was that it produced men on the one hand and virgins on the other. He urged the girls in his charge to fast (one of them starved to death). The sexual organs, said St Methodius, should be closed up so that no sin could enter them. The best marriage, said St Augustine, was an unconsummated one.

Clearly this was theological genocide. So married couples were admonished by the Church to reduce their sexual pleasures to a minimum (a good way of achieving the opposite), and to devote them entirely to reproduction. It refused with disgust any suggestion of the Dionysiac sort that sex could be divine. Babies were a *consolation* for a filthy act. Thus did a Western world obsessed with sex on the peculiar grounds of it being shameful come into being. From sex theology to pornography was but a little hop.

The medieval cult of Mary as Mother of God tried to sugar the bitter pill with feminine compassion but it also carried the lesson that women could best fulfill their higher destiny by becoming wives not of men but Christ. Under this lay a glaring internal contradiction, best expressed by Samuel Butler in *The Way of all Flesh*—"It was a woman and not a man who was filled most completely with the wholeness of the Deity" (a reference to the Annunciation). What higher destiny could there be than divine impregnation? But the theological reply was that the womb has here been used for *its first and last truly good purpose*. So she can be Mother of God but not a priestess—another belly blow at Isis.

Animals, women, birth, digestive functions—all are potential objects of disgust. Wherever a "blind" biological impulse comes under review there is repugnance and distaste. The mind quickly becomes man's *only rescue from filthy biology.*

The "body" is soon a dumb zone cut off from the "mind" and potentially wild as it stumbles from desire to lust without guidance or meaning. St Augustine put it succinctly and crudely: "As I turned myself onto myself, and said to myself, 'Who art thou?', and I answered, 'A man', behold, in me present themselves to me soul, and body, one without, one within."

The schizo-formula was repeated by Paul—the inner is invisible (spiritual), the outer visible (mortal). Which is as much as to say, inside is life, outside death. So only in *withdrawal* from physiological processes can the truth be found. As for women, they do best if they follow men. Lacking wombs, men have fewer blind biological processes and more mind. It follows that men should dedicate themselves to God rather than to women.

Not that early Christian thinkers accepted Divine Birth as a finished Hellenic dish. They made adjustments. In the second century AD Justin Martyr agreed that Apollo, Bacchus and Perseus had indeed been born of mothers impregnated by the divine spirit but added that the mothers could therefore no longer be described as virgins, while Mary Mother of God hadn't been impregnated, simply filled with Christ, so she had remained a virgin.

Origen's interpretation was more scholarly but the same. He said that Christ's birth was similar to Plato's, whose father Ariston had been "visited" by Apollo. During his visit Apollo advised Ariston not to consummate his marriage to Perdictione in order that she could give birth to Plato without a preliminary sex act. Mary's conception, on the other hand, was "spontaneous", Origen said.

In another fourth-century version of the same tale Lactantius argued that she had been fertilized in the classical tradition by the wind or Boreas, like the twelve mares of Erichthonius.

After Christ you couldn't be born divine, at least no Christian could, but you *could* reestablish contact with a lost divinity by rooting out those desires in yourself which took you to the nasty core of biological function. St John Chrysostom, also in the fourth century, put the matter boldly: "Suddenly their happy lives were over, they had lost the beauty and honor of virginity. They were made subject to death. Do you see where marriage took its origin? For where there is death, there too is sexual coupling; and where there is no death, there is no sexual coupling whatever."

* * *

These may seem sad views of life yet they all derived, if in a quite mad way, from the Mysteries, whose techniques for the storage of sexual vigor were no doubt kinder and at least effective. There is a technique, said to be of Chinese origin, which involves the continual delaying of sexual emissions through long periods of love-making. Orgasm-withholding is a rich source of levitational dreams. Or, in the case of an orgasm, the sperm is imagined by the male to be drawn back into the testicles.

The early Christians, like the media today, didn't know where to put their faces when they heard this kind of thing. Instead of studying the matter in an Hellenic spirit they tucked up their habits and fled. When such notions could be traced to a human that offending body was cast to the flames.

But even Christian priests developed Tantric ideas of their own. In the sixteenth century the Adamites and the Brethren and Sisters of the Free Spirit practiced sex as a divine exercise. That is, it became worship, transforming every cell in the body. Since Christian theology abjured the physiological these attempts to bring Christianity down from the head were quickly snuffed out.

The priest near Florence who lived freely with nuns of his choice in the same period got off with a defrocking, partly because extra-cathedral sex was so common that you had to be a fool to get caught.

St John Chrysostom's sickly statement about marriage which I quoted above was a typically gross effort to purvey a precious hermetic idea. He failed to point out that the suppression of sexual energy could also lead to a demonic preoccupation with it, as in

189

the case of our Theban hermit who dreamed on a regular basis of girls sitting on his knee and ogling him with vicious and successful persistence. The mind has to be diverted from desire as it does from food during a fast. There is a painless and body-friendly way for all such methods.

The Gnostic arguments were different but only in degree. They declared Christ to be pure spirit, therefore beyond all Birth, Visitations, Annunciations, Divine Impregnations or Crucifixions. Matter in Gnostic eyes was by its nature un-spiritual, so that nothing in the habitat could be other than mortal, and Christ never had been mortal. This became what we now call the Greek Orthodox view.

The Roman church countered this, no doubt with some reluctance, by emphasizing Christ's humanity. But this had its dangers too. The Arians held that Christ was as much a man as any other, and that he was chosen for his divine role only at his baptism. This was heresy for Rome because it went too far the other way.

Was Mary simply the human mother of Christ the man, or the human mother of a divine Christ, or the divine mother of a divine Christ? Was she, as Theotokos argued, no less than the Mother of God?

Constantinople buzzed with ridiculous puzzles of this nature. Yet they were real enough for priests and friars because to them fell the job of instilling revulsion for sex into people who married and bore children and went about their daily business, busily and happily indulging their healthy desires. How far could theology advocate death in life without producing a depressive mankind of the sort we have today? If you went to Mani extremes and said that matter was the Devil's work, what kind of God did that leave you with—a God who had knowingly created the devil?

In AD 431 Cyril of Alexandria laid it down at Ephesus, as a matter of Church doctrine, that Mary was finally and without doubt, despite all apparent oddities in the argument, Mother of God. And he excommunicated Nestorius, the patriarch of Constantinople, for asking the rather appropriate question, how could God have been a baby?

When subtle and demanding esoteric techniques are put in the hands of people who don't understand them and have no one to guide them the effect is to enrage the body and disorder the mind. Bitter dispute, harassment, burnings and massacre result. Armed with an absurd code which fails to make head or tail of what penances and fasts are all about, the Christian tottered like a drunkard, platitudinizing about purity and grace.

The state of his sewage arrangements, his awful plagues, his revulsion from personal cleanliness as well as from the sex he frequently had too much of (like Philip II of Spain, who wore out three wives with his sexual importunities), his petty hatreds and denunciations were the real barometers of how much purity he attained.

The fire of war and madness, not love, was the result of his clumsy hermetic excursions. Erasmus once warned his fellow Christians that their wars of words could easily becomes wars of swords. And they did. We aptly call them the *religious* wars.

SEVENTEEN

What The Devil Created The Mind Can Mend

In fact war entered the Christian system as *a vehicle of enlightenment*. The idea of life as a dark conflictual zone favored the use of war as quest, a necessary means of change that drew the successful combatant ever nearer the promised light. No one can say that we haven't been at it ever since.

When the first imperial Christians junked the reincarnation idea as an easily disposable feature of the "old" religion they unconsciously turned their renunciation program, hypocritical as it was, into a sort of day-by-day suicide. You were now allotted one life only and in this life you had to decide between the path to heaven or the path to hell. All life was thus concentrated in an after-life choice, not on any benefit or grace that might accrue here and now. So all the time you were here you were somewhere else, and present time was spent in future speculation.

As a way of writing off the habitat it was impeccable. Nature was now an incidental background to your drama, not only the nature outside but the one that gave you sexual appetites. You could befoul your environment, hide your body not only from the elements but from your own gaze, because you belonged to neither.

So you missed the obvious connection between your sewage and your plagues, between your willful ignorance of your own body and the high mortality rate.

Since this one life of yours was of only incidental importance, being a mere ante-chamber to heavenly delights or the most gruesome eternal tortures, you did everything as it were absently, overlooking yourself as a live thing. A death religion therefore came about, one that led inexorably to wars of every variety, until the whole habitat threatened to be engulfed by it.

With engaging credulity we say that our mortality rate is commendably lower than that of medieval times but we miss out the genocide of twentieth-century wars as if they were a few duels. We attribute medieval deficiency in modern health norms to superstition or hide-bound ordinances such as that which forbade the holy to look on their own bodies, particularly if they were serpents or woman. Dark houses with tiny windows shut fast at night, no idea (until the seventeenth century) of the possibility of what we call infection, a long dulled wait for the Second Coming—we can call up dumb pictures of medieval life from our popular-lore department as if we all had history degrees. Yet we are unable to attribute our modern genocides to the very same theology those people were trying to realize. All doctrines get trimmed here and freshened there in the course of time. Each generation does it, and concludes that it has removed the doctrine. Not a bit of it. The doctrine was only strengthened. And the changes take so much time---as in the case of hospital hygiene, for instance. It took until the twentieth century. When first told that you must wash your hands before and after an operation and throw away the surgical debris doctors laughed! So we omit our genocide figures, which run into hundreds of millions (enough for a millennium of Black Deaths), and say "that isn't mortality, it's war".

Disease or war, the origin is the same. In Hippocrates's time life expectancy was greater than in medieval times because the theology was different. Not that there wasn't mortality trouble in his time too, otherwise neither his lectures nor the cypress-shaded healing place at Epidauros would have been necessary. But our present mortality-rate is the highest ever recorded since this tragic primate started walking on two paws. He has had a balance problem ever since.

But—again I must say it—we shouldn't be hard on an animal which got lost in a strange habitat and has been earnestly trying to find his way ever since. In so doing he has made, we have to admit it, many marvels, many splendors and miracles which still make our hearts beat faster, even as our imaginations, together with our lungs, close up.

The fact that today we find him standing forlorn in a dense un-breathable fog of his own making shouldn't tempt us to lose faith. We would then be falling into the most spineless of all the evangelical decretals—that failure is a moral punishment.

No, the sheer enormity, consistency, passion of his total failure, in which we sit choking and hawking today, is a pointer to his, well, sincerity.

Of course it would be also very foolish, if not polemical to the point of showing off, to say that the word "modern" was interchangeable with "genocidal", apart from not being very original. We do do an awful lot of peaceful things, after all. We have rehab programs for the victims of war, family life and the volatile aspects of the necessarily free market, we have museums, vast libraries and musicals.

The fact remains that our mortality figures *have* gone up an awful lot. Could it be, *dare* it be that in the theology which brought this new phase of civilization into being in the third century after Christ there was an underlying *doctrine of war at any price*, an insistence that conflict is the spice and meaning of life, namely the Crusading Spirit (sack and misappropriation on behalf of Our Lady)?

Of course if you are going to advocate struggle as a way of life you won't say it in so many words, particularly if you think (as both Hitler and Churchill did) that the struggle is going to be as swift as a blitz. You simply revive the idea of the quest and the fearless spiritual warrior, and in the end you will stir the population from its lazy habit of working eight hours a day into the higher energy of pure destruction.

There was nothing in Christ that you could call an incitement to war, apart from that almost-aside in which he said "I bring not peace but the sword" (meaning, "your old perceptions have to go and courage is required").

But the Greeks were a very fierce people. They fought without quarter. And to inherit their religion, without inheriting that too would have been impossible.

At first sight it seems impossible that Socrates, whose mission was to bring sanity into that fierce world, could bequeath the very same ferocity, not the sanity, to the Christian civilization. Again we must make allowances for the fact that everything he said was misunderstood and therefore twisted into its opposite. His description of the philosopher (i.e. initiated master) as "half dead" argued for Christians a punitive program in which this life should be taken as an interim trial to be hurriedly brought to conclusion in a verdict of heaven or hell. He wasn't referring to the habitat, the world of light and colors, when he said "half dead". Far from despising present life Socrates saw it as a version and reflection of the Elysium after death. He meant the perceptions. Being unable to perceive like others, he could no longer share much with them. We must understand the offer he made—that all you need is a mind to find your own salvation, the power to *think*, with which power every human creature is felicitously endowed—slave, criminal or beggar. With this alone you may rid yourselves of the perceptions you have never thought it possible to question because they were "reality" for you.

It presented an irresistibly precious chalice to the Christians, which they irresistibly misunderstood to the last detail. In a short time the chalice was minus not only Christ (who had no time for after-life heaven and hells) but Socrates too.

If you didn't believe that Christ was divine you got burned. If you believed that matter was through and through evil, ditto. If you believed that matter was through and through divine, ditto. If you believed that Christ was matter divine or otherwise, ditto. Life was a gasoline tank with a lighted taper hovering over it.

This civilization was based so squarely on alienation as a principle of life that it felt free to strike the habitat dead, defile and terrify animal life wherever it crept, turn its genocidal obsessions on to its own species, kill millions of others once they had come of age and further millions before they left the womb: free to play the maniac because the habitat was a snare and illusion that threatened to bring low the mind!

* * *

All this defining of how much sex you could have, how divine Mary was, how much a naughty temptation nature was, how the parts of the Holy Trinity were related to each other, was clearly an effort to create new laws, a shared language for an altogether new civilization. All the decrees and decretals and councils were showered on us so that the old world would be lost to memory altogether.

But what a shower it was! Even the word "faith", from the Latin for trust or confidence, is a strange one when applied to, of all things, religion. It led to the quaint idea of "believing" in God, a verbal Credo much like a legal document or oath of allegiance.

The first to use the words "Catholic Faith" was Nicholas of Amiens, in a paper addressed to the Pope. His extraordinary argument was that Christian theology was the most advanced form of mathematics available to mankind!

Like Alain de Lille, Nicholas tried to define the Church in terms so firm and precise that hopefully the great heretical movements would be silenced. Armed with Aristotelian logic, Euclidean geometry and Numbers, the Church would settle theological arguments for good. Which it did—but with the sword.

The world buzzed with exciting analysis as an instrument of changing it all—while the perceptions remained exactly where they were, that is, committed to war. Of course there were also those, like Peter Abelard and Bernard of Clairvaux, who said you couldn't analyze God. But the other school prevailed. One of its adherents was Clarembald of Chartres. He called it *intellectabilitas* or intellectuability. God could be thought about as precisely as a thing could be measured and weighed. Indeed, this was the meaning of theology. It was the application of mathematics to the spiritual universe. He should have said that this was a definition of *Christian* theology.

The Spaniard Ramon Lull, born in 1235, travelled everywhere in Europe and North Africa. His ideas were still influential during the French Revolution. In his *Ars Magna* he argues that being enlightened was the same as being Christian. The more scientific knowledge there was, the more Christians would come into being. The Christian faith would spread as the New Knowledge was accumulated by inquiring Christian minds. It would be a vast organ of wisdom capable of solving every problem, including religious ones.

And again there was Roger Bacon describing in detail the future marvels authored by Christ alone—vehicles sea-borne, vehicles mobile on hard ground, vehicles air borne and submarine. His was a more hopeful sign for Christianity and human life was presented in Bacon's *Libro del Gentil* when he argued that discussions between Jews, Christians and Muslims could do only good (they were soon scotched) because the Christian world needed to nourish itself with knowledge of various worlds. He looked forward to one language, one faith, one knowledge recognized by all the peoples of the earth. The human mind would by that time have found its common rational language (we are there).

Few medieval scholars, even Anselm of Canterbury with his brain-twisting ontological proof of God, saw the implications of trying to mathematize religious experience into concepts as neat as equations. The more Schoolmen endeavored to prove, demonstrate and argue the existence of God and the nature of the Devil, the more they demonstrated that there was no religious experience at all behind what they said. Experience needs nothing to substantiate it. I don't need to argue that the tree I see is a tree. I say "I see it, if you can't you're blind."

It is why religion causes so much trouble, why we fight over it and despair of other people's and can't apparently do without it, least of all when we adopt one of its atheist theologies.

The Christian religion sank beneath *the desire to understand*. Anselm of Canterbury even said it—*credo ut intelligam*—"I believe in order to understand". Over the coming centuries this neat statement turned into the unwritten (because universally agreed) "I will give up religion in order to understand".

If only the Master—Socrates— could have spoken with them, ironically, quietly from his shady Athenian corner. He might have shown them that they would change nothing by disputation, that his own method hadn't in any sense been disputative. All he had done was ask leading questions and imperceptibly the disciple had been drawn to witness his own perceptions, and leave the world to look after itself.

His leading questions *were based entirely on the reactions to them*, stage by stage. They were only "leading" because they extracted from this reaction the basis of the next question, so that the disciple felt he had the knowledge already in him and that Socrates had only elicited it.

It wasn't disputation from fixed points of view at all, nor was it analysis of a fixed point of view. It came from and returned to *perception alone*, not to systems of thought.

So if Socrates confronted one of our physicists who wanted to talk about God's Mind today he would quietly ask him what the mind was and when the physicist had explained that he was referring to the human mind he would only have to ask "Then how can God have one?"

In other words he would look at the physicist's perception and not at his speculations at all.

Even church liturgy began to reflect the intelligibility-mania with its questions and answers (catechism) and explanatory readings from scriptural texts. At the ringing of a tiny bell there was one devout moment of consecration—brief enough in all conscience— when even those pacing round the church might pause from talk.

What a paradox it was that Christ, so painstakingly un-intellectual in his sermons, should be handed over to academe. You must twist the Gospels out of all context to squeeze a drop of distaste for the habitat out of them. Women, animals and children are everywhere present. The Pharisees and Sadducees are upbraided for their calculating attitudes. Birds in the air, beasts in the field are analogies for the human.

Dead-habitat doctrine is sometimes called Manicheeism. St Augustine started as a Manichee but later renounced it with great eloquence. But neither he nor most other Christian thinkers managed to shake it quite off. The Persian theologian Manes introduced the doctrine to Christians in the third century. He was executed in AD 277, for theology is a risky business.

His basic tenet was that the habitat, and the physiological functions that belong to it, are not simply inferior but *devoid of divinity*, indeed the work of the devil. He dropped a Persian seed into the confused Christian mind and its somber flowers sprang up for centuries.

Some people believe that this evil-matter idea started with Zoroaster, the Persian prophet who lived about thirteen centuries before Manes. Certainly Zoroaster claimed that men could and should engage themselves in the work of changing the world. And he may well have been the first thinker we know of to say that the habitat needed revising.

But the more probable truth is that horror of the habitat and the consequent need to re-design it is never far from the stricken human mind at any epoch.

Not that the Persians or Christians said that the habitat had been *created* bad. In the Persian version of the Adam and Eve story darkness and falsehood are states that have taken possession of the human mind. It was thus human perception which had gone wrong. God or Ahura Mazda created the world pure and wise but Angra Mainyu, lord of darkness, undid that divine work. Therefore matter, though created by God, ceased to be in a proper sense His handiwork. In order to reach the light again, humans had to work. The efforts of Angra Mainyu had to be undone.

In a visionary account by a Zoroastrian named Arda Viraf, written after the birth of Christ, the bad deeds we commit in our youth are represented as a stinking old woman full of blotches, our good deeds as a beautiful girl with nice breasts. Hell is a frightful pit, also stinking.

In his vision of hell Viraf sees a man with a snake crawling up his anus and emerging from his mouth—the soul is being punished for sodomy. A woman drinks male urine and eats male excrement because in life she approached water and fire while menstruating. Another woman hangs by her breasts while being eaten by wild beasts from below as her reward for adultery.

Christianity drew back from this kind of thing. It might agree with the Persian doctrine that man had to struggle for grace but it was obliged to argue that grace had become easier through Christ's mediation. While some taste of hell was necessary it had to be balanced by a promise of heaven that lay on the other side of the "strait gate" offered by Christ.

* * *

We all know when we say of someone "he's a puritan" that it indicates disapproval of certain sexual conduct.

But this disapproval was a small part of the total Puritan program. It did succeed in changing human sexuality but not at all in reducing sexual obsessions, as it aimed to do. So the success of *this* clause was ambiguous. But the rest of its program was so successful that human life was changed more radically than it had ever been since the human primate first existed. It produced what we call the "modern" man.

If all we know today about puritanism is its sexual clause it means only that its other ideas became so accepted that they *passed into our perceptions.* We no longer consider "Hard work brings proportionate rewards" a revolutionary statement. It is obvious, trite, although quite untrue of the vast majority of mankind.

So "puritan" could at this point drop out of the language, were it not for the fact that puritan rules about sexual behavior provoked the greatest unrest, and that this unrest is still universal because it centers on that sensitive question of human "animality" at its very source.

Puritanism was in fact a dynamic movement which had supporters all over Christendom. A Puritan was usually a quite striking person when he began to appear in Shakespeare's England. He or she stood out for integrity and straight-dealing, rather as communists in the 1930s did, and they got a lot of support this way. They were the politically correct people and it didn't do to offend them, more especially as they identified themselves with the City or money interests, understanding that money was the most mobile and flexible way to bring the "old" society, based on the inheritance principle, down.

The Puritans were really the extreme wing of the Protestant church. To break away from Rome wasn't enough. Man had to break away from man as he had hitherto developed. Their program was designed to produce a second, new hominid. "New" and "modern" began their journey as OK epithets.

Puritans demanded to be free yet morally responsible for themselves. Everywhere they looked they saw corruption (transactions based on intimate association, not principle) and were prepared to leave their own country and create a society based on principle, not inheritance, far away. And this also they did. And in turn that nation became the most powerful in the world.

They wanted a hominid whose life was based on work and conscience, a watchful creature who left nothing to chance or inherited instinct or family habit or—that most dangerous of all zones—pleasure of a sensual nature. Churches must be stripped of frescoes and images of Our Lady and all those other sops to the senses (colorful vestments, canopied altars, incense) which distracted from the pure act of inward prayer. The "English" revolution two decades or so after Shakespeare's death did the job violently, replacing the monarchy with a Protector and attacking the old venality by means of a new one.

The Puritan attack on human sexuality was a crucial item in its program, perhaps the most important. It saw in sex a shameful display of animal pleasure which befogged and degraded the vigilant mind, and was therefore a chief source of the scheming, lying, bribing, flattering and depraving that prevented true religion. It was just no good going to church and taking the same corrupt soul back home with you afterwards. *The human anatomy had to be overhauled* and to start the operation with an attack on its sexual instinct was right because there lay the dark, blind source of all its follies.

The Puritans made war on public flirtation, kissing and suggestive glances. They wished to throw a cloak of shame round the sex act—not difficult to do where the human's most sensitive and biologically sorrow-laden area was concerned.

But this is dangerous work. You are close, in sexuality, to the source of human dementia. If you make sex a clandestine act you may succeed in driving the "animal" underground, but the risks are great. The restricting must begin in childhood, for there—so the Puritans said—was where the original sin was most manifest, being least controlled by shame. In this way the passions are diverted from the love object, in the first instance the mother and especially her breasts. But it isn't matters of conscience or worship that the thwarted passions now turn to but lurid dreams of rape, mutilation, incarceration and murder for orgasm.

Not that we have thrown off the Puritan program even in our sexual behavior. We may be in revolt against its sexual clause, we may demand to be free but this is because *our perceptions have been successfully imprisoned.* We can no more return to sexual self-abandon and spontaneity by wishing it than we can walk comfortably on all fours.

The hub of that clever, persistent and determined program was self-consciousness, which the "modern" man has in excess. It was thought that if only the human could become aware of what he instinctively ("blindly") did, the animal in him would disappear. Well, the animal can't be revived by self-conscious mate-hunting and deliberately un-clandestine sex and glad promiscuity. It only drives the suppressed animal further down. The more you revolt against the Puritan sex-clause the more you fulfill it. You talk and think so much about sex that you are well-nigh incapable of that intimacy, familiarity and sheer private joy on which marital love depends. In fact, these things may disgust you.

It is always hoped that the adolescent will settle down into marriage and child-rearing once the early experiments are over. But the experiments so complicate the problem—there have been so many of them—that family life is now more or less out as a viable "institution". The poor animal within must go on prowling, hoping, licking the wounds of the last affair.

It illustrates how we see live events with dead perceptions. It doesn't make any difference what we *think*, much less what we *want*. If the perceptions we inherit have disgust packaged in them we can only watch ourselves do what we vowed in youth we never would do: we were going to fall in love, marry, have children and that was going to be that, if only biological facts would walk away.

Sometimes it happens that a couple learns animal spontaneity, rather as mating pigeons do, when confined in the dark with a week's supply of food. They discover that to have the same mate is to possess the whole range of sensual pleasures. The whole Puritan picture of "attractive" or "beautiful" people goes by the board as a mental aberration.

But then the Puritan doctrine was deeply pessimistic. It didn't like the human because he was an animal. And like the Manichee the Puritan balanced this pessimism with its opposite—the cheerful assertion of a choice between good and evil. We can't buy grace with money, they said, and priests can't get us into heaven or hell. So it is up to us.

The program said that prosperity, security and health were *spiritual rewards for industry*. The program looked at the fields and meadows and saw waste everywhere. It saw waste in the laborer because he worked according to the season and not his needs. It saw villages where nothing had "changed" for centuries so that the inhabitants might just as well have been animals (in the Puritan sense of "passive"). And it vowed to uproot everything and everybody.

* * *

It was no coincidence that medieval Oxford, with men like Roger Bacon, William of Ockham and John Wyclif about, paid particular attention to the *practical* side of changing the world, and that the first industries should come about in England six or seven centuries later. The one led directly to the other.

We are so Puritan that we have long forgotten our origins. A small but vigorous movement of highly energetic men undertook the work of so changing life—not simply in one country but the world—that man would at last become detached. We may see this now as a reckless alienation program but it lay in an ardent desire to achieve at last the promised New Knowledge which depended on a clear mind untroubled by sickening lusts. Above all, it understood that it was human perception, not behavior, that had to be attacked. Freedom was the goal and it was only a pity they didn't recognize to what extent they were kicking away the last ladder to sanity.

Puritanism has many various medieval roots. If you argue that God is far distant from the world, as Duns Scotus did, it somewhat reduces Church authority. The Pope can hardly be seen as His Vicar in this case. Man, said Duns Scotus, must show the utmost purity and integrity in the conduct of his life, leaving nothing to a corrupt priesthood. Some centuries later the Bohemian John Hus and Martin Luther protested that the papacy was a hindrance to Christian life.

William of Ockham taught at Oxford between 1318 and 1324. He scorned fellow theologians as a gluttonous gang of rascals. He openly declared (three centuries before Henry VIII) that the Pope was mad for power. He said that moral and political and even theological doctrines were as remote from God as the men who thought them up. The notions of priests and scholars had nothing immutable or inscrutable about them. Life was in the hands of men *to do what they could and would with*. If they didn't exercise their freedom they enslaved themselves to people who did—to popes and emperors and above all theologians who tried to speak about and on behalf of God. All the names we use like "God" and "soul" and "divine" and "immortal" and "redemption" and "grace"—in fact all the words we use about anything—are simply *convenient terms* which have no more significance outside human life than the size of our shoes.

This "nominalism", as Ockham's doctrine came to be called, saw concepts, however majestic their appeal, simply as tools we need to conduct our lives with.

His ideas naturally had a shocking impact since Christendom was busy constructing names for everything under the sun, and endowing them with an everlasting and indestructible significance. We today who live comfortably with words like objectivity, scientific advancement, fact, truth, progress, detachment, pure research and democracy should know what Ockham was talking about.

* * *

Abstract name-giving looks very much like an effort to create an Ideal World over and above the crude, repulsive habitat (within and without). It was evident in the way medieval education was organized. The "carnal" studies were separated from the "divine" studies and the whole curriculum emphasized *abstract systemization*. A few Latin and fewer Greek authors were read but they were largely dressed down for their voluptuous temptations. Latin was the sacred tongue in which theology was written and prayers said, while "romance", namely the vernacular tongue, was fit only for clowns and noblemen—an attitude that persists to this day in our medical and pharmaceutical schools (the straight use of the word "poison"—that is, the original meaning of the word *virus*, namely "poison"—would hardly have the social standing of *virus* today. Nor would "brown grease" sound as classy as *lipofuscum*, or "itch" *psoriasis*).

One of the most reckless things the Church of Rome ever did was, not many years ago, to abandon Latin and substitute *secular languages* (as all vernaculars have become) to express the mystery of its liturgy. Thus the pharmaceutical industry was much wiser.

The Abbot of Cluny gave up reading Virgil, officially the most acceptable of the Roman writers, after a dream about an ancient vase full of serpents. After all, loving accounts of the habitat had to be treated with watchful suspicion.

Only one man from the ancient world was given ecclesiastical status—Aristotle. The calm and order of his thought had a tremendous attraction for people who so deeply lacked those qualities. Even Duns Scotus, who saw God as absolutely free, and very far from mankind, argued that He could not defy the rules of logic!

The basic instruction for a young monk was in grammar, rhetoric and dialectics or logical argumentation. If he showed aptitude he could go on to astronomy, geometry and music, and he could study Aristotle in depth.

Before AD 1200 the only part of Aristotle's work known to Christians was his Dialectics, but after that his Physics, Metaphysics and Ethics (sometimes highly inaccurate because they were translated from Arab versions and not from the original Greek) began circulating the monasteries and universities.

This was the first framework of *our* education, an academic or abstract system which has to be learned as if it had never originated in the thoughts of men but represents an irrefutable, absolute and everlasting body of principles on which all reality is founded.

In medieval times you argued about what Aristotle's words meant but you didn't question that the meaning was absolutely and indisputably right. And if you could demonstrate that any argument you put forward, however whimsical, was supported by Aristotelian argument you had won the day.

It was a great comfort, this certainty in the midst of straw-sucking puzzlement.

The private education received at home by gentlemen until well on into the nineteenth century concentrated on the Greek and Latin authors in order to teach the values of civilization, which these gentlemen would hopefully personify in their adult conduct. In this sense Christendom always knew how squarely it was founded on ancient Greece, even to the smallest details of behavior.

Our data-knowledge which has now been substituted for this as the basis of education is really the "carnal" studies taken to the medieval conclusion of a Complete Knowledge which is however being added to all the time, though its premises are never questioned or even thought to exist.

A medieval monk's chief pursuit, if he showed aptitude for learning instead of farm work, was to copy the Holy Writ and manuscripts in as fine a manner as possible, thus adding to the monastery library which would one day contain all knowledge. Before the thirteenth century a reasonably complete library was thought to contain all essential knowledge, so that a scholar like Dante who had studied every one of the texts might be said to "know everything".

But the division of learning into carnal and divine was a ticklish one. It involved a typical Christian schizophrenia such that when you were being carnal, say as a mathematician, you were deserting the divine, and when you were being divine you were deserting practical realities. You went from the carnal class where He didn't exist straight into a divine class where He threatened you with heavy assignments of hail maries if you were carnal.

The basis of puritanism (as a feature of all Western religion) was thus prepared. In the seventeenth century this fatal schizophrenia was refined by Descartes into a philosophy. He was a mathematician (carnal) as well as philosopher (divine) and laid it down that to be objective means to be *destitute of passion*. The relationship between Puritanism and science was now prepared too.

If we want a strict definition of Puritanism we ought to say that *its policy was to draw science out of its purely speculative stage into practical life*. In a certain way the Puritan temper *was* the scientific temper— extreme detachment from all natural phenomena, especially the passions within and any suggestion of personality in the research, for the good reason that the goal was mental illumination devoid of any animal presence whatever. So we find that practical science was pioneered *in those countries which had the strongest Puritan movements*. Likewise the so-called Industrial Revolution happened in a Protestant country, Britain, while the purely Catholic nations were the last in Europe to be industrialized.

* * *

If you suspect human intimacy as a dangerous echo of the animal within and wish to substitute for it a grandiose program of behavior calculated to the last detail, clearly nothing the village or the agrarian system offer you is going to serve.

The weekly or monthly local market is the very expression of intimacy, an exchange of goods produced within a few miles. Familiar faces are brought together, personal stories exchanged. There is little unexpected in that pre-industrial world except the birth and death on which religion concentrates.

You can say that the old system was still a form of capitalism but it had very few points in common with the later industrial system, which depended squarely on applied concepts, numerical assessments, population statistics, all formulated and discussed at great length in England and France during the hundred or so years before that "industrial revolution" began.

The last human links with the habitat were gradually cut. Products were packaged as if destined for no place in particular and any in general. The modern farmer has no more similarity to his agrarian predecessor than computer chips have to counting beads.

Capital is a very shrewd concept for taking away the human hand from all transactions. It is the store of money required to realize production systems that will have no reference to any one locality or person, any one group or religion or community. It cuts across all.

Now tell me that the Puritans were unwise to canvas support in the City rather than in the great aristocratic houses or parliament. Tell me that theologians are divorced from practical life!

Capitalism achieves the program of detachment without words or police or admonition. It was the worst conceivable plan for a primate biologically saddled with an alienation problem.

Of course there were cries of horror throughout the nineteenth century about what was happening. But no one could avoid the alienation principle. It claimed, like a virus, all the alternatives to capitalism—from Fabianism to Marxism. There were some remarkably clever and dedicated communists but their dream of the new society remained based on abstract analysis, even to the point of planning deliberately what the industrial revolution did haphazardly, namely the use of workers as a "means to the end". Communism was to be, par excellence, the scientific management of human life.

The first Puritan revolution, which deposed and executed Charles I, led straight to the steam or industrial revolution a century and a half later. The new class of morally vigilant managers (that is, vigilant for their own profit) were Puritan without even knowing it. Lord Byron's wife was described as a "rigid" Puritan. Said Edward Trelawny, who knew her, "They are a brave and undaunted sect in self reliance on their superiority over all other people, and fear nothing." The old lords and ladies weren't taken off in tumbrils as they were in France but roped into the new money-making game. You have a daughter, I have the cash.

Nothing short of pogrom-sized concepts across the length and breadth of England could achieve what that steam revolution achieved—a swift effective blackout of all the old habitat-enclosed intimacies and conflicts serenely ritualized by time. "Industry" meant literally a life based on diligent effort. A new human was indeed produced.

* * *

The historians have done one of their best revisionist jobs on the steam revolution, but not out of willful design. It was because they belonged to the class that benefited most from it. An amusing exercise is to pick up a cheap one-volume edition of Trevelyan's *History of England* and try to find material on the Luddites and the Peterloo Massacres, those desperate revolts against the use of a whole class of laborers as a low-wage, sweated force for the quick production of low-priced, quick-selling commodities. Women and children were sacrificed with the utmost evangelical zeal. Charles Dickens dedicated his whole writing life to describing this frightful dress rehearsal for the Nazi forced-labor camps, in that worst period of industrial capitalism, the first half of the nineteenth century.

The way our present system came about has never really been faced. Humans had to be wrenched, twisted, pushed and humiliated into it—quite literally without anywhere else to go, and a fate of death by exposure or death by starvation. Dickens's *Little Dorrit* converted George Bernard Shaw to socialism, and it was England that Marx and Engels chose as the seat of their researches. Many a continental communist in the twentieth century was first converted by *The Condition of the English Working Classes*.

The Luddites and the Massacres will be found in Trevelyan's index alright but the text kind of wings over them. Still, his revisionism didn't go to the point of a recent (1993) British historian who announced, apropos of his new History of the World, that if there was a trend at all in human history it was toward a growing capacity to control the environment. This is equivalent to revising the present while it's happening.

Originally "holocaust" meant a burnt offering. The first generations to be thrown into mines and sweated in mills to the point where even the best of them drank gin to feel any life at all were intended as a burned sacrifice to future affluence just as, again in the twentieth century, the Jewish massacres were for the integrity of the Nordic soul. It is quite wonderful what the stricken human brain will think up.

After World War Two this same holocaust was extended to the habitat. Since animals were theologically non-existent, except in so far as they were divinely designed for human nourishment, the torture of fowl and livestock on a scale even the Nazis would have been staggered by was a logical extension. Bashevis Singer's comparison of this to the Final Solution was really saying that a certain natural or biological Nazism had seized hold of the human species.

Deprived of light and air, living in their own excrement, the animals designed for meat fulfill the hell to which they were intellectually relegated millennia before. Pigs will go mad and eat each other's tails, chickens will peck each other to death and what you do in this case, purely in a scientific spirit of course, is to remove the tails and the beaks, i.e. reduce even further the faculties by which they live.

Dr Tom Regan (*The Case for Animal Rights*) says that 64 million animals die by laboratory experiment annually, and 5 billion animals are killed for food annually.

In the year 2006-2007 Britain conducted over three million experiments on animals, an all-time high for this greatest of all medical make-believes—that other animals are a physical paradigm for humans.

* * *

There should be no doubt in our minds by now that the Nazi death camps and our animal death camps are theologically connected.

Yet this theology had a hard passage. Witness the fact that it took so many centuries to be physically applied, and that where dead-habitat doctrine was preached in medieval times it was persecuted. Some heretical sects, notably the Cathars of Languedoc, were more than partial toward it, and they were step by step eradicated by means of torture, immurings, razing of homes and villages. Bezier in the south-west of France was where they were politely invited to settle, and then excised.

Christians generally, including the Inquisitors themselves, were by no means agreed about the role or origin of the Devil. While everyone might agree that he was a Fallen Angel there were various opinions as to how much power he had. Some even said that he, not God, had created the earth.

But in one matter there *was* agreement—that while God might be far distant from the habitat the Devil was *all too close*. While you needed effort, vigilance and sacrifice to reach God, you needed none at all to reach Old Nick.

We mustn't believe, however, that dead-habitat doctrines produced bad men. As the ancient Romans used to say, *the senate is a beast, senators are good men.* On the contrary, the doctrines spurred the desire to do good, to overcome the calamity of birth and the calamity of nature.

The Knights Templar felt that good and evil were equal forces, hence their black and white flag. They too were exterminated by the Church in the first years of the fourteenth century. The Bogomilists of the Balkans, the Cathars and the Albigensians of France were the declared enemies of the Church as an institution not of Christ but the Devil posing in his name as the true religion.

These "heresies" created a most dynamic energy and fervor and each introduced a special way of life, disregarding civil law. The higher Cathars eschewed all meat and ended their lives by gradually abstaining from food and drink altogether. Nobles and peasants alike were moved by them to follow the "good men" (real Christians) and abandon the "bad men" (priests). The Cathars held with the Gnostics that Christ could never have been human, namely tainted with diabolical flesh. He was pure spirit, and only *mistaken* for human.

The Church (in so far as it had any official doctrine at all) was deeply confused by all this. It distrusted both the "pagan" attachment to the habitat and the Manichee school of rejection. The Toulouse Inquisition saw the Cathar doctrine as saying that Christ existed only as a sort of ghost, therefore unreal—despite their own use of the words "Holy Ghost"!

Medieval thinkers wisely saw the danger of splitting God from nature—of robbing the earth and human flesh of all sweetness. The Inquisition emphasized the Devil and hellfire from time to time but never did it take a decided Manichee stand and declare that matter was the Devil's creation, and God excluded from it. Being the children of the classical world, which had celebrated the sweetness without denying the darkness, Christians weren't wholly strangers to a balanced attitude.

But there was a drawback about sweetness for them—it might present a temptation to forget God. Loving the habitat, enjoying one's "animal" desires could take the attention away from what lay *beyond* the habitat, *beyond* desire.

Wherever the Christian turned his *Socratic perceptions* caught him. They bound him to what in effect was no religion at all because there was no experience of love in it. God belonged to the mind, not to the earth. The dreaded "blindness" of brutes and infidels made you go for talk and explanation in all things. In the one fatal error of the Socratic mystery, that the conscious mind could go it alone without the presence of the Master, lay the sword of terrors on which Christendom impaled herself.

A movement of tight mental control such as the Puritans offered was bound to succeed. Our age of technology, leaning on the arm of chemical and electric-shock psychiatry, was in the bag a millennium ago.

Eighteen

From Ancient Rome To The Duchy Of Sadism

Our word "fake" may or may not derive from *fakir* or dervish of the Sufi order. Either way it is our general view of hermetic practices. But when we see an actual *fakir* walking over red-hot coals with composure or drawing needles through his cheeks with a gaze of joy we are inclined to take him more seriously. And the fact that these self-inflictions leave no scars or blood or burns makes us think a bit too. Our minds go swiftly to the artful tergiversations of showbiz magic. But the phenomenon has been observed and double-blind tested too many times for Puritan doubts to be upholdable.

It was thus too with the Christian martyrs. They died joyfully before men's eyes. They faced lions not with babble theology but love. Even the most jaded of Romans was struck by this. Other Roman sects—the Mithraists and the devotees of Jupiter Dolichenus, for instance—were generally more popular than the Christians but martyrdom bestowed the coup de grace. News of it spread to the military garrisons, especially that at Lyon, where the Christian faith took hold as easily as beforehand it had been resisted. Here were warriors indeed!

Romans often complained about the "squalor" of those fervid martyrs, especially the upper classes, who remembered the serenity and sweetness of the old Hellenic worship. Flagellants looked like barbarians to them, one more proof of the decline of the imperial city. Even other Christians—for instance, those few patrician Romans who had been converted—sometimes agreed.

So it was that the sect began to train itself in the bland Roman art of adaptation. It took on the burden of social respectability. But this had a serious diluting effect on the religion. The emperor Constantine murdered his wife Faustina and his son Crispus *after* the Council of Niceae in AD 325. In his wars against the Gauls he shocked "even the heathen" by sacrificing kings and thousands of prisoners to wild animals. No fire of love burning in *him*.

Also the military support for the new faith had its negative effect. St Cyprian called Christian baptism the *sacramentum*, meaning military oath. Other terms were drawn from social and commercial life as if the new religion was from the beginning set on a self-secularizing course. The words "Holy Communion" came from the Latin *communio* or gathering. The new church was denoted by the word *ecclesia*, a Greek word meaning something like our modern "parliament". The holy texts became "the scriptures" from *scriptura*, the account books used by the state in tax assessment. The epistles were the new "testament" or testimony—will in the legal sense. "Liturgy" came from a Greek word meaning the voluntary taxation expected by Athens from its most prominent citizens between 400 and 500 BC. "Convent" was from *conventus*, meaning both chamber of commerce and quarter-session.

"There is neither Jew nor Greek," Paul said, "neither bondman nor freeman, neither male nor female; for ye are all one in Christ Jesus," not that this was the way it worked out, given the later Jewish ghettoes, the persecution of Hellenic forms of worship, the hounding and murder of fellow-Christians who begged to differ on points of theology and the exclusion of women from the priesthood.

When you try to refurbish an old society it has a nasty way of jumping back at you. And there were ugly things ready to jump back. Any study of imperial life in the second and third centuries

BC reveals them and we will also recognize ourselves too, our own decline and fall, our own dementia. The old Roman way of perceiving things persisted in the new Christian mind and there was no way it could be otherwise, however many oaths of allegiance, credos and such you signed. By the first century BC the Greek games began to look tame to Romans. Organized encounters between humans and infuriated animals, and between humans told to fight each other to the kill, on pain of death, took their place. Romans of all classes spent days at the arena. Mini-massacres were devised with the utmost care. The blood was quickly covered with sand. When any attempt was made to revive the old games (for instance, by Sulla, Pompey, Caesar, Augustus) the reaction was bored. Augustus permitted magistrates to finance only one *munus* (officially "festival" but actually human sacrifice) a year. Caesar did the same. But in Augustus's case it wasn't to reduce the number of sacrifices but to institute his own gladiatorial shows, under imperial auspices.

There were agents (in Rome, *procuratores*, in the provinces *lanistae*) who hired out troupes of trained gladiators for the best price going. At least half the men in each troupe were expected to die in the course of a single *munus*. The gladiators were recruited from prisoners of war, from men already sentenced to death, from young noblemen in disgrace, from slaves and people in need of money or risk.

The blood festivals could last from dawn to dusk, sometimes into the night. In one of Domitian's spectacles a dwarf was pitted against a woman, for the laughs. Each fight was followed with as much collective passion as a football match today, and bets were laid as to which of a pair or group would die. There could be a draw, and sometimes two contestants killed each other simultaneously.

Sometimes a combatant, seriously wounded, surrendered, and then it was up to the victor to decide whether this man should be finished off or spared—unless the emperor was present, in which case it was he who decided.

But there were combats in which no mercy was permitted—all the combatants had to die. A live gladiator was substituted for a dead one at once, until only one remained alive.

At dawn convicted criminals (and in later imperial times Christians of both sexes) were herded into the arena where wild animals mauled them to death. At noon groups of convicted criminals were broken up into pairs: one member of each pair was armed, the other not, and the duty of the armed one was to kill the other, after which he was disarmed and in turn killed.

Just as the refined cruelties of the bullfight disgust many Spaniards today, so in Rome there were those who recoiled from the "games". But spectacles of this kind have an enduring appeal. Anyone who has heard the shrill cries of excitement at a Spanish bullfight when the first blood spills may have recognized in it a strange crooning, the same perhaps that went up in former Christian times at the fall of a head, at the first flames of the stake, at a quartering, at a tearing-out of entrails with the bare hands (the punishment for treason in Tudor times), at a fight to the death between humans, cocks, bears, dogs.

In view of our theological training we are likely to put this down to some lingering *animal* cruelty in the human but among other animals there seems to be no such bleak and black ecstasy. Sometimes, for instance in the cat species, a strangely hypnotized gloating may possess the animal during or after a kill. But we know of no example among animals of deliberate kills for the pure purposes of pleasure, unless we are talking of "higher" primates in close physical proximity to Homo Assassino.

This is because no other species has developed the spectator-faculty to such a degree. The human sits or stands, immobile, while his ears and eyes alone are engaged. Films show every manner of cruelty and suffering in visual detail.

In the 1930s the Spanish bullfight found a new status—not among the *plebs*, as it might have in Rome, but among literary people like Gertrude Stein and Ernest Hemingway. Stein described Hemingway, her literary follower, as "yellow" and "frail", not at all in line with his own child-like fictions: she wondered why he always had to hide himself behind these dreams of "masculine" glory.

Apparently the bullfight gave people a *real life* feeling, and those most in need of it were naturally the most effete. Even Ford Madox

217

Ford, once described as the last pre-Raphaelite, put in a word for the bullfights of Provençe, where he lived as a small farmer in his last years.

This foreign enthusiasm irritated those who had been watching bullfights all their lives, like Pablo Picasso. He angrily insisted that the bullfight was a *ritual*, not the brutal exhibition foreign bullfight enthusiasts considered it (the expression "blood ritual" was then coming into vogue).

This cerebral saber-rattling went together with a fashionable interest in the insipid fantasies of the Marquis de Sade. Appropriately, his style of writing was logical and cool. The more voluptuous the cruelty he described, the more icily rational his style. His general theme was that if we sin sexually, even to the last exquisite pleasure of murdering the beloved, we become free of that which binds our hearts in chains. It has to be the beloved we murder because we are trying to break the thing in us that most shackles us to life, namely the fire of love. One of the characters in his *La Philosophie du Boudoir* asks indignantly why private persons should be indicted for murder when governments murder at will.

Iconoclasm in a poor mind has trite effects, as in the following de Sade statement: "It is nature I wish to outrage. I would like to ruin her plans, block her advance, insult all her works".

Child-like rubbish though it is, it personifies a civilization. It figures much more than we like to be aware of in science. Our use of the word "sadism" to describe the mental pleasure of inflicting pain is really a misuse of the Marquis's name, since his doctrine was one of release and purification through specifically physical cruelty exercised on the love object *in a detached manner*. Those who practice the pose of "scientific detachment" have been responsible for the most fearful tortures of animals devised by the human brain.

At first glance this centuries-old mania for looking at human actions from a certain safe distance, with only the eyes moving, could hardly have been connected with Hellenic life, with its interest in action and display. But it did arise from its thought, like a benign tumor from living tissue. The doctrine that the flesh, the "animal" part of us, was to be *overcome* in order to reach the truth made "detachment" attractive to an increasing number. This had back-firing effects. The organism, if its mind starts floating helplessly in an orbit high above the despised physiological functions, must search for all kinds of re-entry systems, to get back to a sense of hot contact, even twisted ones. The murder and mutilation in the hamadryas enclosure at the London zoo in the time of Solly Zuckerman were a last-ditch release for brains cheated of the responses for which they were designed.

And our bloody operations are the same.

* * *

By Shakespeare's time, a millennium and a half after the Roman blood games, England no longer, as the historians say, "acknowledged Rome as her spiritual capital". The aristocracy was bled of its Catholics by Henry VIII. He confiscated the old Church lands into Crown and private property. It was the first of the alienating revolutions that took Europe into modern times. From King Henry's time on you could no longer expect alms and shelter at monasteries, or even find refuge in a church. The orders of the monks and friars were suppressed. It was a profitable business. Henry sold much of the abbey lands to his favorites, and speculators bought from them. The old system of education, in the hands of the monasteries, fell to pieces and instead of subsiding new schools, apart from a college here and there (Christ Church in Oxford and Jesus and Trinity colleges in Cambridge), Henry and his ministers let the thing become a commercial spree.

This revolution was such a success that by Elizabeth's time Catholics had to pay fines for not attending Protestant services, and the newly rich were naturally Protestant. Here was where the Puritans came in. Nothing short of the purification of the human being within could result in pure behavior without. The fact that they virtually supplied Elizabeth's purse helped their influence.

Shakespeare was no Puritan. He was involved in one or two shady agrarian deals in the Stratford on Avon area and had to be careful of their scrutiny. Also he had much to fear from their opposition to

219

the theatre, which they saw as abundantly licentious, equating the drama of the time (not always unreasonably) with the bear-baiting arena.

An extra chill of loneliness enters the English mind about Shakespeare's time, especially as the Puritan is advocating greater severance from the habitat than the easygoing "old" priest ever has, with his sale of days and weeks of grace in the after-life.

For Hamlet there are no connections any more—his father murdered by his mother's new husband, his mother a pawn in a stranger's political machinations, his friends bought, his fiancée convinced that he's crazy. A whole order has collapsed. It has made him an eccentric. Thus he keeps his sanity in a now alien world where all the loyalties have gone.

It is worthwhile taking a special look at England here because she played a big part with France in the deliberate alienation of the human being from the habitat and thus the spread of dementia. The English were an especially pragmatic people and it fell to them to realize the alienation theology in economic terms, while the French put paid to the "old" society militarily (Napoleon even sold Venice to the Austrians—so much for the millennium-old Golden Book of noble names!).

London in Tudor times had the famous Beargarden, a round theater with three galleries and an arena where animals—not only bears—were tortured and ridiculed and put to fighting each other. It was in a part of London called at that time "the Liberty of the Clink", containing a prison or "clink" and numberless brothels and taverns. The man in charge of the animals at the Beargarden was called the Master of Her Majesty's Game, and he got five pounds sterling every time the Queen herself attended one of the performances.

Having seen a captive bear being baited in Kurdistan I know how it looks. The poor animal tries to arouse compassion in the frightful hearts of its primate oppressors with pathetic whimpers and beseeching eyes but the oppressors are alienated beyond recall.

At the Beargarden in London dogs were incited to do the baiting, as they were used to maul bulls to death. Or the victim might be a horse or ape. One bear was nicknamed "Harry Hunks" and for the amusement of audiences was whipped until the blood ran down his shoulders. A horse with an ape tied to its back was baited by dogs (a Spaniard present wrote home that the sound of the ape's screams and the sight of the dogs "hanging from the ears and neck of the pony" were "very laughable"). The audience betted on the outcome as ancient Roman audiences did in the arena.

What can be said of such beings except that they are in an advanced state of dementia?

Much the same fascination with crime and cruelty drew Londoners into buildings almost identical to the Beargarden for the performance of plays, and sometimes plays alternated with baitings (the skeleton of a bear was found under the recently excavated Rose Theatre, where Shakespeare may have performed).

Greene, Marlowe, Nashe—the so-called "university men" of the Elizabethan theater—presented human terrors of every kind. Sweet Will's work had little of the raw brutality of Marlowe's. At Philip Henslowe's theater at Newington Butts the takings during June 1594 for Shakespeare's *Titus Andronicus* were twelve shillings as against a now lost play from another hand called *Bellendon* which took seventeen shillings. *Hamlet*, a finer play than *Andronicus*, took eight shillings, *The Taming of the Shrew* nine shillings (in *Andronicus* there were several shillingsworth more of crime).

Paradoxically, only the Puritans came out against cruelty— whether in the Beargarden or the drama. The two most ardent Puritans of the day, Philip Stubbes and John Northbrooke, were appalled by it and heartily contemptuous of the fact that Queen Elizabeth enjoyed both kinds of theater. But their denunciations were less because cruelty was wrong than that it was an aspect of lust. Philip Stubbes hated drama because of its "wanton gestures", "bawdie speeches", "kissing and bussing", "clipping and culling", "winkinge and glancynge of wanton eyes".

Much cruelty was in fact banished from public life by the Puritan example. Entire populations can now be disposed of without any undue cruelty of temperament on the part of those who conceive, prepare or perpetrate the crime, as in the Holocaust. Hitler taught that any sympathetic feeling toward the Jews must be suppressed because it was solely a job to be done—one of self-cleansing.

In the same way millions of animals may be used for the purposes of laboratory experiment in any manner or degree, unhindered by law, and again without cruel intent or much thought whatever because "animals don't feel".

The Puritan did much to make human life less overtly cruel but it failed to introduce a life that was kinder. The same cruelties could now be performed on an infinitely vaster scale, only, as we now say, "clinically". It was just a word but in man's history a word is enough to achieve what the heart and conscience should never have countenanced. The quite useless experimentation on animals which all medical doctors approve by the very nature of having qualified continues simply because of the huge trade in the capture and mutilation of beasts from all over the planet.

In France today it is said that the bullfight has reached an even meaner level of cruelty than those in Spain by dint of persecuting the bulls behind the scenes so that by the time they reach the public eye they are mad with grief and weakness.

NINETEEN

Fighting The Good Fight Until Everything Is Dead

Now I am coming to modern times and leaving our monks and their Greek masters far behind in a cloud of exhaust fumes. Let us see just how much perceptions have changed in these last five centuries, and how the exhaust fumes came into being.

I shall first take a particular individual who lived through the so-called "English" or Cromwell's short-lived revolution, when he abolished kings and queens. So-called Puritans were now thick on the scene.

Samuel Pepys was born fifteen years after Shakespeare died. As a child he was a fairly "hot" Puritan, as it was called—like his parents and cousins. He witnessed without pity Charles I's beheading at Charing Cross.

Pepys no doubt cultivated the precise speech and nasal accent fashionable in Puritans at the time (from which the nasal bias of American speech today derives). He was a tempestuously sensual man and the inner struggle this forced on him was at times quite painful.

As a Cambridge undergraduate he behaved like the sons of rich or titled parents though his origins were humble. That is, he got helplessly drunk and was once reprimanded in front of the college's assembled Fellows. He sang a lewd song forty times over in a Cambridge whorehouse. His eye was always glad and roving and thanks to his secret diary (written in one of the earliest shorthand systems—Thomas Shelton's "tachygraphy") we have an account of his extramarital flirtations and affairs.

In the England of his time kissing on the mouth was an accepted form of greeting even between strangers (this lasted among working people until well into the twentieth century) but caused sophisticated horror among visiting Spaniards at Queen Elizabeth's court. This old inherited English sensuousness went together in the Puritan with tight moral attitudes ever on the watch for lapses within and without, and of course this made the sensuousness all the more fevered. The Puritan and the Profligate nourished each other in one and the same person (note the origin of our "permissive" sex). Pepys drank and sang and played his flageolet with his work-superiors but soon began to note in his diary that he couldn't bear the thick heads in the morning, the vomiting etc. On the last day of 1661 he made a solemn vow to cut out theater-going and wine. But the following day, attracted by a handbill advertising a performance of *The Spanish Curate*, he went off to see it in the company of the young William Penn (who later took Quakerism to America and had a state named after him). Theater was like wine for Pepys. He needed it for his health.

He and his wife Elizabeth quarreled and romped alternately. When he scolded her once for the untidiness of the house she called him a "pricklouse". He did his best to leave her behind whenever he had a commission outside London, especially if there was a chance of meeting attractive wenches. He was unsafe with maids, cooks, ladies' companions. Each year he recorded his determination to reform, to come clean with his wife, to give up wine, to eschew taverns and whores, but only when his wife found him dallying with her maid was a brief reformation forced upon him—at the point of a red hot poker which he awoke one morning to find a few inches from his nose and in his wife's hand.

At bottom Puritan reform is always *self-reform*. Lust made purity necessary, self-indulgence made self-sacrifice necessary, soft attitudes made hard ones necessary. The mind was always in judgment of itself, withdrawing and condoning, freezing and commending. By a peculiar process of self-immolating steps the Puritan climbed to grace, his eyes on heaven and a bad smell under his nose.

A certain core of unrelenting hardness, a kind of irritated unspoken distaste for living things—developed in him, latent and almost unconscious, as his sympathetic bond with other creatures eroded.

Those people who still escaped the Puritan influence, in the landed aristocracy and the laboring classes, lost their sympathetic bond much more slowly. Only World War Two wiped it out.

The Puritan was a model for the future factory owner, able to watch with equanimity the reduction of rural scenes to bleak treeless smoky wastes.

Puritans were a ferment in English life for centuries, frequently disregarded but never forgotten. Just as in Elizabethan times they challenged and checked the monarchy through their influence in the City so a century later they abolished the monarchy altogether and put Cromwell where the king had been. During his revolution, which came to a head in the winter of 1640, mobs went round London shouting "Reformation!". The following year there were barricades along the Chelsea road, and Hyde Park Corner became a fortress. On an icy morning at the end of January 1649 Charles I was beheaded publicly. He and his court were considered to be in the same category as theaters and ornate churches, incense and sensuality.

Cromwell's regime didn't last long but it was no failure. He introduced a new efficiency and exactitude in government and it looked as if the Reformed Society might at last be in our midst. There were now to be no surplices in church, no organs or choirs or Madonnas or frescoes. Speech must be reserved, sober and exact. From this time the word "old" took on a pejorative meaning, "new" became hyperbolic.

People soon tired of it. In ten years the regime and the Protector were gone. Far from being a principled society the new one was just as corrupt as the old. The Protector had become a sort of king (shortly before his death he was thinking of becoming one in fact). People said of his "Reformation" that it had turned into a "Deformation". It left behind a mood of sullen suspicion toward everything decorative, flamboyant or elegant, in manners and clothes as in church furniture. Most of those who had been "hot" Puritans were now hot Royalists, yet not the same royalists they had been before, just as Charles II wasn't the king Charles I had been. The monarchy had changed. The Dutch ambassador remarked that these days he didn't know whether to apply to the king or parliament for executive decisions.

* * *

Without this Puritan background neither England's later Age of Reason with its sentimental novels and fainting heroines and genteel classes at their "tay" and coffee, nor the most powerful mercantile empire in existence, could have come about. The downright Dr Johnson, firm in grammatical as in theological principle, was the literary lion of *this* time, rather than the witty and satirical type personified by his namesake Ben at the time of Elizabeth and James.

Cromwell's revolution was a premature attempt to industrialize England. What we call the Industrial Revolution really took place over three centuries and should be seen in three stages: 1) Henry's VIII's break from Rome; 2) Cromwell's destruction of royal prerogative in favor of parliament's; 3) the steam revolution 1780-1820.

By the time of the steam revolution Puritanism had already eroded the paternal relationship between landowner and laborer, and it was the landowners' brutal "enclosure" (theft) of common grazing land that provided the new factories with sweated labor.

The very idea of industries arose from *the Puritan idea of thrift or economy*. Every acre must now be measured, every action of man or animal must be accountable in terms of yield. The astute Karl Polanyi, back in the 1940s, was the first to realize that for the first time human labor became a commodity on the market like Brussels sprouts and spring onions, in a haunting echo of ancient Greek slavery.

But it was dire necessity that produced this last steam-phase of the industrial program. That necessity was provided by the Napoleonic Wars and the blockade of English ports. It was a choice between increasing home production or military defeat. If only the two sides had seen that their aims of producing a self-alienated mankind were identical much time might have been saved, though in that case we should probably all be dead by mass suicide by now, as opposed to half dead by oxygen depletion. After all "production"—without any regard whatever for the people who did all the work—would have run out of human beings fit for any kind of work at all.

Yes, the Puritans wished to reform human life to the finest detail: dancing, card playing, drinking ale, dressing up (and the dressing up of church or liturgy) had to be excised because they were reliable ways of getting to hell, while work and regular reading of the Bible were ways to heaven.

Not that Puritans were against the idea of a ruling class (they were mostly members of it themselves) but they thought that rulers should be capable, practical and pure in heart and deed. Above all government money (e.g. for the financing of the standing army) must no longer be in the hands of a king and his court but a parliamentary assembly of the Pure.

There was something irresistible in these ideas that affected even the aristocracy. The Puritan technique too was irresistible. Plant disgust in the most incorrigibly sensual nobleman and you could depend on its doing its lonely work unaided, burrowing like a worm into the brain until, by a process of daily irritation, the Puritan-Profligate conflict had come into being inside his hitherto bleary mind.

Puritans were adept at triggering off that little mechanism. Fear was its chief weapon. If they could once induce disgust toward the sex-reflex (much helped by the terror of syphilis which was now widespread among the gentry) or the digestive reflex or even the autonomic sweating action of the skin, a victory had been won. The mind turned a disapproving eye on the self, and soon every reflex-action came under frightened surveillance.

So it is in the eighteenth century, the Age of Reason, that we first hear of people stinking. Shakespeare refers in a sonnet to his lover's bad breath but by the eighteenth century the whole person is giving offence. A lady tells Dr Johnson to his face that he stinks and this occasions one of his few limp replies: "Madam, I stink, you smell."

If you told people for long enough that they stank and that fleas in their wigs were a disgrace they became in the end enthusiastic ablutionists like the Victorians. So the alienation principle came full circle: it started in our cloistered medieval friends as a horrified distaste for the naked body (Queen Isabella of Spain told Chistopher Columbus to scold the American Indians for washing so much) and, ending in stench and itching in hair public and pubic, completed itself in—the American bathroom.

The industrialization of Britain could never have happened without these preliminary *changes in the brain*, which made it possible for scores of landowners to take over common land not legally theirs, depriving laborers whose faces they had known from childhood of the free pasturage and tillage on which their survival depended. A wealthy class came into existence which observed no responsibility to those who created their wealth for them. A half century of intense parliamentary activity was necessary to enforce such conscience by law, between 1870 and 1890. Such "paternalism" no longer came, shall we say, naturally.

As a system of drilling the human being into an altogether new state of mind which could take nothing for granted, and in which vigilance was the prime feature, it was ideal. Strict hours of work and the fact that your right to live depended on the degree to which you worked and the type of work you did—such things had never been heard of before. Inevitably they made deep inroads into the untidy, unpredictable and disordered zone of the primal reflexes, and within a few years of the appearance of the first steam-driven looms a Non-Biological Species really seemed a possibility. It was easy to predict the day when the female of the species would have "forgotten" how to care for the young, and the male to have "forgotten" how to care for her.

Some historians say that the first step toward industry happened as a result of a canny London lawyer who owned a country estate. He noticed how much seed was wasted when it was broadcast. Laborers were in the habit of casting it in big handfuls irrespective of the places where it fell, so that too much seed choked growth here and too little grew elsewhere. He observed too that the traditional plough wasted much of the horse's strength, and turned the soil over inadequately, owing to un-thoughtful design. In other words, with less labor there could be more food. Thus it was the land that was industrialized first. The industrial idea was then extended to the equally wasteful cottage industries which duplicated goods that could come from one deftly placed factory.

Such calculations were unthinkable for the old type of laborer. The habitat was unlimited for him, the hours he spent in the fields passed easily. There was enough food for everyone. He went to bed at dusk and rose with dawn and saw no reason why what had been good enough for his forbears should ever be changed.

One of our favorite popular-lore yarns is that the first industries came about as a result of an interest in "progress", or an even vaguer "spirit of industry", much like the "spirit of democracy" that was supposed to have hit ancient Athens. The story goes that industries brought in "democracy" or government by the majority, quite as if the spirit of industry was identical with the spirit to be represented by politicians (of all people). The truth was that the political system had to be adjusted to the existence of a new wealthy class, called "middle" because it was neither landowning nor laboring, and which demanded a degree of control over society proportionate to its degree of control over the labor force (which was tyrannical).

The clever-dick story here is that steam-mechanized industries came about because of the increase of population, which required faster food production. But populations had increased many times before, in ancient as in modern times, and nobody had sat down and thought up steam.

Puritans believed in work, in step-by-step self-advancement. Hence the increasing importance of the word "progress" in the nineteenth century. To reach a state of grace you couldn't remain still. The movement alone was good for you.

God watched you in the world He created for you. He expected you to do something with that world, puzzle it out, discover its operating principles and thereby make a success of your life rather than simply leave it there.

The Puritan was alert. He was likely to have a greater bent for analysis than others. He could more easily than others break his inherited bonds with those around him in the service of an idea. But he was also more likely to be a person of integrity and stick to his principles.

He made it possible for whole populations to come into being which would behave and even try to think and feel according to what *should* be. The ethical blueprint which people began to carry around in their brains was like a new invisible witness, a one-man judge and jury watching with critical eye not only other people's behavior but the torrent of feelings and unseemly thoughts within. A collected, in-charge-of-myself expression of face was used for the public thoroughfare. This was "living in front of a mirror" (D.H.Lawrence's description of American life, but true of all modern humanity).

Evangelism, as Puritanism came to be called in its new nineteenth-century edition, transformed England from what must surely have been, if we are to believe Thomas Hardy's accounts of its last days, an idyll (though we must be careful of the word "idyll" wherever there is human presence) into a smutty production-center. What looks to us like remorseless greed in the owners of coalmines or factories where sweated adult and child labor was employed was simply *applied evangelism.* The more degraded the workers, the more tales circulated in the new middle classes that these women and children and broken men were degraded "by nature". Unctious gossip claimed that these men and women copulated at whim in the mines, got dead drunk in the gin shops at the end of a day's work. The evangelist attitude was that yet harder work was the only means to grace for such people. Yet those same wretched people had not many years before led perfectly orderly lives as country folk.

Eating, drinking, touching, seeing, hearing, sexually desiring—all were enslaving for the Puritan and had now matured into work schedules which had to be met irrespective of sickness or weakness or youth or the need to feed and nurse the young.

* * *

Let us look more closely at the Puritan's horrified recoil from natural impulses. John Brinsley, in his *Ludus Literarius*, published in Shakespeare's time, regarded the birch (blows received from it were called "the jerks") as a divinely appointed instrument to "cure the evil of their" (children's) "condition, to drive out that folly which is bound in their hearts, to save their souls from hell, to give them wisdom; so it is to be used as God's instrument for these purposes. To spare them in these cases is to hate them."

Childhood was the period when original sin exposed itself frankly. "What is youth", asked Lewes Bayly in his *Practice of Pietie*, "but an untamed beast, all whose actions are rash, and rude, not capable of good counsel when it is given; and ape-like, delighting in nothing but in toys and baubles?"

It was the heart of Puritan thinking—a taming process that would make a cleaner and straighter world. One had to be cruel to be kind ("spare the rod and spoil the child"). From this thought came the later "the means justify the end", developed in the eighteenth century and the basis of many a massacre in the twentieth.

Detachment here is achieved by *an ideal*. The pleasure felt by ancient Roman spectators of gladiators fighting each other to the death is now consciously applied to *uprooting* pleasure.

What is the effect of such ideas on the new-born? The tiny creature can't talk or walk, only distinguish objects that appeal to its simplest and most immediate appetites, such as the maternal breast. Here reflexes are all there are, so we liken the newborn organism to an animal which steadily "develops". The Puritan suggestion is that the baby isn't properly speaking a human but one that has *to learn how to reason* in order to become one.

The newborn child receives far more information than meets our morbidly detached eye. It will imitate its mother's facial movements at six days old, indicating that it already has perceptual and learning powers. It has seen no mirror, yet it will transpose its observation of the mother's tongue-movements into a similar delicate movement of its own.

The newborn child, for all its identification with the mother, is more aware of the world than may appear. It reacts to noises from different areas in a room, it draws back from threatening objects, it can distinguish soft from hard and shows fear of dangerous heights. Babies avoid too much heat or too much cold. That is, they decipher and act on information. Even the embryo in the womb responds to external dangers. Its "scream of pain" during abortion is often cited. The embryo is aware of noise and heat. The Puritan version is that this is a virtually dead cellular form.

Clearly, our relegation of the living embryo and even the baby to an inanimate limbo is a result of our inherited distaste for whatever isn't the mind. Only when the child begins demonstrating mind is it said to be becoming properly conscious.

Some psycho-biologists are baffled by the slow growth of the human baby compared to the quick growth of other animals. Why are we, considered the most advanced of the animals, the least in this one respect? The answer is obvious but not one to occur to psycho-biologists. It is that a newborn's information is unusable in a mind-oriented world. Secondly, the first demand we make on a baby, within a very few weeks of its birth, is that it engage the tender rational part of its brain to a far greater degree than that required in other species, which means an actual *interruption of growth*.

The child must respond to its own world with all its inherited information and it must simultaneously join in the adult war *against* this information. The conditions for walking schizophrenia are already in place. After all, quick animal growth demands that the organism be whole, not divided into warring parts.

The baby has to learn to recognize linguistic sounds in the mother's mouth and differentiate expressions of face from each other. It must begin with simple vowels such as "ma" and "pa" and with muscular movements such as smiles and frowns. It cannot be expected to communicate urgent feelings to adults so far from its world of inherited information that they understand only highly articulated, conscious messages.

The subtle information the child wishes to convey is thereby lost. Its expressions and sounds and movements fall on blind eyes and deaf ears, despite the closest bond in nature. This sense of obstacle will continue through life. The expectation of non-response will become resident in the brain. Wherever there is a high degree of technology this biological schizophrenia becomes ever more acute. Where both advances and responses are misunderstood health will suffer. Sophisticated adult ills such as stomach ulcers, cardiac disturbances, essential hypertension and various forms of cancer may afflict the child even in the first year of life.

The warmth, smell and tactile wonder of the mother's skin, the ecstatically consoling nourishment of the breast—these are the baby's voluptuous world. But it must grow in a world which regards all this as the Lowest, while Thought is the Highest, and the mother will be unconsciously teaching this.

Sometimes old inherited memories in a baby will try to assert themselves but, finding no response, they withdraw again. The six-day baby will walk with support but by the age of eight weeks it has lost this capacity. At least a year must pass before it will try again. A newborn child will take an offered ball in the first week after birth but rarely do so again for several months. It will turn for certain sounds and this ability too will be lost for some time. This is frequently presented in psychobiology as a "mystery".

Instead of leaping about and scaling trees and sunning themselves on rocks, the parents and neighbors are busy serving highly complex mental systems unknown to the child. The child is thus slow of growth because he or she must adjust to a secondary human habitat, not to the inherited world animals know about within days or hours of birth.

In most births the child's transition from blood nourishment to air nourishment receives little special attention. Otto Frank described this shock in terms of *dyspnoea*, that suffocating first gasp of life which is also a first intimation of death. All anxiety, he said, is birth anxiety in origin: it recalls that first experience of a dreaded contrary world. On that first bridge into life, Frank says, we have a first taste of our later tragedies.

In the early months we must learn *how to live out-of-synch*. And we must learn to regard this as the only sane way of living.

At this point we need civilization. Without that safe, eternal-seeming home we can't become specifically human. A civilization offers a sensuous education in which cousins, brothers, aunts, grandmothers move like gods in a solemn, dramatic, vigorous charade. The tiny family unit of our alienation society is quite inadequate to provide this.

* * *

The fact that this new alienated mode of life spread through the whole world attests not only to the extraordinary appeal of the Puritan program but to the fact that the human mind everywhere was already half way to meeting it anyway. All over the globe, even in the East, even in the Catholic countries of the West, that same spirit was present in some form, recoiling with disgust from both the "wild" outer habitat and from the steaming caldron of physiological functions within.

In India the higher Hindu castes traditionally found kissing on the mouth repugnant even in the act of sex and avoided taking food or drink in the houses of lower castes, meat eaters or Europeans. In the lectures and letters of Swami Vivekananda you will find ecstatic references to the self as divine side by side with descriptions of the world as a "mud patch" and daily life as dull, monotonous and "prosaic" (i.e. without divinity). You had to choose, he said, between a "happy" life in which you married and enjoyed the senses, or a "great" life in which you gave up the senses. Life wasn't designed for happiness, he said.

Puritanism existed in the days of Constantine, and in ancient Persia. Catholic countries had their versions of the same distaste, the same longing for non-biological existence on biological earth. The same process went on in French thought as in English, producing an identical new middle class. In fact the two revolutions, the one steam and the other republican, were so much aspects of the same movement that France and England might have been one land. In the eighteenth century London and Paris were closely linked in ideas, such that a suddenly successful English author like Lawrence Sterne was within days acclaimed in Paris, and received there as he had been in London.

Rationalists in both countries attacked despotism, the use of torture, the death penalty for all but the most heinous crimes. They disdained witch-trials, which were now beginning to peter out. Life was indeed changing. Even in Spain the burning of heretics was now a rarity.

Adam Smith in England and the *philosophes* in France made people think about the *practical* features of a new society based on hard work rather than privilege. In both countries, as early as 1748, new methods of plowing and manufacturing wool and managing labor were being discussed. Labor was seen, for the first time, as a commodity subject to "law", much as the earth was subject to the law of gravity. Diderot's *Encyclopedia of the Sciences* buzzed with new thought. The idea that market fluctuations or "economics", as it came to be called, were a science like physics was aired long before the first factory or steam engine came into being. In fact, it led to these (again we must recall Einstein's "First the theory, then the fact").

So neither the Industrial Revolution in Britain nor the French Revolution was a sudden affair. They were products of discussions and arguments. All revolutions come about in this way: from the slow working of new ideas.

The French revolution unearthed astonishing cruelty, as if the genteel manners of the eighteenth century had been a suppression for decorative purposes of a nastiness natural to the human primate. An aspect of this was the growing *cult of detachment* which accompanied the encyclopedism and utopianism. It made remorseless human acts possible. You only had to have a moral argument for a detached blood lust to be released. Describe hundreds of people as belonging to a culpable class or a wrong religion or inferior race and their death or torture can be perpetrated by surprisingly nice people who are after all only doing what is *morally right*, and preparing a *better* world. Puritanism, while reducing the eruption of cruelty in social and private life, simultaneously threw it a marvelous sop of justification, such that millions would in the twentieth century be killed where dozens or hundreds had been killed before, in "modern" wars such as only visionaries had dreamt of, full of massacres organized with the utmost thoroughness on the highest moral grounds, with perfectly meaningless moral slogans playing the same role as the Holy Banner under which Christian towns and churches had been pillaged and razed by Christians in the Crusades.

The Reign of Terror in Paris was a preview of what the human brain could and would subsequently do in manifold forms in the twentieth century. It showed that ancient Roman habits had not only survived but were now a few steps forward in maniacal intensity. Those who watched the loaded tumbrels and the tumbling heads and screamed their delight in Paris were, no less than ancient Romans, at a blood sport. But we mustn't overlook the fact that behind this madness was the idea of *a future society*—the achievement of which justified all degrees of excess. Without this enthronement of ideas as higher than life ("idealism") there would have been no cruelty. Without doctrines describing the *ancien regime* as stagnant and blind, and the new revolutionary regime as scientifically informed and rational, not a man or woman would have stirred against the privileged classes—especially as the "new" society was the invention of these classes! Aristocratic heads were cut off with no regard for the fact that the revolution had been born and nurtured in the aristocratic salons. The Marquis of Condorcet, one of the most eloquent of the idealists, as he was one of the earliest pundits of the idea of progress, had to run away from the Terror, and committed suicide.

A fact we may not find pleasing, despite the historical evidence behind it, is that idealism always sooner or later *wallows in blood*.

If you regard yourself as enlightened and wish to bring your light to other people (whom you, by deduction, regard as in darkness) it isn't long before you see their resistance to your ideas as an act of enjoying the darkness, and want to drop bombs on them. Hardly one pogrom or massacre or burning hasn't been based on this idea of its victims being locked in dark and devilish blind impulses which mark them out as inferior organisms. The ridiculous survival-of-the fittest idea (never Darwin's, by the way) was an intellectual extension of this dementia.

Puritan principles, confirmed by the wealth to which they led, put the monarchy in Queen Victoria's time on a firmer and more popular basis than ever before. An elaborate legal and administrative system came about. Detailed supervision of roads, sewage, housing, water supply, transport, hospital care and human welfare were now urgently necessary in order to clear up the demented mess left by the "industrial spirit".

New ideas, experiments, projects spawned from the zeal. They aroused horror too. John Ruskin asked what was going to happen *afterwards*—except "noise, emptiness and imbecility"? The new middle class, he said, couldn't even speak English properly. The only time they showed warmth of feeling was when self-gain was the subject. The country had taken a wrong turning.

The bitterest enemies of industrial machinery were the first workers, back in the late eighteenth century. Ned Lud, a laborer, wrecked some of his master's weaving frames and was thought soft in the head for doing so. He was appalled at the new looms invented that did the work faster at the cost of its beauty. Our popular lore has absorbed this travesty of real history as "fact", so that so-called Luddism is now a useful pejorative term to shroud a new vandalizing industrial project in a cloak of righteousness. Even the Brontë sisters, otherwise sympathetic to the less fortunate, disapproved of the roving bands of laborers who in the second decade of the nineteenth century wrecked or set fire to looms and factories.

Luddism has a long history in Europe and was once officially backed. Inventors were traditionally regarded as fiends (*pace* Livermore!). The inventor of a loom more efficient than the traditional one was put to death at Danzig in 1529. For a new process in dyeing yarns in 1533 another man was executed. In the same century mechanized printing presses caused riots few disapproved of. Luddism was an instinctive conviction that in the end the old inherited ways of life would erode and give way to lawlessness.

Thomas Paine was one of those ardent advocates of working mens' rights who were really bosses in sheep's clothing. He saw God as a kind of divine thinker who expected His human creations to decipher His sublime riddles. The habitat was now a Laboratory Bench. Logically enough he emigrated to America where the idea of the world being a divinely appointed workbench was already under way. But his new countrymen ostracized him for being an atheist (in revolutionary Paris not many years before he had been arrested for *not* being one). An irony was indeed at work here. The new Puritanism, while a theology, also presented a mathematical universe brought into being by Pure Thought, so that the word divine was beginning to sound decidedly foreign to it. Little wonder that the Quakers disapproved of Paine.

Yet, apart from his bold rationalist views about the Old Testament, his ideas fitted well in his new home. Both the "untamed" habitat and "Old" Europe were to be superseded. They represented a blindly inherited field of helpless action (George Washington used the word "chaos" to describe Europe). Control was the key to all. The New World would bring humankind into an unconditioned state of rational free choice. Money, not inherited status or the power of personality, would be the passport to status. A new wealthy class quickly came into being, wealthier than the wealthiest of the Old World. The conclusion that God had at last found His country and His people, and that He was pouring down His blessings on them in gratitude could hardly be avoided. Denial of the progress-ideology began to seem a treasonable offence.

The United States was *the third side* to the triangle of which the steam and the French revolution were the other sides. The American Revolution was simply the transference of steam and Jacobinism to a new continent, in the earnest belief that if you physically left the old regime behind its dementia would somehow walk away.

For more than half a millenium the Christian world worked to get that triangle into place. Whether we are talking about John Wyclif or Hus or Luther or Cromwell it is reform—*making something all over again*—that constitutes the dominant idea. Whether the Puritan in his many disguises attacks Roman corruption or royal prerogative or the use of Latin in the celebration of the Mass he insists that only *a new society* is a sure guarantee of their destruction.

Even at the risk of dividing Christendom into two mutually hostile theological zones, and thus weakening its power to survive Turkish attack, the "old" Catholic world had been swept away by the new Reformed or Protestant one. From the sixteenth century on, reforming in every department of life became a maniacal quest. By the nineteenth it looked as if the actual face of nature was going to change—rivers placed where there had been none, hills removed and smoky towns erected in areas which were now recalled, in nostalgic reminiscence, as pastoral heavens. By this century the old world seemed a thing condemned to die, and it was being finished off gleefully in every manner—at the coal face as in the trenches.

Old England was by now a ghost. Arnold Toynbee wrote that the nineteenth century created wealth but not well-being. In that century the new men of industry were scrupulous in their dealings with each other. Their homes were impeccably clean. A prayer before meals was *de rigueur*. Many of the New Men were "Methodists", adhering to a decided "method" of worship originally established by a "holy club" of founders in Oxford back in 1729.

Without Wesley and Witfield the idea of new methods in every field of life from agriculture to dress could hardly have swept the land. Like every great system that has been presented to humanity this one was through and through theological, not at all an unprincipled drive for wealth at all costs. It involved passions, ones of faith and not essentially gain. That was only the cream on top. The monks had promised that the world would be turned on its head by Christianity and this was it.

The basic idea of the evangelical cleansing process is that inside the human lies a foul caldron of temptation which manifests in any form of easy-going association such as you could recognize in the kissing of strangers or gossiping in lanes or drinking tea from the saucer instead of the cup or calling things by names so local the next village thinks them strange or throwing old shoes at a departing relative about to take a long journey.

Thus it was that the village-dweller, like Dickens's Pip in *Great Expectations*, on the first awed leg of his pilgrimage to London, began to feel shame toward his past, its accents and simplicities and—so it seemed now—innocence. The binding unconscious forms bestowed by civilization loosen their hold on him. His previous self seems a blind, automatic one, his old style of speech ignorance. In the nineteenth and twentieth centuries this had happened all over the globe, little by little, escalating in the last half century with a furious force. *There* lies the undoing of the civilization we know we have lost, *there* lies the change of perception which is both a loss of the previous phase and a preparation for the new one. It is how all civilizations corrode and not all the backward-looking and admonitory and bewailing speeches in the world can undo that corrosion, for it has taken place in an area over which *the conscious mind has no control whatever.*

Years later, as a confirmed city-dweller, the liberated one begins the reverse process of looking back on his village with longing, he considers the old habits charming or "closer to the earth". By this time the village is an economic backwater frozen into its required period—Medieval, Rebirth or Georgian. A third process now begins—the travel package. The village becomes a television costume drama not yet shot.

Roofs that don't leak, shoes that don't let water and pockets full of cash—these were promises held out to us and who is to say that they shouldn't have beguiled us? The theology beats time to the rhythm of the washing machine, the flashing of the television screen, and it promises nothing short of that bliss of freedom offered by all mysteries and initiations.

Technology is the visiting angel, its annunciation a bank loan. It guarantees health, a lower infant mortality rate and self-respect. At first the results are spectacular. A new bustle seizes town and country. They rise eagerly for the day's work, rest without care at night. But soon the family, religion, language, nervous system begin to fragmentate. Ideas are the new currency. Is a certain trade-union action right or wrong? a government tax oppressive? the schoolteacher expert enough? Tempers rise. Simultaneously there are Luddite reactions too—the old religion must be upheld, someone else's religion must be assailed. An ethnic "clash" takes place, then a war. Graves are desecrated. A riot here, a strike there. No one is safe.

So we come full circle: the first steam sent people into mines where, in order to provide the base material of steam, they choked dust all day and never saw the light. Or they sweated in mills and factories until they were stunted. Today we *all* breathe foul air, are *all* starved of the light, are *all* in some way stunted.

But still and all it was *child-like enthusiasm* that brought all this into being. And this enthusiasm was global, otherwise it wouldn't have spread like a summer fire. The monks were perfectly right when they said that they were fulfilling a need in all mankind for one society.

Losing the old habits of life is at first quite extraordinarily exhilarating. The old village-feeling that "nothing happens" gives way to a certain buzz in the air, a sense of potential activity. You no longer stare by the hour at the dusty road for the approach of a carriage or car, you no longer eat the occupants with your eyes as they speed unheedingly past.

Railway and steamship transportation, newspaper production, the telegraph, factory-made food, trade unions, water conduits, city lighting, street cleaning, public education—even the poorest were breathless with excitement at all this activity.

Everywhere in Europe, as the inventions spread in Dickens's time, the idea of the Advance of Man came with them. The future would provide more comfort and vitality, more civic order, more peace among nations. From London to St Petersburg it was assumed that the more education people got the more refined they would become.

The idea that in the next century Europe would all but cave in under the weight of its millions of dead, its cities half destroyed, would have been laughable for all but visionaries. As to foreseeing Hitler, that too would have been vouchsafed only to the mystical or psychic types. When the visiting Narendranath Datta, a devotee of Ramakrishna and better known as the monk Vivekananda, warned a London journalist in 1903 of the frightful carnage that would in not many years overtake Europe the journalist wrote an urbane, wryly amused article describing the conversation as illuminating except in this one particular, where clearly the noted seer had gone off the rails.

For too long everyone had lived in a misty mythical daydream. A Victorian put it nicely:

Fine age is ours and marvellous—setting free
Hopes that were bending into gray despairs,
Winnowing iron like chaff, outspeeding the airs,
Conquering with smoky flag the winds at sea,
Flinging with thunderous wheels immeasurably
Knowledge like daily light; so that man stares,
Planet-struck with his work-day world, nor dares
Repeat the old babble of what "would never be".

And this is how London's new mass-circulation magazines of the time ("penny plain, tuppence colored") seemed to another Victorian: "The little child, lighted by the single wick of a small lamp, sits at this moment perched above the great steam press of the 'Penny Magazine', feeding it from morning to night with blank paper, which at almost every pulsation of the engine, comes out stamped on both sides with engravings, and with pages of plain, useful, harmless knowledge, which, by making the lower orders acquainted with foreign lands, foreign productions, various states of society etc tend practically to inculcate 'Glory to God in the highest, and on earth peace—good will towards men'."

But the euphoric perfume, rising from transient middle-class luxuries, turned to foulness indeed. George Bernard Shaw and Beatrice and Sydney Webb in the Fabian movement worked hard to pull the wool from people's eyes. Shaw's *Man and Superman*, written in 1903, described "the illusion of progress" as a hindrance to biological evolution. His *Heartbreak House* was withheld from presentation during World War One because, in his words, "when men are heroically dying for their country, it is not the time to shew their lovers and wives and fathers and mothers how they are being sacrificed to the blunders of boobies, the cupidity of capitalists, the ambitions of conquerors, the electioneering of demagogues, the Pharisaism of patriots, the lusts and lies and rancours and bloodthirsts that love war because it opens their prison doors, and sets them in the thrones of power and popularity". Tolstoy repeated the message as ferociously in his *Fruits of Enlightenment*.

In the "old" world, before cities were lighted and heated and transportation was freely available, men sat in cafés bored, played cards by the hour. The "new" world of Paris, Vienna, London, Milan roared and sparkled---what encounters were possible, what unexpected bustling scenes at every corner! Emil Verhaeren, the Belgian poet, composed hymns to machines and wept when the Zeppelin crashed. Stefan Zweig, an ardent devotee of the new world (which, after all, had come about so smoothly in his native Austria, minus the holocaust factor) translated Verhaeren's hymns into German and propagated the poet's name wherever he went. William Blake's sorrowing prophecy about the "dark satanic mills" of his time were now considered at best pathetic.

It was so clear: the "inventions" (dynamite not included) would ensure an era of intelligence and quality in all classes. Political revolutions would become unnecessary. Poverty, injustice and bad behavior would no longer feature in Christian society.

The unbelievable wanton mass-killing of the 1914-1918 war was done with the machines these "poets" had been singing hymns of praise to. Without the production of iron goods and new communication networks the carnage couldn't have taken place. Emil Verhaeren lost his faith in machines—and of course in mankind. The peculiar deterioration of society that accompanied every "scientific advance" could no longer be disregarded. But since the deterioration could hardly be put down to science, on ideological grounds, it had to be put down to human folly. "It isn't science but the way men use it that's bad" originated as a cliché at that time, to become the fixed popular-lore idea it is today.

Likewise Stefan Zweig drew in his horns. He began to say that the advance of mankind had taken place too quickly and would require some decades of adjustment (another by now senile canard). However, when Jews began to be insulted in German streets, then dragged from their homes, then forbidden to go to the theaters and opera houses (which they subsidized), when they could no longer sit in cafés or even on park benches, when his own house in Salzburg was searched and his books (probably the top sellers of the world) were burned and forbidden, he at last lost faith too, and a few months before the first encouraging news of a Nazi setback came from North Africa in 1942 he committed suicide together with his young wife.

TWENTY

Master Of Systems But Not Of Self

It is so easy to get ourselves into a commotion about all the mistakes we have made, the absurdities and wanton bullet-headedness that led us into this dead-end street where the question rises in the sky in dark and not golden letters, "What next?". To judge by the number of deserts in the world that were once fine arable or wooded land, other civilizations have got it wrong too.

Maurice Maeterlinck thought that the termite civilization was the earliest, most complex and intelligent of any known to us. At least, it had *once* been a civilization. And this had actually *produced new organisms.*

The more I learned about termites the more I felt that they too had known the beguilement of alienation and, like us, hadn't counted the cost. They too had gone the path of reflex-erosion.

Most termites, even the "tyrants" who exploit termite workers to the point of collapse, became pared down in the course of time (millions of years?) to automatic organisms that no longer have wings to fly with, eyes to see with or sexual organs to make love with.

They so succeeded in regarding themselves as non-biological that they ceased to be insects. Wings, eyes and sex organs would have impeded the survival of their constructed world—their termite-made stronghold. Intimacy stood in their way. The sick, tired and feeble were eliminated in the termite community.

There is little in the soldier-termites' lives that reminds us even of insects. They know how to dig, construct, store, defend in the most remarkable manner but the play we associate with animal life has gone.

Though the soldiers and workers of the termite colony are blind they can detect the infiltration of light at a depth of twelve inches under the earth. Despite their deafness they can receive messages relayed to them from the other end of the colony and through obstacles, even steel ones. They show ingenuity in their building of intricate forms which no one has taught them, and which they cannot have inherited from their parents, who are unable to do such things and whose work-lives involve neither soldiering nor working. It is high tech of a dazzling order, far beyond anything attained by the human.

The "king" and "queen" are the only sexually equipped termites, and they also have wings. After all, if there were no contact with the habitat there would be no reproduction. So the sex becomes ritualized into a mechanical form. The moment they fly—it may be no more than a yard—they seek to settle on the ground again, the male close to the female. Once settled, they shed their wings and never fly again. There seems to be no animal joy in the flight. And perhaps there is as little joy in the sex.

After copulation the colony is built, or rather the "gardens" are prepared. These will provide offspring with incubation and food. The termite world, like our own, is all a highly sophisticated secondary habitat.

The offspring in no way resemble the parents, being *biologically* that which the termitary system requires them to be—soldiers and workers. They are already wingless, sexless etc. Surely all this has been thought out, an intelligence has been at work allotting to each type of ant its function, and this intelligence has found a way of making that function inheritable?

The colony contains so many features which remind us of the human being that it is a great wonder that only two humans,

Maeterlinck and Eugene Marais, wrote almost identical monographs about it (Marais complained that Maeterlinck had plagiarized him).

The termitary is fairly resistant to weather and predator insects. Even the aggressive flesh-eating ant can rarely find ingress and if he does he sometimes becomes a peaceful inhabitant. Life is so fixed and secure that to all intents and purposes other animals might not exist.

Because descriptions of termitaries are human they are bound to be largely wrong. On the one hand we seem to have here a slave community, on the other hand they may gradually have done away with sense- and sex-organs in order to substitute a rarified life of which we have no inkling.

Our technology too is a biological endeavor. Every species is preoccupied, sometimes obsessed, with the problem of survival but this isn't always to do with predators and food supply. The termitary civilization may have been similar to the human one in having to face *brain problems*. Termites too may have succeeded in severing themselves from the hazards and thus the consolations of the habitat.

It is tantamount to re-designing the organism. And the organism can change in a surprisingly short time if the habitat is hard and demanding enough.

We could one day lose our sense organs and our sexuality just as we lost our refined sense of smell, touch and hearing. That they are an impediment to work, like sickness, is a thought that may occur to us from time to time.

There are hints of this change in the high level of divorce, the low sperm count in certain areas and the prevalence of random heterosexual sex in spite of AIDS. To make this new sexual set-up possible a "permissive" period was necessary. The permission to have limitless loveless sex had to be given. The wrenching of the sex-motive from love, and its new identification with pornography, are preliminaries of the erosion of the sex drive.

The hidden demand in a termite system is that the individual with his (now aberrant) sexual desires sacrifice them for the system.

247

After all, his individual reflexes are of less and less use. There is a point at which they clearly run counter to his new social habits, and even law and order. The heavily biological nature of childbirth is now, almost, an infringement of the principle of equality. Abortion is to assert that equality.

He/she copes with depression, sleeplessness, nervous "breakdown", impotence, intractable pain and other symptoms of walking dementia. The belief is that these are interim disadvantages which later and better systems will rectify. But the truth is that the organism may adapt surreptitiously, unknown to its owner, by dispensing with strong sense organs as sources of misery, so that passion becomes a thing of the past, both as anger and self-immolating love.

There is another complication. Life in the systems makes life in the systems seem the only life there could be. The child perceives traffic lights, asphalt walks, airports and self-propelling vehicles of every kind as more real than the once real primary habitat. His reactions to systems are if anything sounder than his reactions to natural or primal events like sexual advances. These secondary reflexes grow as his primary ones collapse. He crosses streets expertly, is calm and unconcerned traveling at eight hundred miles an hour five miles above the earth. Yet these are responses toward stimuli for which he isn't physiologically designed. In simple terms he is responding to a world that, in being quite beyond his control (viz. the plane in which he travels), gives him a message "You have nothing to do with this" simultaneously as he is in the act of trying to humanize the experience for himself (by reading, playing, during the flight).

Residential areas, airports and high-rises simply do not say "Welcome" to the body's autonomic machinery. The teenager could of course respond to the friendly beckoning of "nature" but he has lost the reflexes by means of which to do this. Thousands of different plant species become merged for him/her in a green, functionless background, at best pleasing to the eye. The weather is related to comfort. As for the animals to be observed, their behavior cannot be deciphered without the help of teachers.

Systems require new reflexes but these are quite unlike the old inherited ones. They fail to provide *guidelines as to how to live*, which makes it impossible to be sane. To the inner-habitat erosion which is already his lot is now added a further depletion of inherited information due to loss of primary stimuli (from "nature"). This "nature" is by now an absurd concept used most in food-ads because it too is in disarray from human predations. The trees, the larvae, the bacteria are losing primal reflexes *in the need to adjust to a new demented habitat.*

More and more in the human being's life has to be talked about, dragged into conscious analysis, which then makes even greater inroads into inherited sources. Suicide may begin to seem the sanest course, unless a multiple-killing spree is chosen instead.

The famous killing rampage on the University of Texas campus at Austin was a media-shock not dissimilar to that caused by President Kennedy's assassination in the same period. The student chose his hour, climbed the tower toward which every path seemed to lead, waited for the surge of students at midday. Those few minutes made up for the erosion of sense and sex faculties in an abstract work-system.

When animals sniff each other they are apprising themselves of the unique personality of the other. The human employs similar methods of informing himself biologically about others but disgust and watchfulness make inroads on these. Where he once had a strong presentiment about someone he now has to attempt a mental analysis based on the other person's appearance. He cerebralizes his conclusion into a "gut feeling" precisely because such feelings (in the solar plexus) *have long since disappeared.* We cover ourselves at a thousand points with this kind of journalese. Writing and singing were never so gutsy as now because the gutsy is a cerebral figment.

Unable any longer to divine other people's nature, he has to take a distant symbolic view of their behavior based purely on his *own* needs. A choreography of behavior comes into being composed of planted smiles, awkwardly un-spontaneous gestures, would-be hearty laughter without abdominal conviction in order to cope with the fearsome divide between "me" and "them". Leisure-time breeds tummy ulcers, work is the balm.

It is the sympathetic bond that has collapsed, this being a physiological, not emotional or sentimental receptor. It doesn't see unreservedly nice or good people everywhere, or believe in them, or even sympathize with them. It is simply aware of them physiologically. It interprets smells, facial features, comportment and presence in a manner understandable to the nervous system, not to the mind.

This is the age of *crooked pictures* of other people, based on the wildest goofy interpretations of their behavior. Killing and assault are natural results of wrong perceiving. In the end Homo Demens lives not with others but his own travesties, so that when others behave differently from his private travesty of them he is bewildered and shaken. After all, his travesties are *reality* for him. He literally makes it up as he goes along.

We may readily imagine what a worldwide source of personal rupture, damage claims, work rivalry and internecine religion this presents.

The Judgment Hall of his mind is a tragically one-man show. The stranger is equivalent to a predator for this bondless brain, causing a prey-flutter of misgiving, even a toxic reaction, at first meeting. In the area of sexual response this may have more extreme choreographic results: the male may try to enact what he feels to be the female expectation of the male, and vice versa, with sickening results in the love-bed. The choreography may go as far as marriage because the ceremony will hopefully turn the choreographed material into real life but divorce, after two weeks, months, years, is the result, making the end as giddily unreal as the beginning.

Paradoxically this may cause a rise in sexual activity, though not in sexual enjoyment, since enjoyment depends squarely on the sympathetic bond. In random sex we are trying to re-create the sympathetic bond in a way we think cannot fail but fail it always does because the Judgment Hall is still—yes, even at the point of orgasm—in session.

A moment's reflection will show us that these physiological changes are of precisely the same order as the pollution, fall-out, soil erosion and ozone holes which also result from complex systems. The habitat has been dragged into the awesome human predicament. It has to cope with a situation for which its "old" organisms are inadequate. The species that are dying out failed to make the adjustment. At a certain point of crisis there may be no possibility of adaptation because *the habitat is no longer in the market for nourishing any organism whatever.*

Twenty One

Divinely High Tech

Which brings us to the most pathetic question ever asked by humans, "What can we do about it?"

This at once presents the difficulty that "we" don't exist. The "we" that will do something about it by putting pressure on governments and recycling bottles and news-print isn't the "we" that drives the car, switches on the central heating and flies at over five hundred miles an hour and enjoys electronic contact with the rest of the world.

Nor is it the "we" that goes on perceiving the world as *all right*. We have no choice but to perceive it this way. Perceptions *must* be old, they *must* lag behind realities, not by decades but centuries.

So we rather pathetically live *by nostalgia*. We must see everything as if it were a hundred years ago, just as we see the sunlight as the *old* sunlight, beneficial to us. We may *think* or *know* that sunlight is at present harmful and that exposure to it invites skin cancer and cataracts in the eye but the sunlight the *perceptions* know cannot contain harm.

After all, we have to make up a reality which is secure, expectable and running along sure lines and here our perceptions are very obliging. They invent helpful mummies and daddies everywhere, strong helpful males and healthy females made for childbirth and child-care.

Television ads live on our perceptions. Again, they have to. What else will they sell to? So they provide us with a nature that is still the old Mother providing whole grains, nuts and golden fruit, the sun still shines clear and unimpeded for the sea resort of our choice and the young are having a fine old time, laughing it up and even splitting their sides with this or that drink or candy bar or sniff of coke or furtive jab in the arm.

We take ye olde perceptions with us to our ecological talk-fests just as we take our cars, our cards and our social security number. *Our every act* is an investment in a world we declare is killing us. So we are dying by our own hands. This much we know but it isn't really suicide because suicide is a voluntary act and there is very little voluntary about us. We have no part in what we daily do!

Nothing is more endearingly pathetic than the "what an awful world our mothers and fathers made for us" talk. They did nothing of the sort. These are *tele-ad* mothers and fathers we are talking about, we need these fictional character-inventions to cover our youthful acts (driving cars, switching on lights and idiot-box, turning up the heat), these acts being precisely those that are killing us, just as it was for Mom and Dad, the real Mom and Dad.

Nobody made this world unless it was you, however little you may be responsible for it. That sentence sounds as logical as 2 + 2 is 5 but this is how perceptions are. They take us by the nose not into logic but lethal outcome.

* * *

In a book called *An Essay on the Chinese Written Character* Ernest Fenollosa analyzed the difference between Chinese and Western ways of thinking. He said that if you asked a Westerner what a word meant he became more and more abstract in his definitions. Asked to define "red" he would first say "Color". Asked what "color" was he would say "A vibration of light". Asked what "vibration" was he would say "A mode of energy". And so it would go until he was talking pure philosophy, despite the fact that he might have no more training in philosophy than a parrot. His education has taught him principles, categories, divisions, summaries by means of which he is able to order his experience *in an intellectual or systematic manner*, that is, reduce it to its universal characteristics. Safe within the Greek tradition he goes from the particular to the universal as his way of explaining the nature of things. *He begins every perception with theory!*

Chinese written characters, on the other hand, give *pictures of things*. Two sloping lines meeting at the top indicate a man (the legs), since his upright position is what chiefly differentiates him from other animals. The sun is a square with a dot in it. The east is denoted by the sun shining through tree branches at sunrise, while in our tradition the east is a geographical concept, an abstract reference without flavor, color, substance, a universal.

But before condemning ourselves for making life abstract we should note that it came from an earnest desire to *understand* matter. Theology—not only Christian but certain Jewish and Muslim thinkers—said that if you detached yourself sufficiently from life, in imitation perhaps of God's supposed distance from his creation, you could achieve special insight into it, perhaps by way of reflection from God's mind.

Let me quote from one of the clever-clever men of the famous Florentine Rebirth that never happened. He is Pico della Mirandola and in his *Oratio de Hominis Dignitate* he has God addressing Adam. And this is what God tells Adam: "I have given you neither a settled home, nor a precisely formed face nor particular gifts, Adam, so that whatever home, face or gifts you choose to adopt may be in accordance with your will and desire." Now if that isn't a portrait of an animal without its original habitat!

Note the lack of a "precisely formed face". It means that it is up to our *will* to form this face. Nothing is inherited. The habitat, within and without, is simply subsidiary material for the human to use in his quest, which is the whole meaning of the earth.

God goes on to tell Adam: "Other species have a definite nature restricted by the laws I have made. You, restricted by nothing, are formed by your own judgment, and this I have bestowed on you. In the middle of the world have I placed you, in order that you may better see all that exists in the world. Neither a heavenly nor an earthly creature have I made you, neither mortal nor immortal, so that, like the lone, gifted painter or sculptor for whom he himself is his model, you may form yourself in whatever manner you choose."

This means you are free! The other animals are "restricted by laws". So you have the freedom, unlike animals, to find out what all those divine laws are about.

And we shall find that the "science" based on this kind of claptrap supposes the very same static, permanent and independent reality which our senses somehow contact, and which our minds are in a position to judge with absolute confidence because those minds are detached from the fixed reality "outside".

Yet one of the scientific disciplines, physics, *finds and constantly says it finds that this is rubbish*. For any philosopher, from Aristotle onward, not to speak of the mystics of the eastern religions, and of Persia and Egypt, it would be rubbish too.

Are we beginning to see why, when we pursue certain "scientific" premises, we are drawn into harmful repercussions which we cannot perceive until after they have happened?

Naturally, if we treat the habitat as if it were dead we are bound to miss out some very big issues—like the abundant life in the habitat. And this is what rebounds on us in the form of droughts and radioactivity above supportable levels and hydrocarbons and inert lakes.

For to see a thing "scientifically" you have to make it dead for yourself. There is no way you can avoid this. You can't study an object without holding it still and thus artificially extrapolating it from the rest of the environment.

It may be a human organ or "supercritical" water (so hot that it has turned into a gas) for the disposal of nuclear waste, but extrapolated it must be, and seen from a distance it must be, and seen without sympathy it must be.

Anyone who has heard surgeons discussing a technical problem over dinner will find with shock that the patient simply doesn't come into it. It can't be otherwise if surgical work is to be done. Whenever we *think*, we must capture the object of our thought and hold it thus. Our mistake, if we are scientists, is to believe that this supplies objective knowledge. Nothing could be more ridiculous.

Our scientific detachment here is a makeshift, an "as if" attitude, both artificial and temporary. The mind which is trying to be detached still belongs to a human animal, and this animal still belongs in the habitat. So it can never step back from the habitat and thus itself. This means that the *object* science is studying doesn't exist. An object is something we can judge from the outside. But we can't get outside the habitat because our human needs lie there.

How can a scientist be other than confused? Everyone clamors for his truths to rid them of their diseases, create greater speeds, lengthen life, ensure less work for higher gains, provide light and warmth at a touch, dispose of sewage and conduct it down tunnels far from eyes and nose.

And behind the "cold" scientific premise there is the enlightenment promise of a "better" world, which means one that will give us more of what we want. We are the customers, therefore the employers.

New computers, aircraft, microsurgical processes, island towns that can be constructed in weeks, chemical food additives—they change our lives so much that we understandably feel a revelation at work. Of course there never *are* revelations, only greater speeds, short cuts where there were once long detours.

We inspire and condition science with our desires, our needs, our perceptions. There is no "objective" study, no "detachment". The words are theological make-believe.

Food, sexual satisfaction, competition, profit, chauvinism, comfort and, not least, war are the actual, operative and determinant motives science is and always will be the servant of. As to *why* we should want these things or whether they are good for us, science's job is not to reason why, it is but to do and... That, after all, was the mandate firmly fixed in the Middle Ages—you mustn't do any speculating.

As for the "enlightenment" idea, we need it as a face saver, a gala balloon for every explosion, every assault on the earth's atmosphere, every death through lead poisoning or irradiation or plutonium leak or pharmaceutical drug, every research fiasco. We have a philosophy of justification at hand for things like the entirely unnecessary bombing of the Monte Cassino monastery and ("to save millions of lives") the most fearful experiment ever enacted on life or habitat, namely the decimation of a city population in eight seconds. We call it Hiroshima. Wars abound in enlightenment rhetoric.

Even science's "peaceful" uses, like the automobile, take on, in time, some of the murderous aspects of war—give humans speed and they will soon be killing each other with it—to the tune of road casualties similar to those sustained in Vietnam-sized wars. There is nothing intrinsic in automobiles that makes them crash into each other at frantic speeds but there is in the human, for he is frantic with fictions and it is these that push the foot down.

But our perceptions tell us that this is enlightenment, movement upward, attainment of goals of which animals have no understanding. We are a special breed, we have ethical yardsticks all our own, nothing outside us can measure us ethically. Unlike the animals we aren't subject to law. Yes, we seem to have taken that little remark of Pico della Mirandola's rather seriously.

An unsightly, stinking, poisoned world faces us with many questions about ourselves.

* * *

Science, we say, has to do with facts. This is rubbish. *It has to do with concepts.* A fact, like an object, is a concept.

Composed as it is only of concepts, science is never the truth about life but a form of truth about concepts, namely things immobilized for a moment by *the imagination*. Mathematics is an extreme example of this procedure, which is why, in line with our inherited theology, it has frequently been called a key to "God's design". It is abstract. So is physics. Yet—a shock here—the concepts and abstractions can be *realized*. They can remove a city at a touch. They can work invisibly, in our bodies, like radiotherapy.

The concepts "work". How then can we say that these concepts aren't real, aren't the truth about life? Try to find artificiality in a jet engine or nuclear explosion!

So because scientific effects alter our lives drastically we say that science commands not simply the truth but also the highest and only truth, compared with which all other forms of truth are subsidiary. There are other forms of truth but they are "subjective", "private", they carry no weight.

Science is spectacular, weighty, because it fulfills something we wanted. If you want flying objects or under-water transport or instant light or systems for raising fabulous weights or digging enormous depths of course you are going to say that the concepts which supply these things have a status no other form of knowledge can compete with.

But truth or falsehood never came into it. When I light someone's cigarette for them they don't say I've done something "true" just because it came off. Nor could a smoker I refused a light to say I had done something false.

As scientists we have to treat life as if it were concepts. We can't get nearer to our subject than a surgeon does to his or her patient. But we can't say that this stance of ours produces the truth any more than the surgeon can say his knife does. We have a theory that works, as a surgeon's knife works. Truth or falsehood don't come into it except in so far as *a theory worked*.

We know that as a *man* the scientist has no magical powers but he has at his fingertips a magical process. Magic is the fulfillment of a human desire in apparent contradiction of the laws of phenomena. And this is precisely what science—in the form of radio communication, cathode rays, radar detection, remote electronic control, magnetic data storage—gives us. Our inherited perceptions say that you can't make yourself heard by someone a mile away but the telephone says you can. You can't fly at five hundred miles an hour but jet flights say you can.

All stage performers in great or small measure touch these magic-sensitive nerves of ours. If scientists touch them it is because they can demonstrate that their results are the fruit of hard, matter-of-fact labor and skeptical appraisal of the "facts", i.e. ideas manifestly *devoid* of magic. They can stoutly deny the magic and yet look like shamans. Devoid of shamanistic powers, indeed fulminating against such powers, they still occupy the empty shaman throne.

You can't expect scientists to *live* in dead matter as well as study it. *Their* fancies and fictions too have to be met, and because they perceive like everybody else these fancies and fictions of theirs are the same as everyone else's. Magical goals provide the drive that sustains them through hours of boring data-compiling and fruitless speculation and failed experiments. The sometimes startling end-result will compensate for all.

Reason cannot itself supply energy. Reason plods and drudges.

But to fly like angels, to materialize in one place while remaining in another, to produce food and commodities without working to get them, to talk to spirits over great distances, to beam deathly rays on evil creatures, to explore the heavenly firmament in the hope of catching sight of Purgatory or Limbo, to abolish pain and suffering, to create a living being by artificial insemination: these were the medieval dreams, this is why we inherited the commodities and gadgets that fulfill them. No "triumph of thought" or "advance of man" is the cause of what we today call science and technology.

It was the medieval idea of a New Knowledge and its child the New World that lay deep in magic that produced all our "technical" wonders. Miraculous events, strange and unexpected performances are its language. Scientific work is dressed up in analytical and technical forms and this makes us believe that it is less autobiographical than other human statements such as those made in romantic fiction, confessions and Broadway musicals. Every human act, like every animal act, arises from the self, and infallibly describes this self. *Science is a detailed biography of the desires, fears, dreams and nightmares of its makers.*

Anyone who sees a film clip of physicists and engineers jumping with glee at a successful nuclear test will at once perceive this background of fantasy pathetically at odds with sanity.

In the smallest scientific thought you have wants, whims, disgusts. If scientific papers are carefully written to remove all suggestion of human presence it is because of the hot presence of emotion, which defies and dethrones detachment.

It is why so many "coldly" analytical people are good candidates for therapy, and frequently go mad or commit suicide. Self-severance from habitat can be taken too far. The popular idea of the "mad" scientist, the "mad" professor, betrays our fear that they will turn their glazed detached eye on *us*.

We naturally think that every other civilization shared our hunger for magic, and the same kind of magic. We say that if ancient Persians had been given the chance of telephonic communication they would have jumped at it. We assume that had the ancient Greeks alighted on the idea of jet propulsion they would have been hopping on to jumbo jets to get to Heliopolis. The same in advanced mathematics: we say the Greeks were within an ace of the truth about numbers but we finished the job ("evolution", "progress").

But the Greeks had goals quite different from ours. The first dissection of animals took place about 500 BC at the hands of a certain Alcmaeon and he described to some extent the function of the brain and the nervous system. But people showed no interest. Likewise Arab information about the skeletal structure of the body and its blood and nerve systems was of no interest to the medieval Christian. We say that the "Copernican revolution" transformed human thought but the heliocentricity of the solar system was known many centuries before Copernicus lived. One idea will create a furor here and total boredom there, according to the needs it satisfies or fails to satisfy. That we revolve round the sun rather than the sun round us was of all things a status one, and the truth was a turn-off.

Whatever the knowledge a civilization collects—from raja yoga in India to Euclidean theory in ancient Greece—it must emanate from a highly specific human desire, otherwise the energy to get it is missing. This desire is rarely the same in different civilizations, or even in different places and times within the same civilization, because human imagination is tireless in its fertility.

We can judge how magic-oriented we are if we examine our attitude to holes in the ozone layer or to global warming. Unless we act now all is lost. The 1987 Montreal conference on global warming predicted future habitat deterioration but only three years later the 1990 London conference announced that there was twice as much deterioration as the prediction had allowed for.

When the scientists bestowed on us these comforts of the kitchen and mobility and the cathode-ray miracle came about in the form of a box, and manifold short cuts devised for our busy daily life and, not least, the latest lethal ways of disposing of each other we were proud of them. Industrialization meant *the primacy of science*, nothing more and nothing less. From the moment of the first steam-driven pistons and mechanical looms it was the scientific disciplines that determined how the human was going to live. And of course the scientists argued that they were indeed responsible for the well-being of the modern world. Now they are learning things they neither predicted nor cared to know about at the time. You invent the car but miss out the fumes. You invent the nuclear bomb and miss out the radiation. So scientists have also lost status for us. We no longer wholeheartedly trust their judgments. But this is solely because they are now unable to offer us ad lib all we want for our profit, comfort or war. We want their errors rectified but it isn't so easy because our lives run on those errors, just as we run on wheels. We say "They will find the answer to the ozone layer holes" while unable to change the lives that make the ozone holes.

Having been hooked into magic blueprints and progress panaceas for a millennium or more we are addicts and will strike in the streets if governments threaten to take them away from us. Surely those same men and women who gave us our present ruined world will now, being brilliant men and women for whom nothing is insoluble, come up with the magical answers that will give us a healthy globe plus all the things we are doing in it?

* * *

When the media and even governments began their Save the Globe campaigns a few years ago a weird thing could be observed— humans too were in a state of ruin. From everywhere came news of terrorism, a rising crime rate, drug-dependence on a massive scale.

The communist world created by Stalin, at least the European and Soviet parts of it, collapsed. The capitalist world was in such debt that its efforts to look triumphant looked simply down at heel. Suddenly everyone was fighting everyone else. Those not engaged in Nazi demonstrations were murdering their neighbors for ethical, ethnic, class or ideological reasons. For the highest civilization there had ever been, the highest human awareness there had ever been, the highest degree of knowledge there had ever been, this was such a mess you wanted to curl up and sleep it off.

Many claim that thirty million people were killed under Stalin with dialectical coolness. If it is true, *a scientific approach would have been adopted*. The men who organized the deaths are said to have confessed that they lied about Stalin's true nature and the Communist Party. But lies aren't a contradiction of the scientific method so long as they don't happen in a premise or experiment. All the scientific method requires is detachment—the results aren't for you to consider, there is nothing in the death or starvation of millions of people that contradicts a calculation you have made that those people didn't count as humans.

The claim constantly made for science that it is detached and non-emotional thus works both ways. It is also a monster with its eyes put out. Its trade is in observation and deduction, not in conscience or even a minimal regard for side-effects from an experiment in the short or long term.

When the detachment theology was first worked out it seemed attractively harmless. Since God was detached from His creation, and since the human mind was the only truth-finding apparatus in that creation, all we had to do was view the creation with God's detachment and the truth about it would be ours.

It may seem odd that this theology was applied most in the twentieth century, i.e. the most atheist and least theological century there has ever been. But this is how our perceptions work. They take no account whatever of what you think and what you decide. They have the miraculous power to transform all that into their own program—again and again and again.

The communist, if he found his equations correct, if certain liquidations of human life were found necessary to attain the dictatorship of the proletariat and the eventual Withering Away of the State, was able to turn his blindness to the suffering into an act of courage. He *believed with all his heart* that scientific management of life would create an eventual perfect state, and that liquidation of certain people was necessary, just as a bloody revolution was (none of your "gradualist" or "parliamentary" weak-kneeism).

Once a communist accepted his formulae as the truth, his critical faculty was snuffed out. "Bourgeois deviationism" really meant the criticism of experimental formulae. Once these had been decided on they mustn't be cracked open. Your factories might be running on lines suitable for a hundred or more years ago, without filterage plants, but the habitat didn't have to be regarded any more than human life did in the Five Year or Ten Year formula. *Matter*, being basic to all scientific work, was simply an intellectual component in an experimental field.

Now we know that a thesis doesn't have to be right, that a bold synthesis can create a mess far beyond its simple terms. The atmosphere of experiment lies over *all* our various regimes. Whether we are talking about global market capitalism, communism or nazism, *alienation* is the theme common to all, in varying degrees of intensity. Labor, capital and the market are "instruments" now, closely connected to the "centers of power". A huge thing called society is overseen by means of statistics, investment analysis, market trends, forecasts. The Nazis flung themselves into the cold analysis with hot emotion, which is why their neighbors were confused by their behavior (you either behaved reasonably or you didn't). In the same way as the communists they turned their acts of cruelty into courage, though with emotion and not coldness. It was a different gimmick. The Final Solution was conducted with the same thoroughness as Stalin's land reforms. Himmler personally lectured his top liquidators on the need to overcome pity in themselves (this was a literary fashion of the time too, surviving today as a limp interest in the Duc de Sade). In the same way the well-to-do characters in Dickens argue against pity for the poor. Communists closed their eyes under Stalin to what happened in the villages whose water and food supply had been cut off. Jews and gypsies were as available for medical experiment under nazism as non-human animals are today. Yes, alienation manifests in fearful ways.

It would surely be better to take a closer look at that insidious detachment theology lying safe within our perceptions, and thus end our helpless devotion to blind goals. But that is easier said than done.

We can still try.

TWENTY TWO

The Wheel On Which Dementia Turns

How on earth did the mess happen as a result purely of definitions? For this is all science is. And all it has ever tried to supply. Combine this chemical with that chemical and a certain result may be expected which neither of the chemicals alone could achieve. Definitions have no revelations to offer, no comment about anything. But what they do have is something remarkably appealing: *they are infallible.*

If you describe the world in terms of straight and curved lines you can go a remarkable distance simply by defining your first premise more and more until you get to an advanced geometry. If your first premise was right and your observations are right and your deductions tally with both you have produced a true proposition. This is why we say in mathematics QED, "which was to be proved". We knew at the beginning what we wanted to prove, and we succeeded, even though what we wanted to prove may have changed as our definitions grew.

It is the sureness of this simple premise-observation-deduction process that will tempt the scientist in unguarded moments (or because he has no training in logic) to believe that he is revealing the absolute truth about things. Science-journalism is full of the crassest suggestions of this kind and they spill over into science itself, more particularly as journalism in large part decides science's goals.

The results are bizarre. Believing that he is about to crack the "problems that have puzzled mankind for millennia", the psycho-biologist (to take one of the aspirants for the mantle of Absolute Truth) will ask questions with no meaning like *Do our senses give us a true picture of reality?* or, to put it in the technical language thought to endow science with (magical) authority, *Do our sense organs provide us with a trustworthy model of the real world?*

"Deep" questions of this sort are asked at the beginning of papers or conferences on, say, the brain hemispheres or the function of the cerebellum or the nature of intentionality, or the universe as an expression of a unified intelligence. Then the research on the subject is trotted out and before we know where we are technical language swamps the questions out of existence while giving the impression that it is dealing with them. All we are doing is extending *our definitions.*

The biologist goes to his conferences with hope in his heart, drawn by cosmic questions which he supposes to be the subjects of debate, and he is likely to emerge with the questions still ringing in his head and not one of them so much as addressed. All he really got out of it was a new technical angle on homoeostasis, namely—to put it crudely—the balance achieved by the various functions within the body in their mutual dependence.

Neurophysiologists argue with each other about the "baffling" problem of what mind as opposed to brain is, or where mind is located in the organism, or whether machines can think, without the smallest effort to define "mind", "brain", or "think". There is rarely in any field except physics a suggestion that the attitude from which an investigation starts, namely the way the investigator perceives, determines the nature of his conclusions.

The tautological or circular truths of science such as "The amygdala is situated in the brain stem and concerns the function of memory" will never lead to *any other* kind of truth. "Two and two makes four" is the basic form of all scientific propositions. The rest is idle speculation and journalism, especially when dealing with the supposed "mysteries" of space and time, which are facets of perception, not of a supposed external world.

Physics is able to have effects on reality because *human perception* is fitted out with machinery for handling the habitat. That is, the perceptions already provide answers to problems (is it water or an oasis I see?), being a function within the habitat, not an outside perceiver who dwells in a reality that "corresponds" to the view within. Perceptions manufacture impressions, and do so according to internal needs.

If as a scientist you wish to get out of this dull tautological prison your only way is to speculate. The authority of your speculations will then depend on your experience and your wisdom but *they will have nothing to do with science*. But scientific "advances" depend on the power to speculate. Still, such flashes even if they pay off will lead inexorably back to more tautological statements, more two-and-two-make-fours, until the next flash.

You can never get into the Off Limits speculation area for the good reason that the concept of matter on which your work is based maroons you outside. As those cunning monks saw, it ties your hands better than manacles.

* * *

The strength of definitions is that they deal with *what no one could disagree about*. We aren't likely to make a song and dance about "motion is relative to the observer, velocity expresses this relation". But we are wrong if we think that this statement fails to arouse emotion.

Let us take a typical scientific analysis and examine the emotions it may arouse in us. Suppose we come across a scientific description of kissing. We read that in kissing someone we are seeking "semiochemical information" about him/her. We establish the degree of biological attraction we feel for him/her by exchanging saliva. Skin smell, derived from pheromones produced by certain glands, is another factor in this information-seeking.

267

That description makes us feel we are viewing our sexual excitements with detachment. We may even feel that it is *the truth* about our love-making, even that our love-making is a kind of illusion, even that love is a grandiose mental construction built on a "mere" chemical event.

A shock to our self-esteem, this. Our love has been trivialized. But this may help us distance ourselves from the love object— override a love we may be ashamed of because it is unrequited. This is the alienation principle again. Detachment liberated us, just as aeons ago similar acts of mental self-withdrawal helped us survive among stronger animals.

At this point we may read that "semiochemicals in the white rat are stimulated by erotic contact". This completes our detachment game. It makes the subtle suggestion that animals are mechanical objects. So we now see ourselves as animals. We view ourselves from the outside, grappling and sweating and gasping in the throes of a "mere" automatic response. We are now ridiculous. Popular-lore or media clichés can now take over: our "romantic" view of love has been "reduced" to "the plain and unadorned facts".

Of course our body chemicals are far from being "plain and unadorned". They behave in a miraculous manner and in such tiny doses as to be hardly measurable. They are properties of intelligence, like all the chemicals secreted in the organism. To say both "being in love" and "chemicals" is to cite *the very same event in different terms*.

This is what the theology absolutely denied. It said that the chemicals are indeed un-exalted, lowly, inferior, above all inert. They are matter. It told the scientist to treat this love material as a mere automatic process, so this is what we get! In accepting this the scientist swallows the theology of inert matter in one unconsidered gulp, when in fact his chemical analysis says nothing about inertness at all. The "detachment" isn't simply a pose but a *highly emotional attitude*.

The word "emotion" is itself a product of this pose. It replaced the word "feeling" in the course of this century. "Emotion" subtly bestows a new distance. It gives the impression of something undisciplined and formless. "Emotion" really means *mental agitation*, being derived from the French *émouvoir*, which in turn is from *mouvoir*, "to move", suggesting restlessly moving thoughts. Our pop verb "to emote" takes this one step further with its suggestion of an empty beating of the air. To be "emotional" is to betray instability, meaning loss of objective judgment.

This is what the monks were getting at. Only by withdrawing from your animal part can you judge properly. "Pure" and "objective" mean freedom from emotion. The claim that science is "down to earth" or "factual" or "non-anecdotal" is simply a repetition of the emotional claim that our rational part purveys truth while our animal part doesn't.

The truth is that the habitat is sending us a thousand messages every moment which our organism—our animal organism—is meticulously constructed to respond to. Every one of these messages within us sets into motion numberless electrochemical activities of which we are mostly unaware.

These are habitat-processes no less than what happens in the veins of a leaf. There is no chance of detaching ourselves from these processes for an instant.

Habitat can only be separated from inhabitant *for the purposes of theory*, or as a concept. We must have theories and concepts. But it is because of our lack of vital primal or instinctive information that we need them. Far from being a "triumph" of human intelligence our ever increasing dependence on reason is a sign of collapse. Far from being a climax of evolutionary effort, our rationalization of every aspect of human life is a last-ditch emergency effort to salvage a measure of sanity.

Nevertheless, even our reasoning faculty is a habitat process. But the monks and Pico della Mirandola said no to this—we were singled out by God to have free minds. Our freedom from animal attachment to the habitat would give us the truth about it.

On the contrary, our detachment is our only means of controlling the habitat, *not a means to truth*. Likewise science is purely an emergency control, *not a purveyor of meaning*.

Even this detachment-emotion of ours has to do with our animal nature, not with "free" thought at all. When a tiger detachedly calculates the distance between itself and its prey, and the angle of approach that its attack will involve, and the necessary speed, it is involved in a lightning scientific study. Afterwards, when it kills and eats its prey, we can say that the speed of its legs and its angle of approach have been successful. They worked—QED.

But can the tiger, its jaws dripping with blood, call this successful attack the "truth" or the "meaning" of anything?

Nor can *we* say that the expansion of a metal on being heated is the truth about the metal or its meaning. All we can say is that, like the tiger, we have made a mental calculation which achieved a fitting result. It is what we mean when we say that science "works": *our animal-demands have been satisfied*—no more than that. We have warmed the lair and feathered the nest.

Every animal lays claim to a certain unique field of perception within the habitat. The frog's eye is aligned to tiny jerky objects while ours is not. Certain animals can detect wavelengths inaudible to us. Whales can hear other whales thousands of miles away. We are each programmed to a specific set of forms and cannot think or feel outside these.

Only humans, as far as we know, claim total understanding. We insist that reality is the same for all creatures and that we can penetrate to "the truth" about it when in fact we have access to a limited mode within the total process, precisely as every other animal does.

* * *

The word "science" itself is full of misleading emotional appeals and amounts to little more than a pompous puff, referring vaguely to almost any form of mental calculation, however shoddy the form or undefined the premises. It endows respectability to nefarious pursuits in need of it, by inferring that the work is above human emotion.

"Scientific" applied to an enterprise means that the enterprise may be considered reputable and therefore endowable, such as keeping cats or sheep awake by means used in war to torture people. You can honorably sight whales, remark on their habits, swim about among them, listen to their calls over sub-aquaceous microphones but only when you take out notebooks and make lists, brand the whales either physically or by appearance-symbols and use instruments, will the media endow you with the puff. Sometimes just instruments will be enough, especially if they come from scientifically accredited sources (your purchase of them shows that you pay your dues). Dabbing nicotine on a mouse's hindquarters five times a day or squirting liquids from one test tube to another are often enough to qualify for the lofty mantle.

It is difficult for an accountant to look or feel detached when totting up someone's income-tax returns but all he has to do is embark on a survey of the spending habits of his clients, quote percentages and trends and seasonal changes, however haphazardly, and he will be counted scientific. Otherwise, if he simply wants to shoot his mouth off about people's spending sprees he will risk identification with preachers, artists, psychics, visionaries, magicians, eccentrics and circus performers, who are clearly non-scientific, however much system, thought, analysis, logic and detachment they may actually employ in their work, and however superior their employment of these faculties may be to that demonstrated by the general level of accredited scientists.

The word "science" consoles us when we wish to believe that something rather unbelievable is true, when our consciences need to be twisted, when we crave security or comfort at any price to habitat or animals therein.

The word "science" also conveys a false picture of a world-community which shares common goals, as if scientists worked in a removed brotherhood and were even a last-appeal tribunal in matters of human perplexity. This is far from being the case. With engaging credulity doctors, biologists, physiologists and physicists complain that their best ideas are hampered by their own scientific kind. They have to submit an outline of their intended researches to a committee unqualified to judge the matter, they are readily treated as cranks or mavericks if their ideas aren't safely within the accredited ground frozen by time and social approval. Having been groomed in the idea that science tells the objective truth about all things and that scientists are by way of being on a Disinterested Search they are ill prepared for the angry politics that detonate in the Halls of Pure Reason. Where indeed are those scientists making "bold experiments", "advancing", "overcoming barriers", "penetrating to new horizons", "making breakthroughs", "gaining new ground", "shattering illusions" and "opening up fresh territory", in the battle language once dear to science journalism? For the most part they are engaged in routine tests of the utmost boredom which would send any thinker into a state of catatonia: institutional standards of proof have to be met, however blindingly trite the opening premise may be.

Derision has throughout the history of science been the principal weapon by which new ideas have been squashed, careers ruined and suicides induced. Every "breakthrough", from the need for clean hands in hospitals to the theories of radioactivity and radio communication and inoculation and electromagnetic functions in the nervous system has each in its turn been ridiculed by those with the best jobs and the greatest power to promote or ruin. Thus a favorite complaint in the Halls of Pure Reason is that you can get a Nobel Prize for promoting an old idea more easily than you can get even experimental facilities for a new one.

Meanwhile the science journalist must continue to give the impression to a public more or less totally uncritical in the matter that the only reason why new ideas are opposed in the Halls is that they have to be tested and this may take some years (to protect the public, you know). Time-serving attitudes then get dressed as healthy skepticism, mealy-mouthed caution in the service of fashion and power is touted as a prudent avoidance of grandiose or visionary claims. Meanwhile the scientific machine grinds on like an outdated and over-staffed civil service, through and through the personification of an *ancien régime* whose bureaucrats fool themselves with images of intellectual grandeur based squarely on social status and size of earnings and media attention. A new "space probe" excites a spokesman to say that he is reminded by it of the excitement that went into Christopher Columbus's voyages of discovery. He omits to add—he probably doesn't know—that those voyages of discovery were designed to find Eden, not more earth. But he has succeeded in his goal of touching off the enlightenment nerve, while the question of the huge funds needed for "space probing" are conveniently uninvestigated.

Stories abound in the Halls of Wisdom about mean tricks. Research facilities which used to be lavish are suddenly switched off with only the most facile explanation. A book is disowned by its publisher after a group of astronomers, led by a Harvard man, goes to said publisher and threatens to boycott his highly profitable textbook department unless he virtually withdraws it. These are hardly selfless struggles in cloisters. The suppression of ideas and research and sometimes careers has apparently grown worse in the last half century of science's greatest "triumphs". Research has become so costly that only huge corporations and governments can afford it, which lays new ideas open to two inhibitors—first power games which carefully exclude faces that don't fit and secondly government interests, especially interests involving military defense, which make huge funds available but also mean that new ideas can always, under cover of Secrecy Acts, be legitimately suppressed. Little wonder that scientists talk about a "self-perpetuating priesthood" in their disciplines and describe their new theories as "heresies" (never mentioning however that they, like all heretics, are believers in the basic theological doctrine).

Any scientist today who feels what is facetiously called in the Halls the "lunatic twinge" and wants to research in forbidden areas would be lunatic indeed not to adopt the same studiously diplomatic tactics as, say, an employee in the higher echelons of a civil service in need of a pay raise. What else does he expect? He derives his livelihood from powerful organizations—is he naively unaware that all such grand units of power have to get their ideas straight and then fix them to last for years, otherwise they cannot be financially self-justifying?

A. N. Whitehead once put it succinctly in a conversation at Cambridge, Mass.—when an idea is new those who guard it will die for it if necessary; later the idea is inherited and its first fervor goes, so it passes into middle age; institutions then organize themselves around it and go on "like the dead knight borne along on his horse".

No more than he reasons himself to the dinner table does a scientist reason himself to his work. What do biologists' references to an "artistic", even "mystical" thrill or an "elegant" experiment mean other than that their brains are *fired by enthusiasm*? That the experimenter is carried beyond himself is obvious, especially when we consider that his aesthetically pleasing experiment may involve the severing or removal of an animal's limb while that creature is awake and aware.

And what are we to say of a biologist experimenting in body electricity who is enthralled to inflict major burns on his animal victims? Can we rightly say he is sane? His detachment amounts to a frenzy. The zeal this detachment evokes will carry men and women into unthinkably bloody programs—animals imprisoned inside contraptions which deliver electric shocks or fling them about continually night and day or subject them to unbearable decibels of sound that destroy their eardrums. Limbs crushed, amputated, one organ substituted for another, spines removed. Is the story that a certain Dement of Stanford University kept a cat without sleep for no fewer than seventy days apocryphal?

* * *

The Swiss psychoanalyst Blüler was the first to coin the word "schizophrenia". That was in 1911. It was he who diagnosed the dancer Nijinsky as mad—in a very few minutes of conversation. Nijinsky was largely docile, perceiving another world than the one he shared with his wife.

Until Blüler's time the term *dementia praecox* was in medically fashionable use. "Schizophrenia" was designed to show that the subject was divided—he found more meaning in his dreams and hallucinations than in the reality shared by the vast majority. Nijinsky simply "switched off".

Let us call this extreme detachment *alienatio demens*—the madness of being alienated from all around one. We all share this to some degree. When we use the phone, fly somewhere, drive a car, watch a television screen, sit before a computer, press buttons to achieve electric or electronic results, live in high-rises, indulge a passion for speed, listen to amplified sounds, we are using new alienation reflexes. We are able to provide our own music at the volume we prefer, we can watch picture shows at home. Everything new edges us to a well-cushioned alienation.

Because we have conditioned ourselves to accept these activities as part of daily life they are trivial for us, that is the amount of detachment they require (and every day strengthen) is unfelt by us. Traveling at seventy or eighty miles an hour has extreme effects on the nervous system but conditioned thinking separates the act from its effect so that we rarely connect it with stress. So many of the things we enjoy involve this same invisible wear-and-tear that we can't detect to what extent alienation is driving us into the last corner.

When we're "detached" it really means that our mental attention has divided itself into two parts, and these two parts then *look at each other*. All animals do it. The weaver bird will rapidly plaid her nest while keeping a danger eye open.

In fact, divided attention is the key to the full use of animal intelligence—quite as much as undivided attention is. Strangely, the two can coincide, as when we listen with undivided attention to a gripping story while driving a car. The mind is able to work in many different simultaneous modes, only one of which need be conscious.

When a surgeon cuts the corpus callosum in the brain, as he sometimes does to control epileptic seizures, he severs the connection between the brain's two hemispheres and creates in his patient two modes of consciousness instead of the usual single stream. The one mode will now be inaccessible to the other. This means that though the patient may see an object and hear the noise it makes he is conscious only of what he sees, unrelated to the sound. Yet, reminded of the sound, he will remember it.

This illustrates that division of attention is an inbuilt faculty and is essential to the complicated process of perceiving things. Without it no animal could enter such demanding situations as decoying prey, rearing young or exchanging sexual signals. The full wealth of the outer habitat pours in on us continually and all animals are equipped with the perceptive machinery to combine various disparate pieces of information (sights, sounds, skin sensations, smells) into one composite picture. Dividing the two brain hemispheres means impairing this composite picture, though the self and the consciousness remain intact.

When Descartes said that the passions were the enemies of "detached" thinking he did so because a passionate mind is *undivided*. Being desperately in love makes it unlikely that we will see the loved one in a detached manner, i.e. with divided attention. All thinking involves division. It depends on a certain distance but this distance is between two factors inside the mind, *not between self and the outside world*.

But we like to feel we are looking at "the world" from a distance, that we are one thing and the world is another. Two impressions are looking at each other within the one brain, namely an impression of the self and an impression of the thing perceived, and the two are so inextricable that they seem the same. However we try, as the Stoics said, we can't separate that self. When they said it had to be in a relation with something in order to be felt they meant that unless you perceive you can't be aware of the self, and that you have no self apart from perceptions.

If our sympathetic bond is in erosion it means that we can witness somebody suffering without perceiving the suffering. We "know" they are suffering—being mauled by a lion or being burned alive in a racing car—but it is an unfeeling awareness. All of us have seen those accident-clips on television where a skier tumbles or a racing car crashes or a high-jumper falls on his back or face. Some of these look serious, if not fatal. These clips will excite ripples of relaxed, generous laughter. A near-fatal accident, sometimes involving babies, is actually seen as a *plaisanterie*. It means that the degree of detachment attained by the human at present is at a dangerous level.

When we divide our minds in science it is in order to do something similar to this. One doesn't identify with the object in any way. This is why science has no interest in values, in qualities of civilization, in the matter of compassion as against cruelty. Where do goals, values, meanings, morals enter a decision as to whether certain metals, when they fail to expand on being heated, are different from other known metals? An inquiry into definitions has nothing to say beyond the act of defining. It can flourish as well in Nazi conditions as it can in Eden.

But the results can produce fearful results. When we hear that the Chernobyl reactor will remain hazardous "for seven billion years" we get a glimpse of *alienatio demens* in action. Even that use of the expression "seven billion years" is a symptom of it, a pathetic attempt to perpetuate our childlike belief that we have the gift of detached authority.

In our concentration on the "outside" world we comfortably overlook that our detachment pose is the villain of the piece and that our divided attention, so necessary for all thought, may have become divided to the point of a raging schizophrenia which obliges us to live in one reality while thinking in another.

TWENTY THREE

Brain Off Its Moorings

If you base a civilization on one central unquestioned idea which is adopted by generation after generation for thousands of years without any awareness that the idea can be challenged, and if that idea is demonstrably wrong, your civilization is clearly heading for trouble.

That idea, in our civilization, can be defined in one word, "mind". The meaning of that word has changed drastically over the last two millennia but the idea behind it hasn't. And this idea says that the human mind was a status symbol. Until modern times people meant by this a divinely endowed status but now we just mean status. That status is a position of command or supremacy in the animal kingdom. The idea behind it says not simply that the human animal is the brightest of all the animals but also that *it isn't an animal at all*. And the more alienated all our modes of thought and conduct become the more this seems to be demonstrably true.

But it is demonstrably false and we know it. But the idea doesn't budge, for all that. We carry it about with us as a spontaneous response, and this response originated that God's special gift to man was to distinguish him utterly from animals, such that he couldn't be considered to belong to Nature so much as to God.

Few of us would say that any more, just as few of us go to church. Which means that a civilization that avows no religion and governs itself as if religion didn't exist is simultaneously based on a purely religious idea.

Yet this status idea, put down clearly by Aristotle in the wake of Socrates, was a sort of afterthought. It didn't come from any vision or revelation such as is the necessary basis of religion but from reflections about the difference between a religious creature, no longer locked in darkness and death, and a non-religious creature which the animal appeared to be.

And however foolishly grandiose this idea may seem it is a very understandable one. A religion excites tremendous enthusiasm. The ceremonies and moving chants and songs, known from babyhood, the deliriously heightened feelings of a crowd in worship make a comparison with the animal natural. This comparison may prompt the utmost heartless contempt as toward a filthy, demonic object. To this day crowds stamp asses to death in parts of Spain as a "festivity".

It is difficult for us to realize that the first humans that ever existed *woke to the world in dementia*, that this and this alone was the mark that distinguished them from other animals and that this alone made them climb from height to height of heady power—all imaginary of course, invented like so much that their powerful imaginations provided them with. Now they are scaling not terrestrial heights any more—their grandiosity has long since outpaced these—but heavenly, inter-planetary, cosmic ones. Nothing short of the most and the biggest and the infinite and the vast will please this impaired creature.

But he survived—than which fact there can be few more miraculous. His very alienation became a source of intense concentration for him so that *mind* became—all too perilously—his all, guiding his limbs to all kinds of feats which he put down to his enormous strength (puny compared with that of so many other animals) whereas *mind* provided the strength, in the form of will, resistance, tenacity. So a facet of dementia became (to the horror of the rest of the animal kingdom) a tornado, finally transforming our portion of the solar system into a laboratory which now actually looks and smells like a madman's creation.

All this is difficult for us because we are so deeply impressed by our own performance. So deeply, in fact, that it isn't a performance for us at all but reality. Being so hypnotized by it, so surrounded by all its works night and day, deafened and excited and distressed by it (but distress confirms its power), we have to say "This is too huge an edifice for me to question".

It is as if the madman who claims he is Caesar so influences his keepers and fellow inmates and ultimately everybody outside his mental institution that he is acknowledged as Caesar by all. So in truth he becomes Caesar. And the demented origin is entirely hidden.

The peculiar power of dementia—the "demonic" energy, as we say—lies in its transference of the sexual drive into all kinds of imaginative and mental forms. This doesn't at all mean that sex was "sublimated" or "canalized". There was no *loss* of sexuality as there was a loss of vision and nasal power, but a great change did come about, just as it does in zoo animals. The murder rampage at the London zoo which I talked about in my first chapter shows to what extent *mind* had entered sexual performance (and therefore male hierarchy) in the captive animal. So it is the other way round—mind (concentration) invades the sexual drive, rather than the latter being in any way weakened.

I mention this now because we have so diluted the word "mind" from its original Greek meaning of "spirit", and so diluted the word "spirit" to a sort of spook status, that the vast force of "mind" in the human structure has been lost to view.

* * *

In its original Greek form (*menos*) the word "mind" meant the vigor or spirit displayed by a human, not his conscious thought as it does for us (though the Greeks could *also* mean that).

The word could be applied to the processes of digestion, glandular secretion, response to sexual stimuli. But we (beginning with Aristotle) have so elevated the word to a status where it means "non-animal" that it now refers to the act of *withdrawing* from unconscious processes rather than *expressing* them.

This brought the word "brain" into circulation. Originally, as the Greek word *bregma*, this meant just the brow or forehead, i.e. a surface—not at all a force, a spirit. If today we use it more and more it is because we think of "mind" as being exclusively located in the brain area, a calculating apparatus in detachment from the rest of the nervous system.

Of course we know that we can't have a thought without electrochemical events happening inside us. We know that the brain depends on blood circulation and the whole nexus of nerves deployed along the spinal column. Yet our *perception* of the matter is that the brain is responsible for conscious thought, and that conscious thought is the chief directing force in life. But consciousness—and this is basically what we mean by "mind"—is deployed everywhere in the organism. There are cells in the brain as there are in the rest of the body and the messages received within and sent out by the brain would be no messages at all unless an equally intelligent cell elsewhere received them.

But we have never been very realistic this way. Always, in this Graeco-Roman civilization of ours, there has been a great disposition to strike poses, which means to look for the power element in everything. Many if not all of the heavenly fights between the Greek gods were *fights over power*. From the beginning of this civilization a more than acceptable level of grandiosity began to appear in our thought-processes, which in turn invited uncontrolled hallucination, to the point where the brain would come off its moorings.

When we believe (hallucinate) that we conduct our lives with conscious, freely chosen thoughts we are making an oblique reference to our degree of alienation from the habitat. So many of the habitat's functions have dried up for us that we understandably get the impression that we are consciously making our lives, for the good reason that we live within a closed man-made "I am Caesar" habitat that has replaced the earlier myriad habitats. Of course those varied habitats continue to exist with their huge differences of temperature and fauna and flora but there is only one Caesar—and that was how we could bring the whole lot to utter ruin.

Having lifted the "mind" out of the human pathological system we start attributing everything that happens in the world to that mind. At the end of the nineteenth century doctors were keen on attributing their patients' symptoms to hysterical origins ("nerves"). This century "mental problems" became distinct from "physical symptoms", and tend to win primacy over the latter. In the 1930s there was a feeble effort to bridge the two in the form of the "psychosomatic" theory, but a bridge implies two separate banks, so that this theory (now part of Popular Lore as an inherited "fact") left the mind-body division intact. Indeed, this theology determined the structure of our medical thinking so thoroughly that we are lucky nowadays to escape our family doctor without a crude counseling lecture based on dimly perceived media hash-ups of psychoanalytical theory.

When Sechenov, Pavlov's teacher, argued that all human activity was in the nature of a reflex no one knew what he was talking about. We would be ignorant of his name today were it not that Pavlov admired him. Sechenov was really saying that cortical or conscious activity is a tiny portion of the massive electrochemical activity we call life and we can neither control the internal operations on which life depends nor act on any conscious analysis of it.

In the smallest matter, for instance breathing, we are governed not by conscious thought but by autonomic action. The moment most of us start thinking about our breath, and receiving instruction about how to do it, its accustomed natural rhythm (almost always traumatic) ceases, often to the point of hyperventilation. Any genuine breath-specialist knows that such a "natural" rhythm has long ceased in the average human.

It is the same with the eyelids. They blink according to laws of their own until we start talking about their frequency per minute. Only when the new facts have been absorbed by means of exercises will the breathing or the eyelids function "naturally" in the new rhythm. In other words, function *requires the thought to be made unconscious.*

This is how a civilization is made. It comes from the act of withdrawing from the habitat (thinking or concentrating) in order to create a new world but then it must build *unconscious forms* which can be inherited. The more successfully it does this the more perfectly will it imitate the habitat and not be at odds with it as our civilization is.

* * *

In its flourishing moments a civilization is an artistic fling. Everything from painted plaster ceilings to finely reticulated fish knives conveys a sense of form. The artifacts are later collected and archived with reverence. At its peak a civilization is blind in the way lovers are blind. Acts of passion (or folly, i.e. passion gone wrong) abound. Love is more important than life.

In a period of fall like the present one we look back on civilization with wonder and misapprehension. Why on earth did Swann throw himself and his fortune and health away on Odette de Crécy whom he knew to be little better than a whore and not his type anyway? Why did his feeling that she was foreign to him actually excite his love into self-sacrificial infatuation? Why did Proust linger so long over perfumes and the touch of things and a barely perceived expression of face instead of developing a good straightforward plot and making his characters do the logical, wide-awake, constructive things which we know the human, and indeed any animal, to be incapable of?

The technological observer looks back on all this dumbly, searching for his own literal truths. How was it those people loved and feared and followed and worshipped and denounced each other so ardently when they could have sat down and simply talked it out? How could they bear the dependency of loving and the disorder of hating?

In civilization we belong so deeply to it that the subtlest glances can become haunting ancestral beguilements, arouse unquenchable sexual longings, their language too deep for the conscious mind. Smells, the touch of hands, the sound of kitchen clatter, laughter in another room, footsteps on stone steps, the crispness of a morning melt together into an assembly which is only named as "civilization" when threatened.

How to glance at the beloved, how to distinguish a fine walk from a gauche one, how to eat and drink, how to sit, take the air, laugh or sigh, how to greet a friend as opposed to a relative, how to give orders or receive them, how to sleep and how to rise from the bed, how to sneeze, cough, clear the throat, how to dally with the young or dandle a baby, how to listen and how to talk, how to kiss, embrace, excite, sustain the lover and be sustained in turn—all this was passed from one generation to the next with no explicit advice. The child observed them in the adult and yearned to be the same, and in the yearning was already the learning. This is how reflexes work.

* * *

I felt that this decline could span centuries, even millennia— that our own civilization was so discontinuous and turbulent from the beginning as to suggest that the decline and fall of the Roman empire simply extended itself through Christianity until, with marvelous glimpses here and there of a civilization that might have been and so many times nearly was, this fall reached its hopefully final low—in this present killer century.

TWENTY FOUR

The Fiction Of Hard Facts

In the twentieth century nothing has more baffled us than the fact that what should be an era of the most advanced civilization, steaming and thumping and roaring away with the spirit of industry, clicking and blinking and humming with electronic subtlety, has turned out to be a mass murder that would have had Attila or Tamberlaine catatonic with terror.

All right, we don't brag any more about being the highest civilization, or even much of a civilization at all. Just the number and extent of our wars rule that out, quite apart from the lethality of our weapons—and the sorrows left behind by Hitler's all too Final Solutions.

Still, we might feel gingerly about facing a certain proposition which I am now going to set down: that this present century has been the climax of a long-laid compulsion *to destroy all living things.*

If we look at the way the techniques of war have developed over the past centuries we shall find that they increased the range rather than the precision of their destructive capacity. Gunpowder, the single most significant event in that history, was developed not for its ability to destroy precise targets when aimed from the barrels of small arms but for its destructive spread, until the final technique of all, this century, involved no cordite whatever but could achieve the disappearance of a city within eight seconds.

Not that the desire to kill all living things was ever a plan. After all, wars are entered into blindly and escalate helplessly. We look in vain for ideas of terrestrial suicide or even ones that vaguely suggest it. And because this is so we are likely to dismiss the suggestion that this is what we humans were out to do.

I repeat, it is human perceptions we must look into, and these become apparent from behavior. After uniformly *destructive* behavior for the last five centuries, and widespread violent skirmishes for a thousand years before that, we should be able to recognize certain consistent ideas. But this doesn't make them easy to accept, precisely because the old perception is intact, with the *design to destroy* lying immaculate within it.

* * *

Of all the words in modern vocabularies one dominates and that is *enemy*. I am going to adapt something Freud said about phobia: the wonder isn't that we are *enemy*-fixated but that we are ever anything else!

The enemy is the one who always stands in our light. Get him out of the way and the light shines on us. Actually, we invent him. After all, no creature is born with this name. But fiction or no fiction we must get rid of him in order to see the light.

The enemy idea was brought to sophistication in medieval speculations about the devil (*diabolos*, from the Greek)—he being the principal one, Satan (from the Hebrew, meaning enemy) or Beelzebub (Hebrew for the fallen "god of the flies" but more exactly a fallen angel) plus all kinds of subsidiary demons (*daemon*, Greek, meaning half-god) and fallen angels who peeped out of the habitat in animal form and would devour you without so much as a thank you. The enemy was the infidel, the heretic, the pagan, the sinner, the witch, even a pot of ripe plums and your lust for them. Good things could become enemies. Cleverness was a snare of pride. Charity was changeable for vanity. Ardor in prayer could address itself equally to Old Nick, who was all too pleased to satisfy self-seeking penitents.

Life was based on the enemy. The enemy kept you from becoming bent. Thus it was that killing became essential for the uncovering of the light. In crusades, persecutions, witch burnings, and the razing of heresy-infected villages, the enemy was dealt a series of Last Blows which would secure the true, clean dispensation everyone was waiting for. But the offending victim always popped up again even from the headless, the charred, the quartered, the disembowelled, the racked-to-death—just as he does from the radiated, the bombarded, the fire-bombed today.

If *enemy* hovers so ubiquitously in the human mind, and is so much at the edge of every half-thought, it is because it means "that which is preventing me from getting forward". So enmity can't be switched off. You must be prepared for it not only in the wars that make your cities shudder and fall and necessitate less formal funerals than are normal (bulldoze them into holes) but also when arms have been laid down and the soldiers gone home. Then the *trivial* murders begin—the group rapes, the random atrocities, the domestic outrages. The enemy is now parents, males, females, lesbians, homosexuals, heterosexuals, whites, blacks, Muslims, Jews, Christians, children, orientals, westerners, there being no category of human, no thought, beyond the haunted brain's capacity to demonize. It is a double process. The self which demonizes another into *enemy* has already turned itself into that enemy's victim, which adds to the smarting wound, then the smart adds to the anger: fist-fights, strangulations, the cutting of throats begin to crowd the imagination, though the enemy may be a neighbor tranquilly cooking borscht and unaware of any enmity whatever.

Nearly all cries for freedom are for freedom from brain ghosts, those persistent ones which can't walk away because they aren't real.

If the Jews and Bolsheviks and gypsies didn't look like fellow humans to the guards of the Nazi death camps it was because their perception of them already contained the Final Solution, namely they saw them as *the last obstacle* to a good clean life. Just a little effort to overcome the first squeamishness was necessary, in the knowledge that after the clean-up the death chambers would no longer have to figure in life. Hitler even told them in his usual unhesitating words to be brave in their utter lack of mercy.

I mention the victims of the Final Solution here not because they have been the only *enemy* in history but because the Holocaust was at the very heart and hub of human dementia.

Christopher Marlowe dramatized such things in *Doctor Faustus* and *Tamberlaine* four centuries ago. His stories were old epics from a legendary time. It might be worth adding that in one performance during the reign of Elizabeth I somebody in the audience got the idea that among the devils onstage was Satan himself. A riot broke out. Was it a preview?

TWENTY FIVE

The Brain Rebellion

Yet at no time even in modern history did *ordinary* people, those who had to produce the food and fight in the wars, show obvious signs of madness.

In fact, until this century, we could rely on a firm ballast of sound-nerved laboring families to compensate for the actions of enlightened people at the top. They made clothing, houses, vehicles. They groomed and fed and stabled the horses and collected the eggs and milked the cows and were sometimes listened to even by the enlightened for their illiterate wisdom.

But after 1945, namely at the end of World War Two, more and more people began to talk about being depressed. Formerly shrugged off as a personal mood that would quickly pass, mental depression now became something that doctors had to cope with. Diagnosing mental distress as "just nerves" would no longer do, though in fact it was the best diagnosis of the lot. The old regime of sound nerves at the bottom of the social scale and a state of hysteria at the top was clearly gone.

These complaints about depression were most frequent in prosperous countries, and increased with the prosperity. As new money circulated so a much larger middle class came into being, with its vulnerability to enlightenment of every kind. "Affluence", the fashionable word, brought a sense of liberation. The old middle class had taken a beating from the war. Less and less did it determine tastes and standards. There was abundant upward mobility if only because the top was much less different from the bottom than it had been in the "old" days. Some Europeans saw this as the Americanization of the West but role models take centuries to get into the perceptions. In fact it was a process that had been going on since medieval times, namely *the fragmentation of authority wherever it put its head.*

Still, the nineteenth-century promise that once everybody had enough money and the chance of a university education, good taste, good manners and good order would prevail looked to war-weary and day-dreaming populations in 1945 as if it might at last be fulfilled. The fact that precisely the opposite happened wasn't noticed for decades. It continued to be said in the 1950s and even as late as the 1970s that Man had at last reached the top of the arc. "Progress" figured so much in political speeches that it began to sound like overture music to the Last Act.

More books were read, more plays and films were seen, more music was heard and more discussion went on. But there were increasing signs that this had nothing to do with the propagation of old middle-class values at all. Most people when they watched a film or read a book or glanced at a newspaper wanted the crime and the calamity. Man, far from having got to the top of any arc, was increasingly fascinated with the darkness at the bottom. It was this rather than the enlightenment promised by Victorians (not, though, by intelligent ones like William Morris) that got to the top of the arc, and today malevolent behavior previously only written about and filmed is realized on the street.

Some people argued that this was the fruit of affluence. But affluence in other centuries had quite opposite effects. Why was the dark side of the brain now so evident, the bright side gone? Mental depression took various forms: it could be groundless fear and anxiety, a simple grey feeling, it could manifest in "healthy" or "normal" people as a love of (someone else's) murder, calamity, torture, hostility, resentment, revenge, punishment, subterfuge, plotting and punishment in every real or dramatized form.

Depressive minds able to supply this were plentiful, and there was no market dearth of nasty stories both fictional and documented. Apparently humanity had finished two world wars only to sit down and think up the most ghoulish atrocities in the hope of selling them to a publisher or film producer, or to just sit down and watch the result. The massive degree of sitting and thinking and watching was alone enough to cause depression. It was as if humanity had lost the use of its hands.

This love of the fearful, the cruel and vindictive was the *active* side of the brain's darkness, and as such comfortable. The other *passive* side—plain mental depression and self-doubt—was something you needed a medical doctor for.

But no doctor pointed out that the two sides, the active and the passive, fed on each other and increased each other.

* * *

This was where the chemical industry came forward: it would give doctors something to administer not as a cure but as a temporary knock-out.

It presented a novel view of medicine but was accepted without a murmur because short of sending millions of people to psychoanalysts, which most of them couldn't afford, there seemed nothing else to do. The pharmacies began filling up like Victorian ladies' drawing rooms.

It became imperative to encourage the light side of the brain, which would then presumably reduce the dark side. So, particularly in the Sixties and Seventies, a kind of therapy began to circulate that was distinct from both chemical/electrical psychiatry and psychoanalysis. It sought to improve self-esteem, optimism, confidence, good will and tolerance because these qualities seemed in abeyance. The personality had to be "integrated", illuminated. There were Yoga classes, Yoga lessons on television. The word guru became accepted English, and Indian ashrams began to appear in the West. The guru was someone capable of putting the brain into a state of radiance.

We began to ask if this sense of light in the brain didn't have a chemical component, and words like "endorphins" and "melatonin" were put about. The endorphins were secreted naturally by the body. They promoted a state of optimism and protected the organism against pain (endo-morphine). They were also essential to the body's immune system (another expression to enter popular medical language). There was the famous Norman Cousins case—he laughed himself back to health by dint of running comic videos on his television-screen all day. Doctors began to look into his case and he was invited to join the medical staff at Stanford University.

The brain itself, not simply thoughts, much less behavior, now came under investigation. At last the human being seemed to be facing the fact that the erosion of certain forces within him might lead not only to his destruction but the world's.

The increased influence of the gurus and therapists meant that people began to look for more than medical repair-systems. The word "God" began entering the mouths of Christians who had never entered a church except at a helplessly early age. On the lips of Indians and Buddhists it had a different ring—released from ethical overtones and the Old Man in the Sky image. A paradoxical situation arose in which as the Churches lost influence a sense of religion increased. More and more people began adopting techniques of Californian progeny—Est, rebirthing, primal or scream therapy, spiritual massage, past-life regression, neurolinguistic programming, hypnotherapy. The tradition wasn't a new one. Back in the Twenties Los Angeles had teemed with cabalists, yogis, astrologers, psychics. Now these things became a service industry. The idea of religion was now connected with health and well-being and a sense of autonomy. If people didn't wish to say "I believe in God" they accepted the inner benefits of doing so. Religion now had its place as a "self-empowerment" therapy, as a passport to success. The fundamentalists began promising health, wealth and happiness as the certain rewards of following the Redeemer (the Redeemer had quite particularly emphasized that he was *not* offering these things). Even Californian masseurs began touting Security, a Good Relationship and Happiness as the fruits of massages that resembled "hands-on" healing sessions.

All this, despite being much more effective than most non-Californians cared to know, tended to overlook the human's inbuilt capacity to recover his sanity and optimism without an arduous self-development program. There were gurus who said as much. The *self*, they said, was the only teacher, and "I the guru am only an analogy for yourself. You have the thing inside you which you foolishly look for outside." Socrates had said it and it was still true.

But it was easier said than done. Most people, if statistics were anything to go by, felt they needed help—from doctors, pharmacists, psychiatrists, family counselors, sects, while others went to aerobic classes, muscle-development clubs, yoga classes, health spas, dietary schools, martial arts groups and sexually indiscriminate swinging parties. There were unmistakable worldwide efforts by the human being to rehabilitate the human being by almost any means available.

Part of this effort took the form of drug use, whether prescription drugs or narcotics. Masses of people were clearly dissatisfied with themselves and their lives and were desperate to take substances that promised to enhance their experiences, their performance and their personality. "Empowerment" became one of the key-words of the therapies but it was equally a goal for those looking for drug-induced trips because they didn't believe that life was as flat and stale as they found it to be.

With the heavy political stigma against drug-addiction it is difficult for us to see that here too, even in self-injection with tainted needles, lies a burning quest in the human for the life of which he feels starved.

Hoaxed into believing that his is a conscious mind within an unconscious body he naturally gropes for a connection with the habitat by means of mental events, which is exactly the wrong way round.

Many people who are unforgiving toward drug-addiction are themselves addicts, but of approved, pharmaceutical forms which have exactly the same goals of removing depression and creating contentment.

* * *

Gradually, since the 1990s chemical or pill psychiatry has taken precedence over counseling. This was partly because a growing number of people complained of depression, "intractable" pain, suicidal desires. But really it was an attempt to recognize, without seeming to, the fact that the human wasn't the *naturally* sane creature he was cracked up to be.

The ever more fashionable word "biological" as a description of the new psychiatric approach confirmed this. Talk therapy was out but on the other hand no one wanted to hand the brain over to the neurologist, who was already beginning to say that serial butchers and sex mutilators had discernibly different brains from other people. The word "biology" suggested things in the brain which no one could call abnormal and which therefore required round-the-clock psychiatric surveillance. Whatever else it was, it was good for business.

More and more the psychiatric belief was that aberrant behavior required chemical adjustment in order (rather vaguely) to "re-establish chemical balance in the brain". But jiggering about with the "neurotransmitter seratonin" is dangerous if only because less is known about the brain than any other part of the body.

Yet the matter is simple, despite the fancy names given to the chemicals of brain manipulation or their description as "elegant" or "state of the art". Each of them in turn is a "miracle" drug when it appears, and gets a media lift-off, even a front page if lucky. In time (but this part is rarely given publicity) it is quietly debunked in the profession on the grounds that the science is moving forward and has left it behind. But in fact the drug was found to be harmful, which doesn't stop it being re-launched under a different name.

Millions of people take these pills and within weeks are no longer authorities on how they feel or what they think because *their perceptions are now distorted*. The organism no longer communicates its distresses so readily to the mind. A serious de-pilotization of the nervous system takes place.

It isn't only the fact that the brain is a bafflingly complicated organ but that it is the cradle of those responses which make it possible for the human to function in the habitat. If the human were just a thinking mind it might be different. Then the so-called neuroleptics or "lobotomy" drugs might have localized effects. But if you interfere with a response or neurotransmitter you upset the balance on which judgment depends. Anyone who has witnessed a psychiatric patient laughing with genuine enjoyment at somebody else's tragedy (a terminal cancer, say) will know what I mean.

It is what the courts call diminished responsibility, which is perhaps why one of the chief of the miracle drugs of recent years, Prozac, has been cited by defense counsels in a number of murder trials.

Seeing depression or alcoholism as chemical un-balance in the brain, a neurotransmitter problem, is a covert acknowledgement of universal dementia but if you chemically lobotomize the brain you drive the dementia deeper because you further deepen the state of alienation from which it all started.

This alienation didn't happen because of any damage to the brain but because of the particular hazards of human-primate existence. Certain situations of terror can drive any animal mad—i.e. *thoughts and impressions alone are enough to derange the brain*, without any structural changes having taken place.

Psychiatry is locked into theology like every other discipline, and as in medicine generally the inherited perception is that the human's "animal" (irrational) side must be tamed or at least put out of view. Lobotomy, by means of pills or electric shocks, is the realization of a doctrine which said "cut the mind from the feelings" as if—again the hidden theology—the mind was the *opposite* of biological, i.e. a special non-animal endowment.

The idea of "putting away" a mentally distressed person dominated eighteenth and nineteenth century attitudes to all aberrant behavior and was an earlier edition of this lobotomy idea. Shackles and chains were appropriate for behavior that couldn't be predicted, even when it obviously came from the lack of a home or decent meal or warm bed.

The theology created millennia of dread toward whatever behavior wasn't socially vetted for its lack of the "wild animal" within.

Psychiatry reacts to this alleged wildness with the same alarm. All passions are suspect for it, and it could without difficulty establish that every living human is ripe for lobotomy on the grounds of the simplest passions that rock us, quite naturally, every day. And it is the patient's fear of passion, on the same theological basis, that makes him such a good candidate for lobotomy or giggle treatment.

So the theology of the Non-Biological Man leads to the further severing of the brain from the habitat it is designed for. The patient starts off with the idea that depression and worry and fear are wrong and have to be excised, with the result that the real dire problem of human dementia is never addressed.

* * *

There was a great sense of triumph in medical circles at the end of the nineteenth century when safe anesthesia came in. Morphine, a constituent of opium, produced a state of pleasant detachment without loss of consciousness or impairment of the logical faculties.

In the Middle Ages snakeroot was a release from *accidie* or depression. In the seventeenth and eighteenth centuries there was a vast amount of wine-drinking in the leisured classes. Memoir after memoir testifies to continual drinking bouts. Tea and coffee drinking spread as a habit, together with chocolate, which contains the natural amphetamine (chemically known as phenylethylamine) used by the Aztecs, from whom the Spaniards adopted it as another quick fix against depression.

Both tea and coffee were at first treated with suspicion, and users were called abusers. In the nineteenth century laudanum or opium became popular, in the intellectual as in the poorer classes. Now in the twentieth century heroin—just over twice as powerful as morphine—has become the long-duration fix. A fix is said to have a "high" or a "low" aspect and to be able to sleep successfully you must apparently find a balance between the two.

Aldous Huxley was supposed to have started a mescaline fashion when he published his *Doors of Perception* but really he was following a tradition that started in the "Age of Enlightenment" two centuries before him. It was no accident that this Enlightenment should coincide with an enormous ingestion of tea, coffee, chocolate and wine, and in its last years an increasing use of opium. The need for rational control created the deeper need to escape it, in an insoluble spiral the peak of which we are living through today.

Laudanum, an alcoholic solution of opium, was in common use in Victorian times, available at the chemist. Morphine was introduced about 1803, its name derived from that of the ancient god of dreams, Morpheus. In parts of England you could buy opium beer. Poppy tea was given to children as a balm. It was the West that introduced opium to the East, not vice versa. The first amphetamines were synthesized in 1887 and finally developed in 1927.

By the twentieth century it was a matter of choosing whether you wanted to go faster or slower, be more awake or less. In the first half of this century alcohol remained the most popular method for giving life the glow it ordinarily lacked but after World War Two the need for every form of life-enhancement increased until hardly anyone lives without some form of stimulant, sedative or hallucinator.

Governments make war on the drug barons. The idea is to limit and finally abolish the supplies but as fast as the supply of one drug diminishes another one appears "on the streets" (we associate drugs with the streets as if drug-ingestion wasn't also a chronic middle-class habit). The demand in all classes is huge, unquenchable. People will risk imprisonment for experiences that their usual lives don't give them. They are on a *brain rebellion*, refusing to take what is supposed to be real life as either natural or true.

* * *

"Narcotic" drugs are said to be taken to "escape" but far from escaping into another world drug-takers testify again and again that they discover the real one and that the normal world of their perceptions doesn't give a true picture of reality at all.

We use the word "narcotic" to encourage this escape idea but many drugs, like cocaine, are non-narcotic in effect. The hallucinations they provoke may unfold startling discoveries about reality which from that time on, even long after the drug has been dropped, change the very form of perception itself. And that was the reason it was taken—*to alter perception.*

At certain points of collapse in civilization, as dementia sweeps back to control human behavior, there is a widespread revulsion from the old perceptions and they are seen—yes, the very sights and sounds—as a prison. Getting out of the prison, however, has to be done carefully. But almost no one knows how. So quick-fix methods prevail.

When the American Indians used the peyote cactus (mescaline) and the Liberty Cap mushroom (psilocybin) in their ceremonies they knew how much to take and how often. The amount taken was tiny, the ingestion slow. Also the ceremony wasn't a daily occurrence.

Such ceremonies were built on experience. In pygmy ceremonies those who go into trance are held and cared for by others, just as it is in similar ceremonies in Pakistan and India.

The physiological process is a simple one, whether a person is taking tranquilizers or heroin or cannabis. We give ourselves an extra supply of endogenous chemicals—i.e. chemicals the body produces of its own accord. But this *lowers our own production of the same chemical.*

Every time we take a tranquilizer or smoke pot or sniff cocaine the organism responds by not producing those elements which the chemical is trying to imitate.

Thus the pain or sleeplessness or anxiety or depression gets worse once the first effects wear off. So at one and the same time you are augmenting the body's natural supplies and also depleting them as you go along.

So you are starting off with a certain *natural* erosion of faculties as a human primate, then you decide, of all disastrous courses, whether with the help of your psychiatrist or a drug dealer, to erode your faculties even further.

Since the brain always tries to achieve balance it stops self-production of a chemical so as to prevent too great a supply at any given time. Our reflexes are weakened because they depend on a steady and balanced reproduction of *endogenous* chemicals. If you take enough of a drug there is a marked slowing-down of these reflexes, almost always unobserved by the user, whether the drug is prescriptive or narcotic. The victim may "forget" how to walk, breathe, mate, eat, judge, behave with integrity. There are choking sensations as the respiratory muscles lose their autonomic motion. *This is the muscular expression of a general autonomic collapse.*

You will hear that certain "character traits" are common to people who fall into drug dependence. They are often "rebellious" types. They tolerate delays in the gratification of their desires with great difficulty, they are impulsive, socially unhappy etc.

But these same traits get soldiers medals. They are the traits of highly intelligent people too. And they *follow* habitual chemical use rather than precede it.

Not that drugs are character-building either. But the "character flaws" are invariably features of the drug, not features of the character.

When someone on XTC throws himself off a roof in the expectation of flying he doesn't fly but he thinks he is going to. No character flaw here. It is simply how he sees things. When he swims far out to sea in the dead of night and can't judge the distance he has gone, and so cannot get back to shore, his mental expectations are due solely to the drug, which has destroyed his brain's proper habitat-responses.

Moral admonition will have small effect on this state. Analysis of childhood events or parental shortcomings can no more alter the effects of a drug than flying in a plane can develop the leg muscles. You have to have a drug-withdrawal program, and this requires special care because it is much like the death journey or journey to the underworld that the Greek mysteries induced, and which all "rebirth" initiations must have in some form. The hand has to be held, the terrified mind night and day consoled. We must remember that the death journey's effect is to make the initiate go deeper into the habitat, not away from it. So a great sense of belonging, arriving home, ensues afterwards.

A lot of doctors urge patients to stop taking tranquilizers, unaware that chemical ingestion creates its own electrochemical need for further ingestion, and that reducing or suddenly stopping the drug creates a need for higher doses.

The withdrawal treatment most likely to succeed is the one that approaches the brain directly, for instance through the use of electrodes emitting high-frequency waves. In a matter of ten days a tranquilizer- or narcotic-dependent patient can kick the dependency. What has unbalanced the brain can only be corrected by direct influence on the brain. In other words certain high-frequency waves can alter the perception "I must have another pill" to the perception "I don't need to take a pill". What the mysteries did was achieve this electronic or acupunctural effect by sensory-deprivation, fasting or breath techniques, that is *by equally physiological means*, never by advice, admonition, verbal exploration or reference to the conscious will. An addict—the drug can be heroin or alcohol or sedatives— can't connect his feelings to the drug because the action of the drug is to reduce, never sharpen responses. The mind may be momentarily sharper, there may be a sense of greater awareness, but it is because the other ("animal") responses are numbed.

Someone who smokes pot regularly will often make a split-second pause when answering questions. For himself he is answering immediately. We know he isn't. His loss of response is unknown to him.

In the case of a heroin overdose, alone or mixed with barbiturates and/or alcohol, the respiratory muscles may cease action altogether. Tranquilizers too may affect these muscles both by depressing the brain centers on which oxygen metabolism depends and by paralyzing the respiratory muscles.

Although cocaine has been taken for respiratory disorders it can also affect the respiratory muscles adversely so that a panic-stricken breathlessness results. Smoking freebase (cocaine returned to its alkaloid form) may actually block oxygen metabolism, which means that the blood no longer carries a sufficient supply of oxygen round the body and the carbon dioxide is no longer properly discharged. The Aztecs who ate the mushroom, like the Bolivians who today chew the coca leaf, were engaged in energetic pursuits which maintained oxygen balance.

Oxygen metabolism is a delicate operation which takes place in the cells by means of an "organelle" which biologists also call the mitochondria. Some people conjecture that this is a key building brick of the body, the "evolutionary" cell because it speaks a DNA language incomprehensible to the rest of the body and is apparently the only "guest" to be allowed to do so, which may mean that it is a bridge to an outside source of information.

This is biology language trying to explain what it stumbles on without understanding. The important fact about the mitochondria is that it is responsible for oxygen metabolism, and that the manipulation of this organelle by means of breathing patterns is one of the chief methods of changing perception. All biology can do is to use its accepted terminology and if "evolution" is the only term to hand it has to be used, however vague, however irrelevant. Like all the other definitions it cannot escape its circle of definitions. The fact that the two words "aspiration" and "inspiration" describe the breath refers to the use to which the breath was put in Greek and to some extent Roman times. It tapped "hermetic" information and the biologist's use of the word "evolution" shows an awareness of this possibility.

To repeat, increasing the supply of a chemical which the body already produces is hazardous: after a while the body relies wholly on the drug to do its work ("dependency") and for this reason any brusque attempt to withdraw from it can be fatal, sometimes through convulsions. Also the body sets up a strong resistance to chemicals, in an effort to maintain balance. A sedative drug (for sleep) will stimulate the reticular activating system in the brain to keep the mind as awake as possible, just to balance matters. When people stop their pills and find that their insomnia comes back they make the mistake of thinking that the pills were effective and that they must resume and even increase the dosage. In fact the sedative provoked the reticular activating system to fight to keep the body awake, while also depleting the body's natural sedatives. Slow, supervised withdrawal may mean years of nervous crisis, sometimes hourly hell, before the brain recovers—I have witnessed fearful withdrawal from pharmaceutical products called harmless.

If a patient in a hospital starts behaving viciously after a "trank" or "strait jacket" injection our theological response is that this indicates inbuilt aggressive tendencies, so we apply more of the "trank". The Cartesian principle that passions fog the Objective Mind is here realized in the lives of millions of people who know nothing about Descartes and couldn't care less.

The theology said that the mind can become sick (in medieval times possessed). By the 1950s any patient too distressed by pain or sleeplessness to state his symptoms intelligibly was in danger of being prescribed one of the mini-anesthesia or benzodiazepene tranquilizers, which came onto the market at that time. The result was that many people found they were led into "neurotic" behavior by the very chemicals they were given to allay it. In 1980 the Institute of Psychiatry in London produced its first papers on this possibility, finding that after regular use of "normal" doses of tranquilizing chemicals the patient frequently manifested neurosis for the first time.

By 1979 thirty million prescriptions a year were being written out in Britain. In the U.S. over two hundred million prescriptions for anti-anxiety chemicals were written in 1986. As for "narcotics", by 1988 five thousand Americans a day were trying cocaine for the first time, thirty percent of all college students used it at some time. At least five thousand doctors were drug-dependent, a million New Yorkers were regular users. Some spent as much as a million dollars a year on some form of narcotic, hallucinant etc. What else was all this but a deep desire to change "my perceptions"? It said plainly, for all to hear, "The world's all right but I ain't."

Barbiturates by this time were found both addictive and dangerous. This is partly why benzodiazapenes came on the market—as a safe depressant alternative. These new long-acting chemicals supposedly had an hypnotic or sleep-inducing effect, in contrast to short-acting chemicals which simply helped you through a crisis. It was claimed that if you wanted to kill a guinea pig with an overdose of benzodiazapenes you would have to bury it in them.

A British psychopharmacologist once suggested (in a March 1988 bulletin to doctors) that the use of benzodiazepine, even if minimal, could lead to antisocial behavior such as shoplifting, while heavy use could lead to baby-and granny-bashing.

But the more usual side effects were behavioral aberrations or "bad" character—outbursts of fury disproportionate to the cause, a tendency to imagine a structure of events which other people didn't perceive, a need for verbal showdowns, over-excitement, a veering of moods from one extreme to another.

As always we have to come back to the apparently lonely world of the human mind. I remember sitting in a San Diego hotel waiting for a cab to take me into Mexico. It was back in the 1980s, most likely. I was watching a CNN interview of a young serial murderer shortly before his execution. He looked to be in his early twenties. And he was saying "Psychiatrists never got one thing right about me." He was from a good family, no problems, nothing to blame his parents for. No question of childhood abuse.

His victims were all in their early teens. He said he wanted to die because no one like him should be alive. He had already chosen his form of execution—hanging. He looked a quiet healthy youth, more sensitive than most: well-spoken, thoughtful.

What then was lacking in the assumptions of psychiatrists and that progeny which we have inherited from Sigmund Freud called "psycho-analysts", namely men and women analyzing "the minds" of others? With what mind do you do that—a human mind, of all minds?

To my knowledge, only one psychiatrist faced this matter squarely and that was R.D.Laing. He sat down with his sufferers, shared their rooms, writhed with them and laughed and cried with them and never held himself separate with a "mind" that could "analyze", of all preposterous claims.

Capturing the Russian serial killer Andrei Chikatillo in 1992 was especially difficult because everyone thought he must be a departure from the norm, on the basis of the theory that the norm is the sane. More than one hundred homosexuals were booked. Not until Lieut. Colonel Burakov called in a psychiatrist who knew something about Western investigations of such crimes did the hunt proper start. A serial killer doing time gave him a tip: look for someone of *moral rectitude*. Chikatillo was a quiet married man with two children, a one-time teacher whose dream was to own an impressive private library. He committed fifty-six (known) murders. He was judged sane and therefore indictable.

Freud (no idealist where humans were concerned) said *homo homini lupus*—man is a wolf and you had better defend yourself against him. That is, watch out for The Enemy.

In other words human passions in no way subsided, the "animal" self wasn't after all in retreat—it was only topsy-turvy now. There is a French saying, *Turn back the steeds of passion and they will return at the gallop.*

You may turn back dementia with the right degree of civilization but if you no longer know how this is done, what techniques were formerly employed, the dementia will return at such a lick that the civilization will be overwhelmed—and for as long as it takes to find those techniques again.

ABOUT THE AUTHOR

Maurice Rowdon was born into a London working class family in 1922. He was a Forward Observation Officer during the Italian campaign in World War Two. He earned degrees in History and Philosophy at Oxford University and published twelve books on animal/human intelligence and war. He lived for four decades in Italy and became widely acclaimed for his sensitive renderings of Italy and its people. A novelist and a prolific playwright he also developed his own hermetic breathing system which he practiced in California. In the last years of his varied career he and his wife lived between London and France. He died in February 2009.

BIBLIOGRAPHY

AESCHYLUS: *Four Plays*, Penguin Viking New York/Penguin Group London 1961.

ARNO J.MAYER; *The Persistence of The Old Regime* (Europe to World War One), Pantheon Books New York 1981

ARNOLD TOYNBEE: *A Study of History*, Oxford University Press 1955.

ARNOLD ZWEIG; *The Living Thoughts of Spinoza*, Cassell Nad Company Ltd 1946

ARTHUR COTTERELL: *The Pimlico Dictionary of Classical Mythologies*, Random House London 2000.

ARTEMIS COOPER: *Cairo in The War, 1939-1945*, Penguin books1998

BERNARD WILLIAMS: *Descartes, The Project of pure Enquiry*, Penguin Books 1978

D.C. LAU: *Lao Tzu (translated)*, Penguin Books London, Viking Penguin New York (twenty reprints 1963-85)

D.D.R OWEN: *Eleanor of Acquitaine, Queen and Legend*, Blackwell Publishers 1993

D.H. LAWRENCE: *Studies in American Classical Literature; Phoenix, the Posthumous Papers; Mornings in Mexico and Etruscan Places; The Short Novels; Twilight in Italy; The Letters*, Heinemann Books London 1939/1961/1967

DAVID HAMMOND: *The Search for Psychic Power*, Hodder and Stoughton Ltd London, 1975.

DAVID LUSCOMBE: *Medieval Thought*, Oxford University Press, 1997

DION FORTUNE THORSONS: *Psychic Self Defense*, Harper Collins 1996

DONALD A.MACKENZIE: *Crete and Hellenic Myths and Legends*, Studio Editions 1994

DONALD MACKINNON: *The Borderlands of Theology*, Lutterworth, London 1968

DR GILLIAN MCKEITH: *Living Food for Health*, Judith Piatkus Ltd London 2000.

DR MELVIN MORSE MD: *Transformed by the Light (The Powerful effects of Near Death Experiences on People's Lives)* Judith Piatkus Ltd., 1993

DR H.C.A.VOGEL: *The Nature Doctor, A Manual of Traditional and Complementary Medicine*, Mainstream Publishing Company (Edinburgh) Ltd. 1990.

EDWARD GIBBON: *Decline and Fall of the Roman Empire*, Frederick Warner and Co. London and New York 1980

EDWARD HUTTON: *Rome*, Hollis and Carter London 1950.

ELIZABETH MARSHALL THOMAS: *The Hidden Life of Dogs*, Weidenfeld and Nicolson 1994

EMMANUEL LE ROY LADURIE: *Montaillou (the world famous portrait of life in a mediaeval village)*, The Scholar Press 1978/ Penguin Books London 1980 1984 1990

EZRA POUND: *ABC of Reading*, Faber and Faber London 1951

FRANCES A. YATES: *The Occult Philosophy in the Elizabethan Age*, Routledge and Kegan Paul 1979

FRANKLIN JONES: *The Method of the Siddhas, Talks with Franklin Jones (Bubba Free John) on the Spiritual technique of the Savours of Mankind* The Dawn Horse Press Los Angeles 1973

FRIEDRICH NIETZSCHE: *Ecce Homo; Human all too Human*,
Penguin Books 1979, 1984

GEORGE BERNARD SHAW: *Prefaces and Plays*, Constable
London 1931-1954

GEORGE HOWE and G.A.HARRER: *A handbook of Classical
Mythology*, George Allen and Unwin 1931

GOPI KRISHNA: *Kundalini The Evolutionary Energy In Man*,
Shambhala Boston and London 1971

GORDON LEFF; *Medieval Thought (St Augustine to Ockham)*,
Pelican Books 1958

GREGOR VON REZZORI: *The Snows of Yesteryear*, Chatto and
Windus 1990

H.D.F. KITTO: *The Greeks*, Penguin Books USA/UK in thirteen
editions (1951-63).

HEGEL: *Lectures on the Philosophy of Religion in one Volume*,
University of California Press Berkeley/Los Angeles/ London
1998

HELEN HILL MILLER: *Greek Horizons*, Charles Scribner New
York 1961

HENRY CHADWICK: *The Early Church*, Penguin Books 1967

HENRY FIELDING: *The History of Tom Jones*, Everyman's Press

HOLGER KERSTEN and ELMAR R. GRUBER: *The Jesus
Conspiracy*, Element Books 1992

HOMER: *The Odyssey*, Oxford University Press 1960.

HULDA REGEHER CLARK: *The Cure for Cancers*, ProMotion
Publishing 1993

ILVA PRIGOGEN and ISABELLE STENGERS: *Order Out Of
Chaos, Man's New Dialogue with Nature*, Bantam Books USA
1984

INGEBORG BACHMANN: *The Thirtieth Year*, Polygon
Edinburgh 1993

J. BRONOWSKI: *William Blake and the Age of Revolution*, Routledge and Kegan Paul Ltd 1972

J.W. GOETHE: *Italian Journey*, Harper Collins 1962

J.W.N SULLIVAN: *The Limitation of Science*, Mentor, Viking Press 1933

JAMES SCUDDAY PERKINS: *Through Death to Rebirth*, The Theosophical Publishing House Wheaton Ill. USA

JAMES SUTHERLAND: *The Oxford Book of Literary Anecdotes*, Oxford University Press 1975

JANE GOODALL: *In the Shadow of Man*, Houghton Mifflin Company Boston 1988.

JEAN-JACQUES ROUSSEAU: *Reveries of the Solitary Walker*, Penguin Books 1979-1987.

JEFFREY MASSON: *Dogs Never Lie About Love*, The Random House Group 1997

JOHN MORTIMER: *Clinging to the Wreckage*, Penguin Books

JOSEPH CONRAD: *Youth: A Narrative/Heart of Darkness/The End of the Tether*, Everyman's Library, Dent and Sons 1967

JOSEPH ROTH: *The Radetzky March*, The Overlook Press, Penguin Books 1995

JOYCE MARLOW: *The Peterloo Massacre*, Readers Union London 1970

KAPIL N. TIWARI: *Suffering: Indian Perspectives*, Motililal Banarsidass, Delhi 1986

KARL POLANY: *The Great Transformation, the political and economic origins of our time*, Victor Gollanz London and Rinehart and Company Inc 1957

KIERKEGAARD: *Fear and Trembling*, The Penguin Group London 1985

KRISHNAMURTI: *Commentaries on Living*, Victor Gollancz Ltd London 1986; *Freedom from the Known*, Harper and Row 1969

LEE SANNELLA M.D.: *The Kundalini Experience, Psychosis, or Transcendence?* Integral Publishing 1987

LYNN MCTAGGART: *What Doctors Don't Tell You*, Harper Collins (Thorsons) 1996.

M. ANDERSON: *Europe in the Eighteenth Century*, Longmans, Green and Co. London.

MARSHAL McLUAN: *The Gutenberg Galaxy*, Routledge and Kegan Paul London 1962, 1967

MAURICE ROWDON: *Lorenzo the Magnificent*t, Weidenfeld London 1974; *Leonardo da Vinci*, Weidenfeld 1975; *The Talking Dogs, Macmillan 1978*

MICHAEL BAIGENT and RICHARD LEIGH: *The Dead Sea Scrolls*, Jonathan Cape London 1991

MICHAEL GRANT: *The Ancient Mediterranean*, Weidenfeld and Nicolson 1969

MICHAEL HERR: *Despatches*, Alfred A. Knopf 1977

MILTON WALDMAN: *Elizabeth and Leicester*, The Albatross Ltd., London and Paris 1947.

NORBERT ELIAS: *The Civilizing Process,* Blackwell Oxford UK Cambridge Mass 1939; *The Symbol Theory*, Sage London 1991

PAUL ELLIOT: *A Narrow Street*, Penguin Books 1947

PHILIPPE DELERM: *The Small Pleasures of Life*, Phoenix House 1998

PIUS II: *Commentaries (Memoirs of a Renaissance Pope)*, George Allen and Unwin Ltd. London 1960.

PLATO: *The last days of Socrates,* Penguin books 1954

QUENTIN CRISP: *Resident Alien (The New York Diaries)*, Harper Collins 1996

RAYMOND A. MOODY, JR.: *Life after Life*, Mockingbird Books 19 reprints 1975-1977.

REV. Dr R. SWINBURNE CLYMER: *Mysteries of Osiris*, The Philosophical Publishing Company, Quartertown, Penna. USA

RICHARD CHURCH: *The Golden Sovereign*, William Heinemann London 1957

ROGER SCRUTON: *Modern Philosophy*, Arrow Books; *Kant*, Oxford University Press 1982

RUPERT SHELDRAKE: *Dogs that Know When Their Owners are Coming Home*, Hutchinson, London 1999

STEPHEN USHER: *The Historians of Greece and Rome* , Hamish Hamilton London 1969

SWAMI RAMA, RUDOLPH BALLENTINE M.D., and ALAN HYMES MD*: Science of Breath*, The Himalayan International Institute 1979 1975

W.G. SEBALD: *Vertigo; The Emigrants; The Rings of Saturn*, The Harvill Press 1990, 1996, 1998

WERNER HEISENBERG*: Physics and Philosophy*, Penguin Books 1990

WILLIAM L. SHIRER: *The Rise and Fall of the Third Reich*, Simon and Schuster Inc 1960

WILLIAM MORRIS*: News from Nowhere*, Penguin Books 1962

WILLIAM SAROYAN: *Best Stories*, Faber and Faber London 1964

INDEX

C

Caesar 22, 184, 216, 280, 281, 282
Caesar Augustus 216
Calvary 184
Cambridge xii, 66, 219, 223, 224, 273
Casanova 76
Casimir Picard 30
Catherine of Siena 113
Catullus 152
Cebes 180
Cecco d'Ascoli 139
Chamber of Commerce and Quarter
      Sessions 215
Character flaws 299
Charles Darwin 29, 30, 33, 37, 237
Charles Dickens 209
Chernobyl reactor 277
Chevalier de Lamarck 28
Child-like enthusiasm 241
Chinese Written Characters 254
Christ 49, 78, 79, 83, 86, 87, 93, 95,
      97, 104, 112, 113, 116, 117, 118,
      121, 122, 123, 129, 132, 134,
      139, 146, 147, 148, 149, 152,
      156, 164, 165, 166, 170, 172,
      173, 174, 175, 177, 180, 181,
      182, 183, 184, 185, 186, 187,
      188, 190, 194, 195, 196, 199,
      200, 212, 215, 219
Christ Church, Oxford 219
Christendom 61, 67, 79, 82, 92, 96,
      119, 120, 140, 148, 149, 151,
      177, 185, 201, 205, 206, 213,
      239
Christianity 82, 83, 90, 91, 93, 94, 95,
      116, 120, 128, 129, 131, 134,
      139, 146, 147, 149, 150, 152,
      170, 183, 184, 189, 197, 200,
      239, 284
Christopher Columbus 120, 272
Christopher Marlowe 288
Churchill 194
C.I.A. 184
Clarembald of Chartres 197

Communio 215
Complex systems 61, 251
Constantine 178, 184, 185, 186, 215,
      235
Conventus 215
Corpus callosum 275
Crispus 215
Cromwell 223, 225, 226, 239
Crucifixions 173, 190
Crusading Spirit 194
Cyprian 187, 215
Cyril of Alexandria 190

D

Daemon 286
Dante Alighieri 152, 166
Danzig 238
Dementia 5, 8, 21, 44, 62, 63, 64, 90,
      101, 103, 109, 143, 167, 168,
      202, 216, 220, 221, 237, 238,
      248, 265, 274, 279, 280, 288,
      295, 296, 298, 304
Democritus 159
de Quincey 28
de Rouge (Egyptologist) 150
Dervish 214
Descartes 10, 134, 207, 276, 302
D.H. Lawrence 67
Diabolos 286
Diderot 235
Diocletian 184, 186
Dionysiac 158, 168, 170, 187
Dionysios Exiguus 163
Divine Impregnations 190
Doctor Faustus 288
Dominicans 142
Domitian 216
Dr Johnson 226, 228
Drug-withdrawal Program 299
Duke of Burgundy 105, 106
Duke of Orleans 105
Duns Scotus 143, 144, 204, 206
Dyeing yarns 238
Dyspnoea 234

Lightning Source UK Ltd.
Milton Keynes UK
30 January 2010

149323UK00002B/2/P